LONG LIVE LATIN

LONG LIVE LATIN

A Latin Miscellany

JOHN GRAY

CANIS PRESS
Kent- UK

Published by Canis Press
Little Hollies
Bonnington, Kent
TN25 7AZ

First published in Great Britain 2004
© John Gray 2004

ISBN 0-9548878-0-8

A Catalogue record of this book is available from the British Library

Design, typesetting and production by
John Saunders Design & Production, Abingdon OX13 5HU
Printed in Great Britain by Biddles Ltd., King's Lynn

FOREWORD

By Frederick Forsyth

All my life I have had a sort of love affair with the English language. More to the point I have reason to be grateful to it, for its employment has given me a comfortable living through journalism and authorship.

I believe it to be the most delicate, most sensitive, most versatile and most flexible vehicle for communication between human beings ever devised. For that reason I rarely presume to use foreign words where a perfect English matcher exists.

That said, there are certain words and phrases that exist outside our language yet which convey meaning with perfect clarity and for which English can, most frustratingly, provide no equivalent as succinct or precise as the foreign word.

Schadenfreude, that disgraceful but delicious and private exultation at the idea of someone coming an awful cropper (usually someone you cannot abide) comes to us from German, yet repeated circumlocutions never quite capture the essence of that pleasure. So Schadenfreude it must remain, along with Angst, Zeitgeist and a few others.

Far more frequently than German we use French words, and all too often out of pretentiousness because a matching word in English would do just as well. Almost without pause, one can think of fifty 'borrowings' from French that are in common usage.

But Latin outstrips them all. Our youngsters have been learning Latin, whether classical or ecclesiastical, since the dark ages. And quite right too. Even as a modern languages scholar at school, I never cease to find my fragile grasp of Latin useful, whether for deciding the meaning of a derivative word or for stumbling through an inscription left behind by those who walked before us in these islands.

I was once told that Winston Churchill, emerging from Harrow with what today we would term no GCSEs, soon recognised his shortcomings and spent many hours as a young officer memorising a book of some 2000 Latin tags. With his awesome memory he never forgot one of them.

But times they are a-changing. It is not an easy language and as we move further into an age when effort of body or mind becomes increasingly to be regarded as a presumptuous expectation Latin has fallen into desuetude. Fortunately this seems set for reversal with cinema and the media's current appetite for Rome and everything Roman, Gladiator, Hannibal, Colosseum, Pompeii and more.

After **Lawyers' Latin** John Gray has now produced **Long Live Latin**. A Miscellany packed with words, phrases and inscriptions which are translated and accompanied by comment and diverse often amusing complementary material, it is immensely readable as well as being informative. An agreeable companion (a *vade mecum?*) it should be at the elbow of anyone who wishes to read widely, solve crosswords, or just be entertained.

So *carpe diem*; let us go out and get a copy.

To Jonathon, Theresa and Anna

ET

CANI INGENTI
BERTIE

ET CANI NOVO PARVOQUE
IVO

CAVE CANEM

CONTENTS

ACKNOWLEDGEMENTS

First and foremost I record my thanks and great debt to His Honour Judge John Weeks QC (*quondam* classical scholar of Worcester College, Oxford) for his uncomplaining reaction to regular consultation particularly for assistance with translation but generally in connection with the production of this book. My great thanks too extends to Jean Frere, Cressida and Jane Annesley for proof reading and valuable advice: to Francis Grew of the Museum of London for knowledgeable help: to Victoria Baines and to Stefan Stanke for correction of linguistic error, for finding some further references and for youthful advice and input. All errors notwithstanding are mine. To David Worthy (who helped me with my Latin when I was aged eleven) for general advice and assistance, to Tom Kemp for undertaking the jacket lettering and design, to my wife, Susan for drawing my dog logo and for drawing my dogs, to John Saunders for his patience and good humour in the course of design and production and last but not least to all those in the Canterbury Cathedral library for providing me endlessly with the Vulgate .

Antoine de Saint-Exupéry extract from 'Wind Sand and Stars' translated by William Rees (Penguin Books, 1995, first published as 'Terre des Hommes', 1959) reproduced by permission of Penguin Books Ltd. Translation copyright William Rees, 1995.

Laurence Binyon extract from 'For The Fallen (September 1914)' reproduced by permission of The Society of Authors as literary representatives of the Estate of Laurence Binyon.

Robin Birley extracts from Roman Records from Vindolanda on Hadrian's Wall reproduced by permission of the author Robin Birley.

G.K. Chesterton extracts from 'Lepanto', 'The Aristocrat' and the phrase 'Blessed is he that expecteth nothing for he shall be gloriously rewarded' reproduced by permission of A.P.Watt Ltd. on behalf of the Royal Literary Fund from 'G.K. Chesterton. Stories, Essays and Poems', Everyman's Library J.M. Dent and Sons 1965.

Walter de la Mare extract from 'Fare Well' reproduced by permission of the Trustees of Walter de la Mare and the Society of Authors as their Literary Representatives.

E.M. Forster extracts from 'Abinger Harvest' and 'Howard's End' reproduced by permission of The Provost and Scholars of King's College, Cambridge and The Society of Authors as the Literary Representatives of the estate of E.M.Forster.

L.P. Hartley extract from 'The Go-Between' reproduced by permission of Penguin Books Ltd. From the Little Oxford Dictionary of Quotations, Oxford University Press 1994.

A.P.Herbert extract from 'Beaucort Revisited' reproduced by permission of A.P. Watt Ltd. on behalf of Teresa Elizabeth Perkins and the Estate of Jocelyn Herbert.

W.F. Jackson-Knight extract translation of Virgil's Aeneid from Penguin Classics 1956, revised 1957) reproduced by permission of Penguin books Ltd.

Rudyard Kipling extract reproduced by permission of A. P. Watt Ltd on behalf of The National Trust for Places of Historic Interest or Natural Beauty.

George Orwell extract from 'Animal Farm' (copyright © George Orwell 1946) reproduced by permission of Bill Hamilton as the Literary Executor of the estate of the Late Sonia Brownell Orwell and Secker & Warburg Ltd.

J.K.Rowling extracts from 'Harrius Potter et Philosophi Lapis' reproduced by permission of the Christopher Little, Literary Agency on the author's behalf. Copyright © J.K. Rowling 1997.

Dr. Roger S. Tomlin for permission to reproduce under the entry for *Vegetus Montani* part of his translation and commentary in 'Britannia' 24 (2003)'.

George Bernard Shaw acknowledgement for the expression 'we learn from experience that men learn very little from experience'. Attributed.

Evelyn Waugh extract from 'Brideshead Revisited: The Sacred and Profane Memories of Captain Charles Ryder' by Evelyn Waugh (Penguin Classics 1999). Copyright 1945 by Evelyn Waugh reproduced by permission of Penguin Books Ltd.

Grateful acknowledgement to Dr. R. S. O. Tomlin, to the Administrators of the Haverfield Bequest, The Roman Inscriptions of Britain, The Journal of Roman Studies, The Temple of Sulis Minerva at Bath (The Oxford University committee for Archaeology) for material used under the heads *Follis, Liquam(en) antipol(itanem), Rufus Callisuni* and *Qui mihi Vilbiam.*

A general grateful thanks to all those concerned with the granting of copyright permissions. Without exception they were helpful, patient and accommodating.

PREFACE

EXORDIUM ET PRAEFATIO

Latin lives on. About us it is everywhere; unavoidable. To know little or nothing of it may too often disappoint. It is in our literature, on tombstones, in and on buildings (especially inscribed above doorways), castles and monuments; on coinage, on commemorative plaques (it has a fine lapidary quality), in churches, in stained glass windows, on medals, in museums, in the blurb that goes with classical music on compact discs, in the classification of plants, animals, birds, reptiles and insects, in the graffiti particularly of Rome, Pompeii and Herculaneum and in horoscopes, with their related Latin signs of the zodiac. We talk unhesitatingly of *agenda, ante natal, et cetera, interim, quota, quorum, veto* etc.; and we like to buy our shares *cum* dividend. And what a large number of Latin words like these qualify as *de facto* English so as to have made appearance in the main text (not in an appendix) of the Oxford Modern English Dictionary. Translation is alternative English. (Examples are in appendix four).

How often do we skip the Latin we find in a book or stare blankly at the inscription we see on a plaque or a coat of arms? (sometimes after a struggle to recall a long forgotten and even then usually insufficient smattering of the language). In ignorance we pass on, deprived of what might have been informative, amusing, pleasing, moving . . . is it not gratifying to know that the inscription beneath the armoured three legged emblem on the Isle of Man coat of arms . . *stabit quocunque jeceris* . . . means 'it will stand whichever way you throw it'? (so verbose in translation). And how many know the meaning of Latin inscriptions cut into the rim of their one pound coins, know why they are there or have even noticed them? In 2004 how many know or have learned the Olympic motto? (*citius* . . see text).

'Long Live Latin' is a personal, sometimes eccentric, miscellany of Latin words, expressions and proper names for those who hanker after an understanding of what may confront them and who would like to learn something of those personalities from antiquity whose names they may stumble across. I have catalogued only a fraction of what might be encountered, set out translation and, where appropriate, added variously comment, related information (I hope interesting and sometimes amusing) and snippets of complementary history and poetry as the spirit moved me. In the case of graffiti good taste has nearly prevailed: in 2,000 years this art form has changed little. Ecclesiastical and biblical Latin has its fair share of space: so much of it for some well worth a reminder; for others an introduction. There is also much ancillary English quotation. Bernard Darwin, in his introduction to the Oxford Dictionary of Quotations 3rd edition wrote: 'Quotation brings to many people one of the intensest joys of living'. I am one of those people. 'Long Live Latin' is light reading quite as much as it is a book of reference.

There has been some Latin in my life since an early age and I enjoyed helping with my children's Latin homework. To promote this out of favour language is however possibly pretentious. I am not a Latin scholar and have had much linguistic help (gratefully acknowledged elsewhere) from the better qualified.

Having practised as a lawyer all my working life, I had become familiar with the Latin which, over the centuries, had been woven into the very fabric of English law. I viewed it with affection. It made for a certain respect, born perhaps of association with the awesome might and splendour of Rome. It brought too interest and a mystique, which brightened and dignified legal proceedings whose potential for degeneration into the monotony of tedious drone is very great. From 1999 onwards, efforts of the powers that be to eliminate its use left me disappointed and indignant.

Use of Latin has become almost politically incorrect. Smacking of elitism, it has been banned by the Treasury and, to repeat, for questionable benefit powerful factions in the law now spurn its centuries-old friend and faithful companion. Its use seems to be frowned upon as asserting a superiority, as being divisive, fuddy-duddy, something for which to apologise: all this the reflection of a generalised dumbing down in a society where increasingly what is excellent and esoteric is deprecated. Nobody must aspire to excellence lest others feel inadequate or uncomfortable: a reaction against academic and artistic endeavour that might stimulate, brighten and reward . . . all driven by the *politically correct*, an imperative norm the source and authority of and for which is too often obscure and questionable. Stripped of its Latin, the language of the law could too often be tediously flat; a publisher's word well known to writers who have received a rejection slip: it means dull, boring, vapid.

Facit indignatio versum (see text). In 2001 I wrote 'Lawyers' Latin'; primarily to help (but also to cheer) young lawyers with little or no knowledge of the language, who might struggle, particularly in the early days of its persecution. Latin in old reported cases will not disappear, though gradually it will crop up less and less. Research drew to my attention abundant Latin unrelated to the law, which reminded me of much that I knew, told me more of what I half knew and introduced me to a great deal that it was a joy to learn. So as to share all this, I sought to broaden 'Lawyers' Latin' and included entries of general interest such as: *afflavit Deus et dissipantur* (God blew and they are scattered) *decus et tutamen* (an ornament and a protection), *et in Arcadia ego* (and I in Arcadia), *Harold Rex interfectus est* (King Harold is slain), *opus Dei* (work of God), *Pater Noster* (Our Father) and *vivat Hispania* (Long live Spain).

It was however thought better to keep to law related Latin in a work the prime objective of which was to help young lawyers in difficult times. I expanded extensively the reject material and this book resulted. It contains therefore only minimal law related Latin; so much of which may be of interest to those who are not lawyers.

We should not deny a language which is so much a part of our heritage born of nearly four hundred years mainly civilising Roman occupation and protection of this island (when the legions left in AD 410 to defend Rome against the marauding Visigoths, the emperor Honorius warned Britons that they must look to their own protection). Rather we should be alerted to the rich fund of wisdom, inspiration and knowledge that comes with what is to be found in a language used for so long in our land: a language revered by past masters of our own tongue; Milton, Pope and Dryden. Lord Byron chose Latin to express his fondest thought and perhaps continuing ambition, *plenus et optabilis coitus* see text. And the law, as *arbiter elegantiae*, retained Latin *inter* many valuable *alia* as a medium for the public expression of indelicate matters which in English might be embarrassing and disagreeable; as indeed frequently does much of the general public: capable of a wide usage the expression *in flagrante delicto* is commonly used euphemistically as a reference to just one activity. Expressed in Latin so much becomes markedly less stark and thereby inoffensive.

The fascinating texts in letters excavated at Vindolanda, a Roman fortress on Hadrian's Wall, are the first record of the everyday life of people living in Britain. As the world agonised over Iraq's Saddam Hussein, President George W. Bush might have liked to emulate Cato (whose every speech to the Roman senate concluded with *delenda est Carthago* 'Carthage must be destroyed') with 'Saddam must be destroyed'. He might too have welcomed support from the views of *Vegetius* and of Oliver Cromwell (military experts in different ways) *si vis pacem, para bellum* and *pax quaeritur bello* 'if you want peace prepare for war' and 'peace is sought by war'. Fragments only of Cato's great oratory survive: yet for one piece of advice to us all he deserves for ever to be remembered: *rem tene, verba sequentur* 'stick to the point and the words will come'.

Latin will surely see a revival; not on account only of a British affinity for things analogous to the wronged underdog, but through a wider realisation of how much it has to offer. In a letter of 1st June 1716 the author Thomas Burnet wrote 'I am now at my leisure hours reading Horace [65 – 8 BC] with some diligence and find the world just the same then as it continues to be now . .' In 2004 I venture to doubt that the world is much different.

I have said nothing of how to pronounce Latin. For this and for a short biographical note on the Roman writers, I refer to James Morwood's Dictionary of Latin Words and Phrases (Oxford University Press 1998). Further, comment in my text upon quotations taken from the Roman writers is sometimes idiosyncratic and/or unrelated to the original Latin context. For a scholarly reference to the classical context in many such cases, I recommend the same work.

My text is alphabetical, so that any expression the reader may wish to look up can readily be found. There is too abundant cross-referencing of related matters. A subject matter index lists most entries under heads: they may thus be traced in the text by reference to subject matter. A partial English index lists words and names which may have been seen in the text and may be used where they are remembered, but the Latin entry or entries under which they appear is/are not.

I wondered about inclusion of classificatory Latin (of plants, birds, fish, reptiles etc). I could have filled several volumes with that. It accounts however for a significant part of the Latin living about us and ought not to be ignored *in toto*. I settled accordingly for just a few sample entries related to familiar things.

Some historical information given may seem not to be wholly accurate. The Roman empire spanned well over a thousand years. There was much change and what may have been true at one point in time may not have been true at another. This is exemplified by comparison of the coin related entries for *denarius* and *follis*.

By attempting to inform, interest and sometimes amuse, this book I hope may go some way to dispel an undeserved hostility towards the Latin language and to swell the numbers of its devotees. But, despite the deplorable decision in 2004 of the AQA (the UK's largest school's examination board) to phase out Latin in 2006, there are signs of a strong come back and support more formidable than mine is at hand. In the Rome of today there are some 50,000 Latin inscriptions. Following Mel Gibson's controversial film 'The Passion' in which Latin was spoken, a resurgence of interest in the language saw the Italian authorities arrange free Latin lessons for tourists and *Il Giornale* declare *Latinum mortuum non est* 'Latin is not dead'. The Vatican too has issued a Latin dictionary which copes with such modern expressions as football and spaceship . . . *pediludium* and *sideralis navis* (literally star or heavenly ship). On David Beckham in tattoo is *ut amem et foveam* 'that I should love and cherish' and *perfecto in spiritu*. One of England's heroes in 2003, which won the rugby union world cup in Australia, was Jonny Wilkinson: was he not *primus inter pares?* And might his motto not be *alta pete?* Rome and Romans are back in vogue and Latin should follow in their wake. BBC TV has featured productions on the Colosseum (with Latin dialogue!) and on Pompeii. In 'What the Romans did For Us' BBC 2 has provided regular and diverting ten minute vignette episodes portraying diverse aspects of Roman life and achievement in Britain. Robert Harris has given us his book 'Pompeii'. In the cinema Hannibal is to follow Gladiator: and Bloomsbury has published J.K. Rowling's 'Harry Potter and The Philosopher's Stone' . . . in Latin! *Harrius Potter et Philosophi Lapis!* What more could Latin hope for than that he 'stick up' for it? And when in later life he becomes, as he surely will, Sir Harry Potter *Latinae defensor (promotor?)* then Latin will certainly flourish again.

Lege feliciter!

October 2004
John Gray

AUTHOR'S NOTE

In the text below: the words 'his' and 'he' include respectively 'her' and 'she'.

An asterisk after the last word of any entry in the text means that it is to be found in Appendix Four, which lists Latin contained in the main text of the Oxford Modern English Dictionary 1992 edition, Latin which on the face of it has been accepted as having become *de facto* English.

HOW TO USE THIS BOOK

Entries of Latin words, phrases, names etc., which may be sought are alphabetical and abundantly cross-referenced to other entries with a nexus.

An index in Latin under subject matter heads commencing at page 207 narrows the field where there is no memory of the first word of a Latin name, word or phrase in the text and is a memory-jogger generally.

An English index commencing at page 213 is not comprehensive and caters for the situation where there is memory of a word appearing in the text but no recollection of the first word of the Latin entry under which it appeared. Eg., one may wish to check when the Treasury abandoned use of Latin tags but have no idea as to which entry contained this information. The word 'Treasury' in this index will reveal the page number and hence the entry under which this appeared.

A

A bove majori discit arare minor 'a young ox learns to plough from an older one'. Applicable to apprenticeship or a barrister's pupillage. The word plough is from old English. As well as referring to equipment used for turning over soil, it meant in the Domesday book an area of land which could be tilled by a team (usually) of eight oxen in a year. The amount of arable land on an estate was, for taxation purposes, assessed by reference to the number of ploughs. See *fas est*.

Ab alio specta, alteri quod feceris 'look for the treatment you have meted out to others'. A warning to all those in authority: from parents and schoolmasters to judges. See too St. Matthew Ch 7 v 1 and 2. "Judge not that you may not be judged. For with what judgement you judge, you shall be judged: and with what measure you mete it shall be measured to you again."

Ab asino lanam 'from an ass wool'. The Roman could not get wool from an ass just as the Englishman cannot get blood out of a stone. This is the Roman reference to attempting the impossible.

Ab honesto virum bonum nihil deterret 'nothing deters a good man from honesty (honour)'. Seneca. Is the old adage, that every man has his price, incorrect? Note Horace *justum et tenacem propositi virum* 'a man who is upright and steadfast of purpose'. See *dona clandestina, laudator temporis, lucri bonus, nec prece nec pretio, non bene, omnia Romae, pecunia non olet, quid enim, probitas laudatur* and *si possis recte*.

Ab incunabulis 'from the cradle'.

Ab initio 'from the start. From inception, the outset or the beginning'.

Ab origine 'from the very beginning'. The aborigines are the original inhabitants of Australia.

Absit invidia 'let bad feeling be absent'. No offence meant (nearly).

Absit omen 'let there be no (ill) omen'. Do not read anything bad or ominous into what I have just said. Latin brevity at its best.

Ab urbe condita 'from the founding of the city'. Abbreviated to AUC, this refers to the founding of Rome (by *Romulus* see below) in 753 BC, upon which Roman dating was based. Caesar landed in Britain in 55 BC or in the Roman year 699 AUC, though the Romans usually dated by reference to the name of the consuls in office at the time. See *AD, AH, Anno Hegirae, Anno Domini* and *consule Planco.*

A capite ad calcem 'from head to heel'. From top to toe.

Accepta aqua lavit manus coram populo dicens innocens ego sum a sanguine justi hominis vos videretis 'he took water and washed his hands in front of the multitude saying, I am innocent of the blood of this just man: witness (the fact)'. Vulgate. St. Matthew Ch 27 v.24. Reaction of Pontius Pilate (Roman governor of Judaea during the reign of the emperor Tiberius) as the mob screamed for Christ's crucifixion. Source of the expression 'I wash my hands of the whole matter'. But how often can we so easily shrug off moral duty? See *ecce homo, Jesus Nazarenus, quid est veritas* and *quod scripsi.*

Acu rem tangere 'to touch the thing with the pin or needle'. To hit the nail on the head. *Rem acu tetigisti* you have touched the thing with a pin or needle. Plautus. Rudens V.ii.19.

AD See *Anno Domini, AH* and *Hegira.*

Ad Calendas (or Kalendas) Graecas 'at the Greek Calends' (Calends being the first of the month in the Roman calendar). Suetonius (*De Vita Caesarum* lives of the Caesars) tells us that the emperor Augustus often wrote 'they will pay at the Greek Kalends, which meant never, because the reckoning by Kalends is a purely Roman convention'. (Augustus 87). See *ides* and *nones.*

Ad captandum vulgus 'to attract or win over the crowd'. Political or other pandering. Appeal to the caprice of the mob. Promises in the nature of bribery made by politicians, particularly in manifestos at election time, are too often made *ad captandum vulgus.* See *belua multorum, faex populi, profanum vulgus* and *mobile vulgus.*

Addendum 'what is to be added' or 'thing to be added'.
Additional matter (plural *addenda*). Something added or to be added.

Adeste fidelis, Laeti triumphantes 'O come all ye faithful, joyful and triumphant'. First lines of an 18th century hymn sung at Christmas. In the English Hymnal: hymns number 28 and 614.

Ad eundem gradum 'at the same step or pace'. To the same degree. A convoy travels at the speed of the slowest ship: a truism applicable in many circumstances.

Ad gustum 'to one's taste'.

Ad hoc 'to or for this'. For this specific purpose. A committee might be set up temporarily '*ad hoc*' to consider some matter. . . . an *ad hoc* committee. Or there may be an *ad hoc* appointment.

Ad hominem 'to the man or person'. Relating to or associated with a particular person. In decision making or argument, relying upon a person's emotions, characteristics or prejudices e.g., 'I don't accept his defence of greedy bankers: he's a greedy banker himself'. His views are *ad hominem.**

Ad horam 'to the hour'. Punctually.

Ad idem 'to the same'. At one. Coincidence of understanding. See *constat, nemine contradicente* and *una voce*.

Ad infinitum 'to an infinite degree. To infinity. Without limit'.

> 'So naturalists observe, a flea
> Hath smaller fleas that on him prey;
> And these have smaller fleas to bite 'em,
> And so proceed *ad infinitum*'.
>   Jonathan Swift 1667-1745.

See *ubi saeva*.

Ad lib. Abbreviated version of *ad libitum*, meaning 'at will, at pleasure'. In English the expression '*ad lib*' has come to refer to a speech or performance without planning or preparation: something improvised or spoken '*ex tempore*' . . . see below. It is also used in some restaurants. E.g., 'coffee *ad lib*' . . . meaning: as many cups as desired with payment only for the first; as much as you please.

Used also in musical scores to indicate that a part so marked may be omitted or that the tempo is in the discretion of the performer.*

Ad majorem Dei gloriam 'for the greater glory of God'. The Christian society of Jesus' motto. Abbreviated to AMDG. The Order is Roman Catholic, founded in 1534 by the Spanish soldier saint, St. Ignatius of Loyola. The Jesuits.

Ad nauseam 'to nausea'.
E.g., The sermon went on and on *ad nauseam*.*

Ad poenitendum properat, cito qui judicat 'he who decides in haste repents quickly'. Publilius Syrus. Not quite the same in English. Act (marry?) in haste repent at leisure. Often thought of as an old English proverb but the true source may be William Congreve's (1670–1729) 'The Old Bachelor.'

Sharper:
'Thus grief still treads upon the heels of pleasure:
Married in haste we may repent at leisure'.
Setter:
'Some by experience find those words misplaced.
At leisure married they repent in haste'.
Congreve's cynicism finds further outlet in the same work.
'Courtship to marriage, as a very witty prologue to a very dull play'.

See *sapientis est proprium nihil.*

Adulescentem verecundum esse debet 'a young man ought to be modest'. Plautus. Horace speaks of *multum demissus homo,* 'a very modest (unassuming) man'.But beware *malus pudor* 'false modesty' Satires 1.3.53. See *quae fuerant vitia mores sunt.*

Ad referendum 'for further consideration'.

Ad rem 'to the matter or thing' . . . in hand. Pertinent, to the point. *Nihil ad rem.* Nothing to the matter (in hand); not to the point; irrelevant.

Ad unguem 'to the fingernail'. To a nicety, to perfection, flawless. No true artist or craftsman has ever produced anything which he thinks to be *ad unguem.* See *fecit, pax possessori, pinxit* and *salus factori.*

Ad unum omnes 'all to one'. All, to a man.

Ad valorem 'to value'. In relation to or in proportion to value. An *ad valorem* duty or tax will vary according to the value of the item or matter taxed.

Adverso flumine 'against the stream'. Roman equivalent of uphill struggle. The opposite is *secundo flumine* . . . with the stream.

Advocatus diaboli 'devil's advocate'. A name given by the Roman Catholic Church to an official formerly appointed to put the case against a proposed beatification or canonisation. His opposite number was called "*Promotor fidei*" . . promotor of the faith. Contemporaneously with the last revision of the Code of Canon Law in 1983, Pope John Paul II abolished these offices and substituted an elaborate investigative procedure in which those questioned must include some who oppose the proposal. The canonists seem to have advised against the adversarial procedure, something familiar in English law.

The expression 'devil's advocate' in popular usage has come to mean one who urges an opposite view; sometimes one who argues for the sake of argument, taking up an unpopular, absurd or unarguable standpoint. See *opus Dei*.

Aedes Christi 'temple or house of Christ'. Official name of Christ Church, Oxford and explanation of its colloquial name 'The House'. Founded in 1525 by Cardinal Wolsey, it was initially called 'Cardinal College'.When Wolsey fell from power it was seized by King Henry VIII and refounded as 'King's College'. In 1545 however he dissolved King's College and founded it as 'Christ Church'. See *Aenei nasi, Coll. Omn. An.* and *Corpus Christi*

Aegrotat 'he is sick'. Used as shorthand for a doctor's note confirming medical excuse for not doing something or for not undertaking some obligation. A certificate that a student (usually a university student) is too ill to take an examination. Also the name given to an examination pass, sometimes awarded when the student is assessed as good enough but had been too unwell to take the examination.*

Aenei nasi 'of the brazen nose'. Words from which the name of Brasenose College, Oxford (known since the late 18ᵗʰ c. as BNC) is derived. The College was founded in 1509 although a medieval Oxford Hall had previously existed on the site since about 1270. The Hall is thought to have had a brass knocker on its door. In the 1330s rebellious students migrated from Oxford to Stamford in Lincolnshire. A house called 'Brazenose' in Stamford was acquired by the College in 1890 and with it came the knocker thought to have been on the door of the Hall. The College was founded as 'The King's Hall and College of Brasenose' (*aula REGI et Collegium Aenei Nasi* abbreviated to *Coll Aenei Nasi*). The brass knocker, with an exaggerated nose in profile, hangs in the College to this day. See *Aedes Christi, Coll. Om. An.* and *Corpus Christi*

Aequo animo 'with an equal mind'. With equanimity. Composed. See *boni viri arbitratus.*

Aere perennius 'more lasting than bronze'. Horace. Odes III. xxx.1. Horace spoke of his poetry being a monument more lasting than bronze; even than the pyramids! Latin at its succinct best. An expression which cries out for use as the trade name for some durable product. Perhaps it already has been. Cf., *Plus uno maneat perenne saeclo* 'may it live and last for more than a century'. Catullus. See *exegi monumentum, immortalia ne speres, non omnis moriar,* and *qui fugiebat.*

Afflavit Deus et dissipantur. 'God blew and they are scattered'. Inscription on one of a number of medals struck after the destruction of the Spanish Armada in 1588. See Winston S. Churchill 'History of the English Speaking Peoples' Vol II page 204.

Adversaries not infrequently both believe God to be with them. 'Gott mit uns' 'God is with us' said an inscription on the belt buckle of a German soldier killed in Normandy in 1945.

The soldier's prayer of La Hire, a stalwart aide to Joan of Arc, is a delight:

'God, I pray you that You will today do for La Hire what You would wish La Hire to do for You, if La Hire were God and You were a man-at-arms'.

Conjectured role reversal with God is to be seen again in the famous epitaph of Martin Elginbrodde:

'Here lie I, Martin Elginbrodde:
Have mercy o' my soul Lord God,
As I wad do, were I Lord God
And ye were Martin Elginbrodde'.

The prayer of the Royalist Sir Jacob Astley before the battle of Edge Hill in the Civil War (1642-1646) is touching.

'O Lord. Thou knowest how busy I must be this day. If I forget Thee, do not Thou forget me'.

Sir Jacob led the last of the King's troops to be defeated: at Stow-on-the-Wold in 1646. He is recorded as having said to his captors:

'Well boys, you have done your work, and may go home and play – unless you fall out with one another'.

See *Exurgat Deus* and *Ditior in toto alter circulus orbe.*

Agaricus campestris 'mushroom of the plain'.Occurs in short grass in May to November. Very edible. Various sources make it fairly clear that in AD 54 the emperor Claudius was poisoned by a 'mushroom meal' arranged by his wife Agrippina to ensure the succession of her son Nero, who had been adopted by Claudius. Later, after Claudius had been deified, Nero joked that mushrooms were the food of gods. See *amanita phalloides.*

Age dum, mora noxia, cras nil 'do it now. Delay is dangerous. There is no tomorrow'. Inscription in glass on the upper floor of the Old Ashmolean in Oxford. Sound learning for children whose regular plea of 'in a minute' translates as *nunquam* (never). A policy of 'never do today what you can do tomorrow' won't do. Not quite the same as 'he who hesitates is lost'. There is however room here for firm resolution 'when in doubt do nothing'. A policy too of 'shall we make a decision only when we have to' can be valuable, especially where family matters are concerned. So often life works itself out and no decision is ultimately necessary. See *carpe diem, dum vivimus, ille potens, omnem crede, quid sit futurum, rapiamus amici occasionem de die* and *vesper in ambiguo* but cf., *cunctator.*

Agenda 'things to be done', matters to be considered. From *agere* to do.*

Age quod agis 'do what you are doing'. Be focused, concentrate and do not be distracted. Good advice for all, particularly the young and ageing.

Agnus Dei 'Lamb of God'. An epithet used by John the Baptist to describe Jesus Christ. 'The next day John seeth Jesus coming towards him, and saith Behold the Lamb of God *(ecce agnus Dei)* which taketh away the sin of the world'. St. John Ch.1 v 29.

The concept is depicted by a lamb (usually with a halo) bearing a banner emblazoned with a cross. This was the emblem of the Knights Templar and is that of the Honourable Society of The Middle Temple (Inn of Court).

The beginning of the Roman Catholic Mass is: *Agnus Dei, qui tollis peccata mundi* . . 'Lamb of God, who takes away the sins of the world'. The *Agnus Dei* is also a particularly popular part of the Verdi requiem and of J.S.Bach's Mass in B minor. Note too:

'And did those feet in ancient time
Walk upon England's mountain's green?
And was the holy Lamb of God
On England's pleasant pastures seen?'
William Blake 1757-1827. From Milton. Music by Sir Charles Hubert Parry 1848-1918.

See *Dies irae* and *ecce Agnus Dei.*

Agricola 'a farmer'or 'tiller of the fields'. Also the name of the Roman general and most famous governor of Roman Britain. Tacitus was his son-in-law and wrote his biography, '*Agricola*', a part of our national story. Cn. Julius Agricola, AD 40-93, was a soldier and man of honour. Translation of Tacitus' biography is available in Penguin Classics with the *Germania*. See *Clodius Albinus, omne ignotum* and *ubi solitudinem*.

AH Abbreviation of *anno Hegirae*. See *Hegira*.

Albus 'white'. Can also mean bright or serene. *Albus* Dumbledore is possibly the greatest wizard of modern times and headmaster of Hogwarts School of Witchcraft and Wizardry in J.K. Rowling's 'Harry Potter and the Philosopher's Stone'. An albino is one whose hair and skin are white due to an absence of pigment which is congenital.

Aliam excute quercum shake 'another oak'. You'll get nothing more out of me. See *pecunia in arboribus* and *quercus*.

Alias 'otherwise' or 'at another time'. In English this has come to be used so as to mean 'otherwise called or known as', referring to another or an adopted name. Eg., the Duke of Wellington *alias* the Iron Duke, Ulysses *alias* Odysseus, Eric Arthur Blair *alias* George Orwell and Charles Dodgson *alias* Lewis Carroll.*

Alibi 'elsewhere'. In thriller novels (and in the law) one suspected of crime is said to have an *alibi* answer if it can be shown that he was somewhere other than at the scene of a crime when it was committed.*

Alieni generis 'of another or different kind'. The fox is not of the dog family; he is of a different species: he is *alieni generis*.

Aliquot 'some, so many'. An *aliquot* part is one of so many. A known fraction and integral part of a whole. When the estate has been valued you will receive your *aliquot* part.*

Aliter 'otherwise'. A beggar is to be pitied: *aliter* if he holds a knife at your throat. See *dis aliter*.

Alma Mater 'nourishing mother'. The expression is used usually in relation to a person's school, college or university.*

Alta pete 'aspire to high things, aim high'. Motto.Try never to settle for second best.

Alter ego 'other I or self'. An expression often used to refer to the same person in a different status, capacity or even personality. Also an inseparable companion. By day he was a gentleman: by night his *alter ego* was that of highwayman. Not quite the same as 'wearing different hats he performed widely different functions'.*

Alumnus 'foster child or pupil'. Used to describe a graduate or former student of a university or academic institution. Plural is *alumni*. Feminine is *alumna* and feminine plural is *alumnae*.*

Amanita phalloides. Latin classificatory name for a species of fungi, namely a toadstool known as Death Cap. It is very poisonous. Found July to October in deciduous woods. People die too regularly an ugly death from eating it. Symptoms do not appear for several hours after consumption and usually lead to death, there being no antidote. See *agaricus campestris*.

Amare et sapere vix deo conceditur 'to be in love and wise is scarce granted even to a god'. Publilius Syrus. Sententiae. A.22.

> 'But love is blind, and lovers cannot see
> The pretty follies that themselves commit'.
> > William Shakespeare Merchant of Venice Act II Sc.2 ll 37-37.
> 'The course of true love never did run smooth'.
> > William Shakespeare. Midsummer's night's Dream. Act I Sc.1 l 134.

See *militat omnis amans*.

Amor nummi 'love of money'. See *crescit amor, dummodo sit dives, esurientes, inopem me, intolerabilius nihil, lucri bonus, nolite thesaurisare, oportet ergo, pecunia non olet, radix malorum* and *si possis recte*.

Amor populi praesidium regis 'the love of the people is the King's protection'. Legend inscribed on the reverse of angels (i.e. gold coins bearing the figure of an angel) of King Charles I minted at the Tower mint between 1625-43. This inscription appears also on the reverse of the Golden Jubilee £5 Crown of H M Queen Elizabeth II minted in 2002 (instead of *Regis* there is an abbreviated form *Reg* this time of *Reginae*). The Times of 1st January 2002 wrongly reported that this inscription had not previously been used on coinage.

The inscription surrounds the Queen seen on horseback (as, similarly, on the 1953 and 1977 five shilling [25p] crowns minted on the occasions respectively of her Coronation and Silver Jubilee). The monarch had not been seen mounted on horseback since King Charles I: a silver half-crown of 1642 from the Truro mint sees him galloping over armaments apparently on a battlefield. For the Oxford Crown Piece see *exurgat Deus*. See also *civium industria floret, decus et tutamen* and *draco dormiens*.

Amor vincit omnia 'love conquers all'.
See the general prologue to Geoffrey Chaucer's Canterbury Tales 162 where this is the inscription on the prioress' brooch: ' . . . brooch of gold full sheene. On which there was first written a crowned A and after, *amor vincit omnia*'. See *labor omnia vincit*.

Anathema sit 'let him be accursed'. I Cor. XVI. 22. *Si quis non amat Dominum Jesum Christum sit anathema Maranatha* 'if any man love not the Lord Jesus Christ let him be *Anathema Maran-atha*'. Vulgate; King James authorised Bible translation in which the last two words appear as set out. *Anathema* means accursed. *Maran-atha* is not an intensifying word. Rather it seems to stand on its own meaning 'Lord cometh' or Lord come' (from the Syriac maran atha). What is to become of the man who leads his life with as much goodness as is reasonably possible for a mere mortal but who cannot with honesty make that leap of faith which takes him to belief and hence to the requisite love: the troubled agnostic who is not proud of his condition? And what does accursed mean? . . . consigned to eternal hell fire and damnation? St. Paul's directive seems to show him as over zealous and perhaps a little unkind.

Andronicus. See *Titus Andronicus.*

Andronicus Livius. Name of the first known Latin author. A Greek of Tarentium, he was taken prisoner of war and taught in Rome where he also produced Latin versions of Greek plays (circa 240 BC).

Anglice in English. See *Gallice* and *Latine dictum.*

Animus 'intention, spirit or mind'. A sense or feeling: often ill feeling or hostility.

Animus furandi 'an intention to steal'.*

Animus possidendi 'an intention to own or possess'.

Animus revertendi 'intention of turning back'.

Anno Domini 'in the year of the Lord'. Abbreviated to AD. Western calendars calculate passage of time from the birth of Christ. For practical purposes the commencement date is arbitrarily accepted, though there is disagreement as to the exact year. Dating in this way was introduced in the 6th century by a Scythian monk, Dionysius Exiguus.

Whilst AD is abbreviated from Latin, BC is English based: Before Christ. Why is a matter of some mystery. Possibly because *ante Christum* (before Christ) is uncomfortably close to antichrist and, confusingly, would have produced AC.

The letters AD should always be placed before the number and the letters BC after the number.

By the time of Julius Caesar 355 days divided into twelve months constituted the Roman calendar (system by which the beginning, length and subdivisions of the year are made up). But this did not relate to the sun or the moon. In 46 BC Caesar gave the year 445 days to right the discrepancy which had evolved: and, from January 1st 45 BC, he fixed a year at 365 days (the days of each month being much the same as in calendars today). This was called the Julian calendar: thereby a solar system year was exceeded by about eleven minutes. A differential of some ten days accumulated by the 16th century. Pope Gregory XIII omitted ten days from the year 1582 and proposed that thereafter three days be omitted every 400 years.

On September 2nd, 1752 England followed the rest of Europe and converted from the Julian to the Gregorian calendar. The effect was that the next day was September 14th and eleven days were lost! There was rioting in the streets; it is said because it was thought by the *mobile vulgus* that their government had thus shortened their lives. Probably, at a time when labourers were paid a daily wage whilst rents were often payable quarterly, this was as much because most were quick to perceive a serious financial loss to themselves.

During the reign of Augustus the months of *sextilis* and *quintilis* were respectively renamed *Augustus* and *Julius* in honour of the emperor himself and of *Julius* Caesar. That *quintilis* and *sextilis* mean the fifth and sixth month whereas July and August are the seventh and eighth months is explained by the fact that the names of the months were given in earlier times, when the Roman calendar had ten months. This legacy persists and the same explains why the months of September, October, November and December (from the Roman *septem octo novem decem*, seven eight nine ten) relate to the ninth to the twelfth months of the year. See *ab urbe condita, AH, Augustus, Caesar* and *Hegira.**

Anno regni 'in the year of the reign'. Used in relation to the passage of years in a monarch's reign and in particular for the dating of statutes. The words appear on the rim of the Silver Jubilee Crown of King George V minted in 1935 to celebrate twenty five years of his reign: *Anno regni XXV*. This is known as The Rocking Horse Crown: for explanation see *draco dormiens*.

Annus horribilis 'a horrible year'. A year of disaster etc. One to forget. Words used by HM Queen Elizabeth II to describe 1992. However, in addressing HM The Queen and guests at the Guildhall luncheon on 4th June in 2002, her Golden Jubilee Year, the Lord Mayor of London expressed the hope on behalf of her loyal subjects present that the year ahead would be an *annus magnificus* a great or splendid year. See *Domine dirige nos*.

Ante cibum 'before food'. Words, often abbreviated to AC, to be found in medical notes or on prescriptions, denoting that something is to be administered or taken before food. See *BD*, *nocte* and *post cibum*.

Ante meridiem 'before noon'. Abbreviated to AM.

Apollinaris medici Titi imperatoris hic cacavit bene 'Apollinaris physician to the emperor Titus had a good crap here'. Well known graffiti from a latrine in Herculaneum. One has to wonder if the graffito-writer really was the emperor's physician. *Medicus* might have been better grammar. Titus was emperor from 79-81 and Mount Vesuvius erupted in 79 burying Herculaneum. See *apud lapidomurenses, cave canem, Colosseum* and *pecunia non olet*.

Apologia pro vita sua 'explanation for his life'. 1864 autobiography of John Henry (Cardinal) Newman. See *profiscere anima christiana* and *novissima hora est*.

A posse ad esse 'from being possible to being real'. From the possible or the theoretical to reality.

A posteriori 'from what follows or comes after'. Proceeding from effects to causes. See *a priori* and *Quinque Viae*.*

Apostrophus. Latin name given to the symbol or character (a reverse C: thus Ɔ) used in Roman numerals. IƆ is alternative to D in meaning 500. Above five hundred the *apostrophus* may be used in the construction of greater numbers. Since Roman numerals are frequently to be seen on buildings and memorials (and since few can remember them much above fifty . . . L) explanation is set out in Appendix 2. See *numerus*.

A priori 'from what comes before'. From what is already known. The expression is usually used in relation to reasoning. *A priori* reasoning is that whereby deductions are made from what went before, ie., prior knowledge, actual or assumed. Reasoning or arguing from cause to effect. See *a posteriori.* *

"Apud Lapidomurenses primo die capita hominum in latrinas detruduntur," dixit Harrio. "an vis sursum ascendere ut rem ipse experiaris?" "Benigne" inquit Harrius, abnuens. "in latrinam nunquam quidquam tam horribile quam caput tuum detrusum est potest fieri aegrescet".

"They stuff people's heads down the toilet the first day at Stonewall" he (Dudley) told Harry.

"Want to come upstairs and practise?"

"No thanks," said Harry. "The poor toilet's never had anything as horrible as your head down it . . . it might be sick".

From J.K.Rowling's Harry Potter and the Philosopher's Stone (Bloomsbury 1999)

Translated by Peter Needham and later published additionally in Latin as '*Harrius Potter et Philosophi Lapis.*' An apposite reminder for adults of how young children speak to one another.

Roman latrines were communal and in the nature of social centres. "Housteads" (the Roman fort of *Ercovicium* on Hadrian's wall and an English Heritage site) boasts the best known Roman latrines. They are very proud of them and have had the social scene depicted in a picture of which a postcard and a larger poster are available. The fort too is the most complete Roman fort in Britain. It has a museum and commands spectacular views. For those thinking to visit the northern frontier of the Roman empire information may be secured by telephone on 01434 344363. *See Apollinaris medici, Brittunculi, caput draconis, draco dormiens nunquam titillandus, draco Malfoy, nimbus* and *pecunia non olet.*

Aquae Sulis. 'Waters of Sulis'. Roman name for the town of Bath, 'Bath Spa'. Famous for the Great Bath containing hot water from a sacred spring in the Roman Temple of Sulis Minerva. Minerva was the Roman goddess of guilds and trade crafts. See *qui mihi.*

Aqua regia 'royal water'. Name given to a mixture of hydrochloric and nitric acids in which the royal *(regius)* metal, gold, has been dissolved. Platinum may also be similarly dissolved. Listed as in English usage in the main text of Chambers Twentieth Century Dictionary 1974: but hyphenated, aqua-regia.

Aqua scutum 'water shield'. In London's Regent Street of 1851 John Emary opened a shop. Shortly after he developed a rain repellent cloth which remained soft and flexible. He re-named his shop 'Aquascutum'. By the reign of Edward VII Aquascutum coats were the height of fashion. The waterproof cloth served for the making of coats for the Crimea and for both world wars. With the trenchcoat, several royal warrants and shops opened all over the world. Aquascutum went from strength to strength. The motto beneath the shield in its coat of arms is *in hoc scuto fidemus* ('we trust in this shield'. The shield shows a crown with rain falling ineffectively about it). Aquascutum's brand concept is: 'Modern British Classics'.

Aqua vitae 'water of life'. Used as a euphemism for hard drink, especially brandy.* See *merobibus*.

Aquila non capit muscas 'an eagle does not catch flies'. Don't waste time with trivia. A reference also to doing what is beneath one; what is *infra dig*. See *infra dignitatem*.

Arbiter elegantiae 'judge of elegance' (good taste). Said by Tacitus (Annals xvi.18) of Petronius Arbiter (died AD 65). Petronius was a man whose energies in the public service as a provincial governor belied his wit and ultra laid back private lifestyle. He was admitted to the inner circle of the emperor Nero's intimates as, Tacitus tells us, *elegantiae arbiter* (both a description and a pun). He is remembered particularly for his long novel (in prose and verse) 'Satyricon' of which only three of some twenty books survive. In this are the entertainingly written descriptions of a dinner party thrown by one Trimalchio, a freedman (former slave) and parvenu of immense wealth. Portrayed is the obscene vulgarity of ostentatious riches, the absurd conversation, the bizarre food served, the outlandish entertainment and drunken behaviour: the awfulness generally of the episode.

Falsely accused of plotting against the emperor, he was ordered by Nero to take his own life. A remarkable spirit shows in his last actions. He opened his veins, then bound them up and wrote of Nero's worst lewdnesses, detailing the acts and identifying the other participants, male and female. He sent this to Nero, then removed the bindings. Tacitus Annals xvi. 18-19. See *cave canem*.

Arcades ambo 'both Arcadians'. Virgil Eclogues vii. 4. Both of them poets or musicians with an Arcadian pastoral bent see *et in Arcadia ego*. Two with common tastes, musical or professional or with like character; 'muckers'. Since Lord Byron's 'Don Juan' (Each pull'd different ways with many an oath. '*Arcades ambo id est*' . . . blackguards both) the expression has come to be associated with scoundrels and bounders.

Arcadia. See *et in Arcadia ego*.

Arcana imperii 'secrets of authority'. State secrets. See *imperium*.

Arcus (pluvius) ' rainbow'.

'My heart leaps up when I behold
A rainbow in the sky.'
    William Wordsworth.

These lines capture so well the joy of the moment (try to express it in other words which are not workaday or banal) as similarly did those of Lord Tennyson in 'The Lady of Shalott.'

'She left the web, she left the loom,
She made three paces thro'the room
She saw the water-lily bloom.'

See *prima luce*.

Argus. See *quis famulus*.

Arma virumque cano 'arms and the man I sing'. The opening words of Virgil's Aeneid. Among the front runners for world's best and most famous opening words in a literary work. The reader is instantly aware that he embarks upon an epic tale of armed struggle and a man's (Aeneas's) valour. John Dryden (1631-1700) translated the opening lines into English verse:

'Arms and the man I sing; who, forced by fate
And haughty Juno's unrelenting hate,
Expelled and exiled, left the Trojan shore'.

It is the story of Aeneas after the fall of Troy. See *fullones ululamque cano*.

Ars gratia artis 'art for art's sake'. Motto of Metro-Goldwyn-Mayer.

Ars longa, vita brevis 'art is long, life is short'. A familiar Latin phrase based on Seneca Dialogi X.1.1. translating from the Greek physician Hippocrates who is saying that the art of healing outlives the doctor. On qualification some doctors still take the Hippocratic oath. For a version of this oath see Appendix 1.

Asterix Gallus 'Asterix the Gaul'. Leading character in a French comic pictorial series of long standing named after him. With bubble dialogue it is published in French *(Gallice)* and Latin *(Latine)*. In the episodes portrayed Romans are variously defeated, outwitted and humiliated by Gauls (Frenchmen!) and in particular by Asterix whose amazing powers and resource are enhanced by a magic Druid potion called Panoramix.

The fictitious Asterix is a name and creation based probably upon the names of those Gallic leaders who had so fiercely resisted Caesar's conquest and who are mentioned in the *commentarii* (see below): Amborix, Cingetorix, Dumnorix and the redoubtable Vercingetorix. See *Caractacus, de Titini, signa inferre* and *Vercingetorix*.

Atque in perpetuum, frater, ave atque vale 'and so my brother, hail and farewell evermore'. Carmina 101. Catullus. c.84 – 54 BC.

Atrium. The part of a Roman house adjoining the entrance and often a central court. The word is used in English to denote a skylit area frequently arising through more than one storey with galleries and adjoining rooms at each level.*

At spes non fracta 'but hope is not yet broken'. See *nil desperandum* and *dum spiro spero*.

Audaces fortuna iuvat 'fortune helps the bold'. See *audentes fortuna iuvat, fortuna favet fortibus* and *macte nova virtute*.

Audentes fortuna iuvat 'fortune helps those who dare'. Virgil. Aeneid x 284. See *fortuna favet fortibus* and *macte nova virtute*. The motto of the SAS (Special Air Service) is 'who dares wins'. And yet the better part of valour is discretion (Shakespeare. Henry IV Part I). Cervantes wrote that valour lay just half way between rashness and cowardice.

In 1757 a British garrison was besieged in Minorca. Admiral John Byng was sent to relieve it. Finding his ill-equipped and inadequate fleet no match for the French, discretion prevailed and he retired: the island was lost. The public outcry at this national disgrace caused the Government to lose its nerve. Despite intercession with the King by Wiliam Pitt, in one of the most disgraceful episodes ever perpetrated by government, Admiral John Byng was court-martialled for cowardice and shot on the quarterdeck of his own flagship. The incident inspired Voltaire's famous observation (in Candide) that: *dans ce pays-ci il est bon de tuer de temps en temps un amiral pour encourager les autres* 'in this country [England] it is thought a good thing to kill an admiral from time to time to encourage the others'.

The inscription in Southall church, Bedfordshire reads: "To the perpetual disgrace of public justice. The Honourable John Byng, Admiral of the Blue, fell a Martyr to Political Persecution on March 14, in the year 1757. When Bravery and Loyalty were insufficient securities for the life and honour of a naval officer." See *decimare*, *qui fugiebat* and *tempori cedere*.

Auditque vocatus Apollo 'and Apollo hears when called upon'. Virgil Georg., IV. 7.

In Greek mythology Apollo was the son of Zeus and Leto, the god of music, song and poetry, of agriculture, prophecy, healing (see appendix 1) and pastoral life (originally the god of light who made plants grow and fruits ripen, but who never married). Cf., *de profundis*.

Augur. A Roman religious official who drew conclusions as to the gods' disposition by observing signs, particularly the behaviour of birds. Cicero spoke of *malis avibus* . . bad birds . . bad omens and Tacitus records [Claudius 22] that if a bird of evil omen perched upon the Capitol, the Emperor Claudius would go to the Rostrum (orator's pulpit in Rome's Forum) in his capacity as *Pontifex Maximus* (Chief Priest), order artisans and slaves to withdraw, and then read out the prescribed incantation of supplication which the people repeated after him. Hence the expression that something augurs well/badly. In Shakespeare, a soothsayer.

The Romans were strong on portents. Cassius Dio, writing early in the third century, gathered together some contemporary accounts of curious phenomena which preceded the eruption of Vesuvius in AD 79. "Numbers of huge men, bigger than humans . . . . were seen on the mountain (Vesuvius), in the country around and in the cities wandering over the earth day and night and also travelling through the air". See *aureus*, *bonis avibus*, *libra*, *rara avis* and *rostra*.*

Augustus 'reverend, venerable'. Taken in 27 BC as a name and title by the first of the Roman emperors, who was born Gaius Octavianus. On the death of Julius Caesar in 44 BC, Octavianus (whose mother Atia was the daughter of Julius Caesar's sister Julia) was aged only nineteen and succeeded remarkably in a power struggle with those who were seasoned soldiers, politicians and intriguers. He found Rome built of brick and left it built of marble. (Suetonius. Augustus 28). A greater than life-sized bronze head of this emperor (found in the Sudan in 1910) is in the British Museum where the visitor can look close up and face to face into the striking alabaster, glass and coral eyes of a man who ruled most of the known world from 31 BC to AD 14. A full list of the Roman emperors who followed is in Appendix five. For an immensely readable and informative portayral of the times, which brings the past to life, read 'Augustus' a novel by Allan Massie Sceptre 1998.

Caesar Augustus (Octavianus) is often confused with Julius Caesar. See *Caesar*.

The name *Augustus* was adopted by most succeeding emperors. See *Aureus, Caesaris Augusti, denarius, consule Planco, et tu Brute, occasionem cognosce, quoad hanc, triumvir* and *Vare*.

Aureus. The highest denomination Roman coin: it was struck in gold. According to Suetonius (*de Vita Caesarum* . . . Lives of the Caesars, Augustus 94 . . . . published in translation by Penguin Classics as 'Suetonius The Twelve Caesars') the emperor Augustus consulted an astrologer called Theogenes and was so impressed that he published his own horoscope and struck a silver coin stamped with his birth sign, capricorn. In the years 18 BC-16 BC he had the same sign struck on the reverse of gold *aurei:* one is exhibited in the Heberden coin room at the Ashmolean Museum in Beaumont Street, Oxford. See *denarius, libra* and *sagittarius*.

Aurora borealis 'dawn of the north'. Sometimes *aurora septentrionalis.* The northern lights. A luminous atmospheric phenomenon of electrical character seen in and around the polar regions of the earth. That in the southern hemisphere is the *aurora australis.*

Ave atque vale 'hullo and goodbye. Hail and farewell'. See *atque in perpetuum.*

Ave Caesar, morituri te salutant 'hail Caesar, those who are about to die salute you'. Gladiators' salute to the Roman Emperor. Suetonius (*De vita Caesarum* lives of the Caesars Claudius XXI. 6). Gladiatorial contests were prime entertainment in the Empire of Imperial Rome and seem to have been very popular with women, special seating in the arenas being reserved for them. Gladiators (along with charioteers. See *circus*) were pin-up boys of the times.

The barbarism of these contests appealed particularly to the notorious emperors Caligula and Commodus (AD 37-41 and 180-192 respectively) and both are recorded as having performed personally in the arena, though with what degree of real risk to themselves is unclear: the historian Cassius Dio however records that Commodus (armed as *secutor*; see below) killed a tiger, a hippopotamus and an elephant. The civilised emperor Marcus Aurelius (AD 161-180) scarcely concealed his distaste for the obscenity of these "games" but it was rumoured that Faustina, his wife, bore Commodus after a liaison with a gladiator.

The *editor,* (sponsor or producer of the show, see below) who might be the Emperor if he had put on the games and was present, had the power of *missio* (the discharge of a defeated but brave and worthy gladiator with his life), though this decision was usually prompted by the reaction of a discerning crowd. Hollywood has it that this was exercised with a thumb up sign: the thumb down sign signifying death. Whether or not this is right appears to be unknown. To close down the thumb (*pollex premere*) was a sign of approbation. To extend and turn it around (*vertere or convertere*) . . . . so that it pointed in what direction? . . . was a sign of disapprobation. Juvenal Book 3. 36 f.

To be a spectator was no guarantee of safety. It was as well to observe decorum and to keep one's voice down. One citizen, whose witty remark at the expense of the emperor Domitian (AD 81–86) was overheard, found himself dragged from his seat and thrown to dogs in the arena. Suetonius. Domitian 10. See *Colosseum, circus, editor, munera nunc, retiarius, secutor* and *silentium.* See it all in the film "Gladiator" which won such acclaim in 2001.

Ave, Dea: moriturus te salutat 'hail Goddess, one about to die greets you'. Title of a well known poem written by Victor Hugo.

> 'La mort et la beauté sont deux choses profondes . . . . .
> Nous sommes tous les deux voisins du ciel, Madam,
> Puisque vous êtes belle, puisque je suis vieux.'
> 'Death and beauty are two subtle things . . .
> We both my lady are neighbours in heaven,
> For you are beautiful and I am old'.

Victor Hugo 1802 – 1885 was a prolific writer of whom Jean Cocteau said: 'Victor Hugo, un fou qui se croyait Victor Hugo' 'Victor Hugo was a madman who thought he was Victor Hugo'. See *ave Caesar.*

Ave Maria 'hail Mary!' The angel's salutation to the Virgin Mary from St. Luke's gospel 1.28: 'And the angel came in unto her and said Hail, thou that art highly favoured, the Lord is with thee; blessed art thou among women. *Ave Maria, gratia plena, Dominus tecum* . . . 'Hail Mary full of grace, the Lord is with thee'. opening words of the Angelic Salutation or Ave Maria, names given to a prayer dating from the eleventh century. *Ave Maria* has been set to music *inter alios* by J.S.Bach whose composition, arranged by Gounod, is sung as an aria. Also words spoken in telling the rosary.

'But all his mind is bent to holiness,
To number *Ave Marias* on his beads'.
    Queen Margaret in William Shakespeare's King Henry VI Part II.

'As him was taught, to kneel down and saye
His *Ave Maria* as he goth by the waye'.
    The Prioress' Tale 20-21. Geoffrey Chaucer. Canterbury Tales.

See *Magnificat and Pater Noster*.

Avete. Utres sumus 'hail we are all leather bottles'. Graffiti on the tavern of Atticus at Pompeii. *Delirium tremens?* See *delirium tremens*.

B

BD. Abbreviation of *bis die* 'twice daily'. Often found in medical notes and on prescriptions, signifying that the dose of a medicine identified is to be given, or that some therapy is to be administered, twice daily. See *ante cibum* and *post cibum*.

Beatae memoriae 'of blessed memory'. Often seen on memorial plaques.

Beati immaculati in via: qui ambulant in lege Domini 'blessed are they that are undefiled in the way: and walk in the law of the Lord'. Psalm 119. Note 'blessed is he that expecteth nothing for he shall be gloriously rewarded'. G.K. Chesterton. The sadness is, that once apprised of this promise, he that expects nothing cannot help expecting something, so that there may be no reward, glorious or at all; and certainly no lovely surprise. Cf., *integer vitae scelerisque purus*.

Beatus ille qui procul negotiis . . . . paterna rura bobus exercet suis 'happy the man who, far away from commerce, tills with his own oxen the fields his father owned'. Horace Epodes ii.1.Cf., Alexander Pope's Ode on Solitude:

> 'Happy the man whose wish and care
> A few paternal acres bound,
> Content to breathe his native air,
>   In his own ground'.

Written when the poet was twelve years old, the last verse is a touching sadness;

> 'Thus let me live unseen, unknown;
> Thus unlamented let me die;
> Steal from the world, and not a stone
>   Tell where I lie'.   See *o fortunatos*

Bellaque matribus detestata 'wars loathed by mothers'. Horace Odes. 1.i.24-25.

A delightful true story tells of an English prisoner of war circa 1944 who was apprehended by guards whilst attempting to escape. Upbraided by the Italian commandant he was told: "if you had gone another twenty metres my men would have had to shoot you . . . and then what could I have said to your mother?'

The Great War of 1914-1918 inspired young men of a doomed generation to write powerfully of so much awfulness in such lovely poetry. It is invidious to single out some, Rupert Brooke, Wilfred Owen, Siegfried Sassoon and Robert Graves.

> 'If I should die, think only this of me:
> That there's some corner in a foreign field
> That is for ever England. There shall be
> In that rich earth a richer dust concealed;
> A dust whom England bore, shaped, made aware,
> Gave, once, her flowers to love, her ways to roam . .'
>   Rupert Brooke. The Soldier.

For more read 'The War Poets' by Robert Giddings. Bloomsbury 1998. See *dulce et decorum.*

Bellis perennis. Latin classificatory name for the common daisy. Grows in grassy places. Very common. Flowers March to October. A joy or a disaster in lawns according to disposition.

Bellum maxime omnium memorabile quae unquam gestae sunt . . . . Hannibale duce Carthaginienses cum populo Romano gessere. 'The war fought against the Roman people by the

Carthaginians led by Hannibal was the most memorable of all wars ever waged'. Livy, Ab Urbe Condita, 21.1. See *cunctator, delenda est Carthago, fides Punica, Hannibal ante portas, nullus amor populus, puella Carthaginis ridebat* and *summa sedes non capit duos.*

Belua multorum capitum 'the monster with many heads'. Horace Epistles I.i.76. The irrational mob. See *ad captandum vulgus, faex populi, mobile vulgus, plebs* and *profanum vulgus.*

Benedicite omnia opera 'all works bless'. A canticle to be said or sung in English at Morning Prayer after the First Lesson from the Old Testament in accordance with the Church of England Book of Common Prayer. 'O all ye works of the Lord, bless ye the Lord; praise him and magnify him for ever'.

Benedicto benedicatur. See *benedictus benedicat.*

Benedictus 'Blessed'. Name given to a prayer taken from St. Luke 1.68 to be said or sung in English after the Second Lesson from the New Testament in accordance with the Church of England Book of Common Prayer. 'Blessed be the Lord God of Israel: for he hath visited and redeemed his people'.

Benedictus benedicat and **Benedicto benedicatur**. Frequently used short forms of grace said by Christians respectively before and after a meal, the exact meaning of which is unknown to a great many. These translate respectively as: 'may the Blessed Lord bless (our meal)' and 'may blessing be given to the Blessed Lord'. Lest these seem disrespectfully short, they are each sometimes followed by the words: *per Jesum Christum Dominum Nostrum . . .* 'through Jesus Christ our Lord'. Some learning surrounds these forms of grace. For an interesting exposition see The College Graces of Oxford and Cambridge by Reginald Adams, The Perpetua Press 1992 at pages 17,18 and 88. See too *oculi omnium . . .* and *quicquid appositum.*

Beneficium accipere libertatem est vendere 'to accept a favour is to sell one's liberty'. Publilius Syrus. Sententiae B.5. Sleaze politicians never learn. See *non bene.*

Bene merentibus 'to the well deserving'. Motto.

Biblia Sacra vulgata 'Holy Bible (sacred books) made common or public'. The common text. The word Bible is from the Greek biblia meaning books. See Vulgate.

Bis dat qui cito dat 'who gives quickly gives twice'. Quoted in Don Quixote by Cervantes. The recipient of spontaneous quickly given charity is so much better off.

Bis pueri senes 'old men are twice boys'. 'Oh, to be seventy again!' Georges Clemenceau 1841 – 1929 on seeing a pretty girl on his eightieth birthday. In James Agate's diary, 19th April 1938.

Blandae mendacia linguae 'falsehoods of a smooth tongue'. Beware the silver tongued advocate. See *homines enim*

Bona fide 'in good faith'. Genuinely, sincerely, honestly without deception.

Bona fides 'good faith'. An honest or sincere intention.*

Bona fortuna 'good luck'.

Bonis avibus 'with good birds'. With good omens. See *augur* and *rara avis*.

Boni viri arbitratus 'the decision of a fair-minded man'. See *aequo animo*.

Bono animo sis 'be of good cheer'.

'Laugh and the world laughs with you,
Weep, and you weep alone;
For the sad old earth must borrow its mirth,
But has trouble enough of its own'.
Solitude. Ella Wheeler Willcox 1855-1919.

The remainder of this poem should be sought out, read and noted. (It is in Everyman's Book of Evergreen Verse edited by David Herbert. J.M. Dent and Sons 1991).

Boudicca. Actual name of Boadicea.
In the hope of preserving his kingdom, Prasutagus, the King of the East Anglian *Iceni* appointed his two daughters and the Emperor Nero as his joint successors. The *Iceni* had managed peaceful co-existence with the Romans. On his death in AD 61 Rome sought to incorporate his kingdom in its empire. His lands were plundered, his widow Queen Boudicca flogged and her daughters were denied their inheritance and raped: these outrages were with the apparent connivance of the Roman procurator (financial administrator in a Roman Province), one Decianus Catus. The Celts were not intimidated. A spontaneous upris-

ing ensued, led by Boudicca who was joined by the *Trinovantes*. In quick succession Colchester *(Camulodunum)*, St. Albans *(Verulamium)* and London *(Londinium)* were sacked with no quarter given: and the Roman 9th legion was virtually annihilated. Suetonius Paulinus, the Roman governor, who had been campaigning in Anglesey, marched south with a large and seasoned force. The rebels were crushed. Tacitus (Annals of Imperial Rome) records (reminiscent of Winston Churchill circa 1940) that before final defeat Boudicca drove round all the tribes in a chariot with her daughters in front of her.

'We British are used to women commanders in war' she cried. 'I am descended from valiant men! But now I fight not for my kingdom and wealth, I fight as one of the people, for my lost freedom, my bruised body and my outraged daughters'.

Even if not familiar with Virgil's *una salus victis nullam sperare salutem* (below) she knew what to expect from Romans she had humbled and bloodied: she took her own life. Survivors however remained fiercely hostile to Rome only to be hunted down and subjected to a terrible vengeance. This bloodshed ended only with the recall of Paulinus (Decianus Catus had fled in disgrace) to Rome, probably following the entreaties of Julius Classicianus, the newly appointed Roman procurator.

Boudicca's resolute face of destiny, shows in a fitting monument (in her chariot on the Thames Embankment close to Big Ben) to her heroic defiance. It symbolises a spirit of freedom and the need to fight injustice and tyranny whatever the odds or the cost. For more read 'Boudicca' by M.J.Trow. Sutton Publishing Ltd. and 'Boudicca' a novel by Manda Scott. Bantam 2004. See *Britannia*, *Classicianus* and *Trajan*.

Bonum vinum laetificat cor hominis 'good wine cheers the heart of man'. Adage well known in France and appearing in calligraphy on the wall of Restaurant Le Roucanel in Larroque 81140, Tarn, France. See in *vino veritas, nunc bibemus, nunc scripsi totum, nunc vino pellite curas, portant armas* and *solis terraeque*.

Brevi manu 'with a short hand'. Summarily; off hand.

Britannia. The Latin name for Britain when she became a Roman Province in about AD 44. The reverse of some of the Emperor Hadrian's coinage (*sestertii*) portrays a personalised *Britannia* in civilian dress holding out a welcoming hand to the Emperor: other of his coins show her seated with a spear and a shield guarding the frontier. She appears also on coinage of the Emperor Antoninus Pius (AD. 138 to 161) who followed Hadrian.

After departure of the Romans in 410, *Britannia* did not appear again until the reigns of Charles I and II when she shows on the reverse side of copper coinage (especially the halfpenny pronounced 'haypeny') seated beside a shield holding a spear in her left hand and an olive branch in her right, the shield emblazoned with the Union Jack.

Britannia's presence on the reverse of copper coinage was then continuous until late in the reign of George III (in 1797 on a great chunk of copper twopenny piece, known as the 'Cartwheel') when her spear was replaced by Neptune's trident and beneath her appeared waves of the sea and a ship on the distant horizon; emphasising Britain's emergence as a seafaring power. In 1740, to celebrate the anniversary of the accession of the House of Hanover, James Thomson had produced the 'Masque of Alfred' (King Alfred had laid the foundations of the English fleet) and written 'Rule *Britannia*' as the finale (music by Augustine Arne): verse two had perhaps had its effect:

'The nations not so blest as thee,
Must, in their turn to tyrants fall;
While thou shalt flourish great and free,
The dread and envy of them all.
Rule, Britannia, rule the waves.
Britons never will be slaves'.

Not until the halfpennies of George IV in 1826 did *Britannia* acquire a plumèd helmet and later a lighthouse replaced the ship. Between 1860 and 1894, on the 'bun' pennies (penny pieces showing the head of the young Queen Victoria in profile with her hair in a bun) there was both a ship and a lighthouse. *Britannia* remained on the reverse of the penny piece until decimal coinage, when it was replaced by the new penny in 1968.

She reappeared however on the reverse of the then new 50p piece (with no sea, ship or lighthouse, but with a lion sat at her feet she held an olive branch) and, in the Autumn of 1987, a new gold bullion coin was introduced, containing one ounce of 22 ct. gold, called 'The *Britannia*': it has a standing *Britannia* on its reverse (like that on florins of Edward VII 1902-1906 inclusive). Since 1997 this coin has been minted sometimes with *Britannia* in a chariot. She most recently appeared, with trident, helmeted and conjoined with Marianne on the 1904-2004 £5 coin minted to celebrate the 100th anniversary of the Entente Cordiale.

Pound notes issued by the Bank of England pre and post World War II bore a portrait of a bare headed and seated Britannia holding a spear in her left hand and an olive branch in her left. These 'Britannia' £1 notes were discontinued and replaced in 1961 by notes bearing a portrait of H M Queen Elizabeth II.

'Rule *Britannia*' is sung each year in the Royal Albert Hall on the last night of the annual (Sir Henry Wood) Promenade Concerts.

Britannia is the personification of Britain and should not be confused with Boadicea. Too many thought wrongly that it was Boadicea (Boudicca) who featured on the reverse of their coinage. See *Boudicca, Carausius* and *Classicianus*.

Brittunculi. Derogatory word for 'the British'. Found in cursive script on Roman letters and documents (written c. 103 AD on thin slivers of wood) excavated at Vindolanda (a Roman fortress with adjoining settlement) south of Hadrian's Wall. Referring evidently to the local tiresome and often bellicose inhabitants, this word is colourfully translated in the nearby museum as: 'The Bloody Brits'. These fascinating letters deal with many matters of everyday life. Their diverse content represents the earliest written comment of anyone living in Britain. Excavation is ongoing. One passage comments delightfully upon the British fighting man:

Ne nudi sint (?)Brittones. Nimium multi equites. Gladis non utantur equites nec residunt Brittunculi ut jaculos mittant 'the Britons are unprotected by armour (?). There are very many cavalry. The cavalry do not use swords nor do the wretched Britons take up fixed positions in order to throw their javelins'.

For further information see 'Roman Records from Vindolanda on Hadrian's Wall' by Robin Birley (Roman Army Museum Publications 1999) and write or telephone: The Vindolanda Trust, Chesterholm Museum, Bardon Mill, Hexham, Northumberland. NE47 7JN. Tel 01434 344277.

In September 2002 English Heritage announced a seven million pound plan to preserve Hadrian's Wall and turn it into a world class visitor attraction as a historical site. There is concern however that the stunning views of the adjoining countryside will be marred unless the sheep who grazed it, seriously depleted by foot and mouth disease, can be reinstated. See *Apud Lapidomurenses, CL Severa Lepidinae, Claudius Karus, renuntium, salus publica* and *veni vidi vici*.

Brutum fulmen 'a senseless (stupid) thunderbolt'. From Pliny. Natural History 11. xliii. An empty threat.

Bufo bufo 'Toad toad'. Latin classificatory name for the common toad. *Rana* is the Latin for a frog.

C

Cadit quaestio 'the question falls'. The question is at an end. There need be no further discussion/argument. Note too *Roma locuta est: causa finita est* 'Rome has spoken; the case is concluded'. St. Augustine of Hippo. Sermons Bk. 1.

Caeca invidia est 'envy is blind'. Livy, XXXVIII. 49.

Caesar. Literally 'head of hair' (abbreviated from *Caesaries*). Name of an ancient and patrician Roman family. Gaius Julius Caesar is the best known bearer of the name (though a number of portrait busts show his hair combed forwards suggesting a paucity of it and his soldiers in the Gallic triumph sang of him as "our bald adulterer" in the bawdy songs which it was their privilege to sing. Suetonius Julius Caesar 39). As title for the supreme ruler it was succeeded by the word *Augustus* and became more often than not the title of a 'number two' ruler.

The emperor Augustus (63 BC–AD 14), the son of Atia, the daughter of Julius Caesar's sister Julia, was born Gaius Octavianus but changed his name to Julius Caesar Octavianus after Julius Caesar's death in 44 BC, when it was revealed that he had been adopted by Julius Caesar and named as his heir. Later he took the title *Caesar Augustus.*

Kaiser and Tsar are each derived from the word Caesar. Each Christmas there will be heard reference to Caesar Augustus at St. Luke Ch. 2 v.1.

> "And it came to pass in those days, that there went out a decree from Caesar Augustus that all the world should be taxed."

It is not possible here to attempt an exposé of the remarkable life of Julius Caesar the soldier, statesman, writer; brilliant, unscrupulous genius. Read Allan Massie's novel 'Caesar' (Sceptre 1994) and Christian Meier's 'Caesar' (Fontana, 1996). See *anno Domini, Augustus, commentarii, et tu Brute, homines enim, ides, reddite ergo, Rubicon, triumviri, Vercingetorix* and *veni, vidi,vici.*

Caesaris Augusti femina mater erat 'the mother of Caesar Augustus was a woman'. Graffiti from a suburban villa at Pompeii. What is the point made? That the emperor is human even if above himself? Between c.34-28 BC *denarii* (see *denarius*) were minted showing him with divine attributes and by 31BC he was being referred to as *Imperator Caesar Divi Filius* 'Commander Caesar Son of God'. He had initially been seen as a *novus homo!* See below. Or was there no point? Was this mere (drunken) drivel?

In 1926 the emperor Hirohito of Japan's younger brother, Prince Chichibu, went up to Magdalen College, Oxford. There is a well known story, apocryphal perhaps, that at dinner with members of the senior common room he was asked how the many Japanese words which followed his name might translate into English. He explained that what they came to was that he was the Son of God. "Well" responded the President of the college, Sir Herbert Warren, "you will meet the sons of many eminent people here at Magdalen". See *Augustus*.

Campus Martius 'field of Mars'. An open area to the north-west of Rome used in early times for exercising and mobilising the army. Mars was the Roman God of war. Later some imposing buildings were erected upon it. Paris has its Parc du Champ de Mars between the Eiffel Tower and the École Militaire.

Canes timidi vehementius latrant 'timid dogs bark more violently'. Also: *canes timidi latrant vehementius quam mordent . . .* 'cowardly dogs bark more violently than they bite'. *Mutatis mutandis* much the same goes for the bullies of the human race. See *canis ingens* and *cave canem*.

Cani ingenti 'to or for the (an) enormous dog'. Dative form of *canis ingens*. See frontispiece and *canis ingens* below. Note also from the frontispiece *et cani novo parvoque Ivo* and 'to Ivo the new and little dog'.

Canis ingens 'enormous dog'. See *cave canem*. See too: *canes timidi, homini fidelissime, quis famulus, semper fidelis* and *tene me ne*.

Canis in praesepi 'dog in a manger'. The dog which denies hay to the oxen: hay which he cannot eat himself.

Cantabit vacuus coram latrone viator 'the one who travels light (with no money) will sing in the presence of the robber'. Juvenal x.22.

Cantabrigiensis 'of Cambridge University'. One who is or has been at that university is a Cantab. See *Oxoniensis*.

Cantate Domino 'sing to the Lord'. Psalm 98; to be said or sung in English (alternative to *Magnificat* see below) after a Lesson from the Old Testament at Evening Prayer in accordance with the Church of England Book of Common prayer. "O sing unto The Lord a new song:

for he hath done marvellous things". See too Psalms 96 and 149.

Cantuar. Preceded by his Christian name, the signature of the Archbishop of Canterbury. Abbreviation of *Cantuariensis* 'of Canterbury'. There appear to have been two Roman names for Canterbury: *Cantuaria* and *Durovernum*. See *Ebor*.

Capistrum maritale 'the matrimonial halter'. Juvenal 6.43. Juvenal uses the expression when writing about a serial adulterer's prospects of changing his ways.

Capitulum hujus Almae Apostolicae et Metropolitanae Ecclesiae Compostellanae sigilli Altaris Beati Jacobi Apostoli custos, ut omnibus Fidelibus et Peregrinis ex toto terrarum Orbe, devotionis affectu vel voti causa, ad limina Apostoli Nostri Hispaniorum Patroni ac Tutelaris SANCTI JACOBI convenientibus, authenticas visitationis litteras expediat, omnibus et singulis praesentes inspecturus, notum facit: (name of pilgrim) hoc sacratissimum Templum pietatis causa devote visitasse. In quorum fidem praesentes litteras, sigillo ejusdem Sanctae Ecclesiae munitas, ei confero.   Datum

Compostellae die . . . mensis . . . . anno Dni *(sic)* . . . . 'The governing body of this Bountiful Apostolic and Metropolitan Church of Compostela being the guardian of the seal of the altar of St. James the Apostle, in order to provide authentic letters of attendance to all the faithful and pilgrims from the whole world who, moved by devotion or on account of a vow have come to the threshold of the Apostle who is our Patron Saint and guardian of Spain make known to each and every person who may inspect these presents that (*name of person*) has devotedly visited this most sacred <u>shrine because of his piety, on the faith of which</u> I give him these present letters stamped with the seal of the same holy church . . . . given at Compostela (date) (name) secretary to the governors'.

Confirmation appearing on the official certificate given at Santiago de Compostela (in north west Spain) to those who have made the pilgrimage there (to St. James) by foot, horse or bicycle (not motorised transport). It is necessary that they should have travelled at least the last hundred kilometers to Santiago and had their pilgrim's passports properly stamped by the refugios (pilgrim's rests) on the route.
St. James was the first apostle to be martyred. Acts 12 1-2. Tradition, beginning in the 7th century, has it that he preached in Spain: and later

29

suggested that he is buried there, his body having been brought from Jerusalem after his martyrdom. The influence of this tradition was enormous. His shrine at Compostela (Santiago de Compostela – 'St. James of Compostela') became one of the great centres of pilgrimage of the middle ages and he was adopted as the symbol of opposition to the heretic moors. The pilgrim's route across France and Northern Spain is heavily trafficked to this day. The shrine is associated with the pilgrim's hat and staff: and the scallop shell emblem of Compostela.

Some who make the journey to the sacred shrine for recreation, adventure or other secular reason may feel, when the Latin is translated, that they ought not in conscience to accept or to retain such a certificate. See *Finis Terrae* and *Roma semel*.

Caput draconis 'head of a dragon'.
Magic password used in J.K. Rowling's Harry Potter and the Philosopher's Stone (Bloomsbury 1999) to expose a hidden passage behind a hanging portrait. Comparable with 'open-sesame' the magic words which made barriers fly open in Ali Baba and the Forty Thieves (from the Arabian Nights). See *apud Lapidomurenses*, and *draco dormiens nunquam titillandus*.

Caractacus (correct name *Caratacus*). British chief who resisted the Roman invasion of AD 43. After defeat and capture of his capital, Colchester (*Camulodunum*), in the presence of the emperor Claudius and of a young soldier and future emperor Vespasian, he escaped and rallied the Welsh tribes (particularly the *Silures*) successfully until defeat in AD 51 after which he fled to Cartimandua, queen of the *Brigantes*. But the defeated have no refuge (Tacitus). She handed him over to his pursuers and with his wife, children and brothers he was taken in chains to Rome: ready for the invariable fate of those vanquished by Roman armies.

In over eight years however his fame had spread and he was to be displayed to the citizens of Rome who were curious to see this renowned enemy. The crowd witnessed a man in manacles approach the emperor's dais with his head held high. There he stopped to address him with a remarkable dignity and forthright eloquence, cogent yet diplomatic (recorded in Tacitus Book 12. 32). The emperor responded with clemency releasing him and his captive entourage: a unique good fortune for an enemy of Rome. No such mercy was extended to the redoubtable Vercingetorix, King of the Arveni, who had resisted Caesar in Gaul before being forced to surrender in 46 BC. The magnanimous and heroic dignity of his acceptance, after the fiercest of struggles, that all was lost is recorded by Caesar himself in the *commentarii* (7.89).

He (*Vercingetorix*) addressed an assembly (of his allies). 'I did not embark upon this war' he said 'for my own ends but in the cause of liberty in our land. As I must now accept my fate, I place myself in your hands. Make amends to the Romans by killing me or surrender me alive as you think best.' He was delivered up alive to Caesar, then taken to Rome where he was humiliatingly paraded in Caesar's Gallic triumph. Pleas by admiring Romans that he was a man worthy of clemency fell upon Caesar's deaf ears and he was put to death in the *tullianum*, the execution dungeon at the foot of the Capitoline Hill where many state prisoners met their end.

Handsome and brave, proud, dignified and formidable, he had done no more than rally the tribes of Gaul against an imperialist invader. Had the roles been reversed one has to wonder what treatment might have been meted out to Caesar. But he was an aggressor seeking conquest and glory; deserving of a come-uppance at the hands of those he oppressed. Caesar had four triumphs celebrating victories over foreign enemies but none relating to his numerous victories over other Romans.

Note that *Caratacus'* father *Cunobelinus* was Shakespeare's Cymbeline. See *Caesar, Cassivellaunus, una salus, veni,vidi, vici* and *vae victis.*

Caratacus. See *Caractacus.*

Carausius (Imperator Caesar Marcus Aurelius Mauseus Carausius Pius Felix). Name of the Roman commander of the British (North Sea) fleet who, in about 286 during the reign of Diocletian, declared himself emperor of Britain and independent of Rome and had minted coins bearing his image struck at various mints in Britain. He was assassinated in 294 and in 296 the emperor Constantius I came personally to Britain to recover his province from the succeeding usurper, Allectus. A unique gold medallion (part of the Beaurains hoard found near Arras in northern France by workmen in 1922, a fraction of which is on view in the Greek and Roman rooms at the British Museum, room 70) shows the emperor entering London and a grateful personalised Britannia receiving him. See *Britannia, Domitianus* and *prima officina.*

Caries 'decay or rot'. One thinks about tooth rot or decay but in his notes or reports for forensic purposes there is a good chance that one's dentist will refer to *caries.*

Carpe diem 'seize the day'. From Horace's Odes 1.xi. 8. *Carpe diem, quam minimum credula postero. . .* enjoy today; 'put as little as possible trust in tomorrow'. Go for it. Don't miss your opportunities: make hay while the sun shines. Cf., *Rapiamus amici occasionem die* friends, let us grab our opportunity from the day. Horace again. '*Carpe diem*' said Sam Torrance on 8ᵗʰ December 2002 speaking to the Sports personality of the year programme invoking the expression as descriptive of the team spirit which had enabled his Europeans to seize the Ryder Cup.

Even in unpromising circumstances *carpe diem*: see *nil desperandum* below and note that the Chinese character for threat can also mean opportunity. Threat, adversity and opportunity may all be challenges which can be seized. But one must first be aware: 'wachet auf' ('uns ruft die Stimme der Wächter') awake (the watchman's voice calls us). J.S.Bach's lively cantata no. 140 alerts and will produce the necessary purposeful mood. See *age dum, eheu fugaces, ille potens, occasionem cognosce, omnem crede, quid sit futurum* and *ut saepe summa*.

Cassivellaunus. Name of the king of the most powerful of the southern tribes, the *Catuvellauni,* who resisted Caesar's second invasion of Britain in 54 BC. He was forced to come to terms. The events are described in detail in Caesar's *commentarii de Bello Gallico* (Penguin Classics. The Conquest of Gaul. Book 4 11-20). See *Caractacus.*

Casta est quam nemo rogavit 'she is chaste whom nobody has asked'. Ovid Amores 1. viii. 43. Very sad. A proposition might be reassuring, even pleasing: and need not be acceded to.

'Say what you will 'tis better to be left than never to have been loved'.
Willliam Congreve 1670-1729. The Way of the World.

But:

'T''is chastity, my brother, chastity.
She that hath that is clad in complete steel.'
Comus. John Milton.

See *quis custodiet.*

Casus belli 'an opportunity of war. A justification for war. Excuse for war'. It has never been clear whether the *casus belli* of the US/British coalition war against Iraq in 2003 (started by the coalition and not an immediate case of self defence) was because Saddam Hussein was allegedly amassing weapons of mass destruction, because he was a bad man from whose oppression the people of Iraq needed to be liberated or because the USA was anxious to exert some control over that country's oil reserves.

Causa causans 'cause causing'. The real, proximate, immediate or main cause. Much used by lawyers concerned with whether a legal wrong is causative of damage so as to entitle an injured claimant (plaintiff) to compensation or any other remedy. See *causa sine qua non*.

Causa sine qua non 'cause without which not'. Fundamental, if sometimes remote, or distant cause of something. Birth or even conception may be said to be a *causa sine qua non* of death: and this could be taken many stages further back: to Adam and Eve? See *sine qua non*.

Caveat 'let him or her beware'. A warning or proviso. To enter a caveat is to put on record a warning.*

Cave 'beware'. One who keeps 'cave' keeps lookout: especially among small schoolchildren for teacher. In first youth many thought it was spelt KV and had no idea as to what those letters might stand for.

Cave canem 'beware the dog'. Warning found on the wall of a Roman house when the city of Pompeii was excavated in 1748, having been buried by lava from mount Vesuvius which erupted in AD 79: an episode which the elder Pliny sailed to witness and was then overcome and killed by the fumes. Pliny the younger witnessed it from elsewhere and wrote descriptions in letters 6, 16 and 20. Note too: Petronius writing in 1st century AD: *Canis ingens, catena vinctus, in pariete erat pinctus superque quadrata littera scriptum 'cave canem'* . . . . 'a huge dog, tied by a chain, was painted on the wall and over it was written in capital letters 'beware of the dog'. Satyricon. Cena Trimalchionis, 29.1. See *arbiter elegantiae, canes timidi, homini fidelissime, quis famulus* and *tene me ne fugia (m)*.

Cavendo tutus 'safe through being wary'. Motto.

Cave ne cadas 'beware lest you fall'. Roman version of, *inter alia*, 'mind the gap'. Used often as a warning in relation to being toppled from positions of power: how are the mighty fallen. See *contritionem praecedit*.

Cave paratus 'beware but be ready'. Motto. See *nunquam paratus* and *semper paratus*.

Cave quid dicis, quando, et cui 'beware what you say, when and to whom'. Avoid gossip and be discreet in what you say.

'For one word a man is often deemed to be wise, and for one word he is often deemed to be foolish. We should be careful indeed of what we say'.

Analects. Confucius.

Yet it was said of King Charles II (reign 1660-1685) that 'he never said a foolish thing and never did a wise one.' See *et semel emissum, nescit vox, paucis verbis* and *vir sapit*.

Cedant arma togae, concedat laurea linguae 'let arms submit to civil power (to the toga, the civilian), let (military) laurels yield to speech'. Cicero. *De temporibus suis* 'about his (my) times'. Famous observation encapsulating Cicero's belief in republicanism and opposition to rule by the military. The first three words are the motto of Wyoming. See Cicero.

Cena Domini 'the Lord's supper'. Sometimes *coena*.

Certum est quia impossibile est 'it is certain because it is impossible'. *Credo quia impossibile est* I believe it because it is impossible. Based on Tertullian *de carne Christi* 5.

Certum est quod certum reddi potest 'something is certain if it is capable of being made certain'. Adopted as a legal maxim for construing documents in which apparent uncertainty can be resolved by further research.

Cestilia, regina Pompeinarum anima dulcis, vale! 'Cestilia, sweet creature queen of Pompeii, goodbye'. Graffiti at Pompeii in the neighbourhood of Tesmo. Bereft young man's suicide note? Better known perhaps, from 'Attis' a poem of the eternally lovelorn poet Catullus (Caius Valerius c. 84-54 BC), is:

Miser a miser, querendum est etiam atque etiam anime
'oh wretched, wretched soul must I again and again lament?'

But Shakespeare wins the day:

'O! how this spring of love resembleth
The uncertain glory of an April day,
Which now shows all the beauty of the sun
And by and by a cloud takes all away!'
    Porteus in The Two Gentlemen of Verona I:iii. 84.

See *amare et sapere, militat omnis amans* and *temporis ars*.

Ceteris paribus 'other things being equal'.

Cf. An abbreviation of *confer*, which means compare.

Cicero. Name of a Roman lawyer, writer, statesman, philosopher: above all orator and advocate. Marcus Tullius Cicero (106-43 BC) lived through the last tumultuous days of the Roman Republic. A great deal of his prolific work has come down to us. He was a man of huge stature to the vicissitudes of whose eventful life it is not possible here to do justice.

In the turmoil which followed Caesar's assassination Cicero was violent and outspoken in his contemptuous denunciation (published in fourteen orations known as the 'Philippics') of Mark Anthony, a self indulgent and ambitious veteran military commander. Cicero did however misjudge the extent to which the young Octavian, (later Augustus) Caesar's heir, was of like mind. While Octavian opposed Anthony the Republic stood a reasonable chance of survival. When Octavian decided (on 27th November 43 BC) that his short term interests at least lay in allying himself with Anthony, Cicero and his fellow republicans opposing Anthony were doomed: their names went straight onto Anthony's proscription list (see *prescriptio* below). Cicero attempted to escape by sea but was intercepted by soldiers. One licensed stroke of a centurion's sword struck the great man down and ended his life. His severed head and hands were sent to Anthony who caused them to be displayed on the rostra (see below) in Rome: a place which in life had seen the orator at the height of his magnificent powers.

For fuller information read 'Cicero and the Roman Republic' F.R. Cowell. Pelican Books 1956 and 'Cicero' by Anthony Everitt, John Murray (Publishers) Ltd. 2001.

There is much quotation from Cicero below: note in particular *homines enim* and see *cedant arma, cogito ergo, cui bono, De Officiis, etiamsi tacent, fasces, fluctus in simpulo, haec studia, homo cui, inter arma, legem breve, legem idcirco, nemo aspicit, nunquam minus, nosce te, novus homo, o tempora, quis umquam, res loquitur, sapientis est, satis cogito diu, sine amicitia, suo cuique, tempori cedere, ut sementem feceris* and *triumviri*.

Circa 'about'. Abbreviated to c. Denotes uncertainty: especially about a date. *Circa (or c.)*AD 1900 . . . around AD 1900.*

Circus 'ring, circle, circus, assembly of spectators'. The meanings of this word spring from its association with entertainment, especially chariot racing. Circus was the name used for the courses to which the

Romans went to see the chariot races. This mass spectacle, financed by the state, was from the earliest of times immensely popular. Crashes at great speed (*naufragia*) were a regular feature: the noise and resulting carnage were all part of the fun and excitement. Charioteers earned vast sums of money with uncertain prospects of living long to enjoy it. Betting was widespread and fierce: and curses (generally written on sheets of lead and usually buried) were directed to charioteers in an endeavour to rig the races. See *defixio* and *qui mihi* below.

The Circus Maximus in Rome is the most famous site: not built over still, its full extent can be seen. It seated more spectators than the Colosseum which provided competing entertainment of a different but even bloodier kind (see *Colosseum*).

Though there are inaccuracies, the multi-Oscar winning epic film version (made by Willliam Wyler in 1959) of the novel 'Ben Hur' puts over well the atmosphere and gripping excitement of the chariot race. That things never were what they used to be is clear from the lament of the poet Juvenal (c. AD 55 – c. AD 130) in his Tenth Satire 80.

'The public has long since cast off its care: the people that once bestowed commands, consulships, legions and all else, now meddles no more and *(duas tantum res anxius optat, Panem et circenses)* longs eagerly for just two things .... bread and circuses'. See *carcares, Colosseum, naufragia, o tempora* and *qui mihi.* *

Citius, altius, fortius 'faster, higher, stronger (braver?)'. The Olympic motto: known to too few.

Civium industria floret civitas 'by the industry of its people the State flourishes'. To celebrate emergence from the austerities of wartime ended in 1945, the Festival of Britain was staged in 1951. *Inter alia* the Royal Festival Hall was built and the Royal Mint issued a proof (finely minted and highly polished) Crown silver coin (five shillings or 25p decimal) bearing the head in profile of King George VI and with the above Latin inscription cut into its rim which was smooth and not milled. The first English Crown had been minted four hundred years earlier in 1551. See *amor populi praesidium regis* and *decus et tutamen.*

Clare constat 'it clearly appears'. A legal writ for succession to property.

Classicianus. Name of the procurator (financial administrator) for the Roman province of Britain *(Britannia)* AD 61- 65.

'London was a Roman town', said Tony Blair, sowing the seeds of

European monetary union in the run up to the June 2001 general election. There is much evidence of this in modern *Londinium* (in particular in the British Museum and in the Museum of London), but a plaque commemorating Gaius Julius Alpinus Classicianus, to be found set in the Roman wall near the statue of Trajan at Tower Hill (see *Trajan* below), is a fascinating example and a credit to those who caused it to be placed there.

Many, tourists and others, must have read the inscription it bears and felt a wish to know more of a humane man evidently *suaviter in modo fortiter in re* (see below) living in barbarous times.

After the defeat of Boadicea (see Boudicca) Roman vengeance more than matched the ferocity of the rebel Britons, as the still bellicose survivors were savagely hunted down. Newly appointed as procurator, Classicianus reported to Rome that a new governor would be more conducive to peace, since the incumbent Paulinus relentlessly pursued brutal revenge.

The Emperor Nero sent a commission of inquiry. In view of his great victory over the rebels, Paulinus' position as governor was maintained but he was recalled shortly after for failing to terminate hostilities.

Tacitus (Annals of Imperial Rome) tells how in the meantime Classicianus (who was by all accounts not an admirer of Paulinus) passed the word to the Britons that they would do well to keep a low profile, bide their time and await the arrival of a new governor. Publius Petronius Turpilianus succeeded Paulinus and in humane and conciliatory partnership with Classicianus restored peace.

The plaque to the memory of Classicianus followed the finding, during building operations at Trinity Place, Minories in the City of London, of his tombstone in two separate broken parts: in 1852 and 1935 (a middle part is missing). These had been built into the 4th century bastions attached to the wall surrounding London and are now in the British Museum.

Classicianus is thought to have been a Gaul, as was his wife, Julia Pacata.

The Roman occupation was the last time that taxes were gathered in Britain on the instructions of an external administration controlling most of Europe. See *Boudicca, Britannia* and *Trajan*.

Claudius Karus Ceriali suo salutem . . . . Brigionus petit a me domine ut eum   tibi commandaret rogo ergo domine si quod a te petierit velis ei subscribere Annio Equestri centurioni

regionario Luguvalio rogo ut eum commem . . . digneris . . . Qui nomine debetorem me tibi obligaturus opto te felicissimum bene valere 'Claudius Karus to his Cerialis greetings . . . Brigionus has asked me, my lord, to recommend him to you. I therefore ask my lord, if you would be willing to support him in what he has requested of you. I ask that you think him fit to commend him to Annius Equester, centurion in charge of the region, at Luguvalium (by doing which) you will place me in debt to you both in his name and my own. I pray that you are in the best of fortune and are in good health. Farewell brother'.

Addressed to the prefect Cerialis, this is the text of one of the fascinating letters excavated at Vindolanda by Hadrian's Wall: the first written record of everyday life in Britain (c. 103 AD) There is insufficient for it to be said that this was a bit of nepotism or old boy networking, but it looks a bit like it.

Taken from 'Roman Records from Vindolanda on Hadrian's Wall' with permission of the author, Robin Birley. See *Brittunculi* and *Cl Severa,*

Cloaca maxima 'largest or main drain or sewer'. Well known name given to the main drain of Rome's sewage disposal system. Built *circa* 100 BC it discharged into the river Tiber. To this day it is part of the city's main drainage system.

Clodius Albinus. Name of the Roman Governor of Britain (province of Britannia) in AD 193 who, after the shocking public murder by the Praetorian Guard of the decent 'slave to emperor' Pertinax, was proclaimed emperor by the legions he commanded. Coinage so depicting him was minted in Britain. The Praetorians however put the Empire up for auction! Didius Julianus, a wealthy senator, was the highest bidder and became emperor. Feeble and without power base he was quickly and bloodlessly (his own execution apart) removed by Septimius Severus at the head of the renowned Pannonian legions. Other aspirants with more or less equivalent military support were Pescennius Niger, governor of Syria and Clodius Albinus. Severus bought time and Clodius' neutrality by calling him Caesar while he took out P. Niger. Clodius was a respected man from patrician stock and a worthy aspirant. It soon became clear however that he played no part in the dynastic plans of Severus. Clodius' army was defeated near Lyons in AD 197 and he committed suicide. Severus caused his naked body to be laid on the ground so that he could ride a horse triumphantly over it: the

severed head was sent to Rome and the torso thrown into the Rhone along with his wife and sons: *in terrorem* actions of barbaric times.
See *agricola, in terrorem, praetor, una salus* and *vae victis.*

CL. Severa Lepidinae suae salutem.
   iii idus Septembres, soror, ad diem solemnem natalem meum rogo libenter facias ut venias ad nos iucundiorem mihi diem interventu tuo factura si venias.
   Cerialem tuum saluta. Aelius meus te et filios salutat.
   Sperabo te, soror,
   Vale soror anima mea, ita valeam, Karissima et have.
   Sulpiciae Lepidinae
   Flavii Cerialis
   A Severa
'Claudia Severa to her Lepidina, greetings. I send you a warm invitation to come to us on September 11th, for my birthday celebrations, to make my day more enjoyable by your presence. Give my greetings to your Cerialis. My Aelius greets you and your sons. I will expect you sister. Farewell sister, my dearest soul, as I hope to prosper and greetings.
Address:
Sulpicia Lepidina, wife of Flavius Cerialis, from Severa'.
Text of a letter written in the summer of AD 103/104 by Claudia Severa, wife of Aelius Brocchus probably commander of a Roman fortress called Briga (near the not then constructed Hadrian's wall) to Lepidina, wife of Flavius Cerialis commander of another nearby fortress, Vindolanda.
   A piece of fascinating domesticity captured from the distant past.
Note that it was customary for Roman men and women of equal social rank to address one another as brother or sister respectively. Severa was not necessarily the blood sister of Lepidina. See eg., *Claudius Karus.*
Taken from 'Roman Records from Vindolanda' with permission of the author, Robin Birley. See *Brittunculi, Claudius Karus and renuntiam.*

Coccinella septempunctata. Latin classificatory name for the seven spotted ladybird. Very common and very desirable in the garden: its larvae eat aphids.

Cogito ergo sum 'I think, therefore I am (I exist)'. Descartes' famous starting point in 'Discourse on Method'. But what are we? Might the dog not think 'I lift my leg, therefore I am'?
   Much earlier Cicero had written *vivere est cogitare* to live is to think.

39

Disputations v.iii. But Seneca wrote *vivere militare est* to live is to do military service! Letters xcv 1.5.

Cognoscenti 'those who know'. Word used in English to describe those knowledgeable in a field, especially art, music and literature. Connoisseurs. Sometimes also those privy to confidential or classified knowledge. Those 'in the know'. The singular is *cognoscente*.

Coll. Om. An. 'All Souls College' (Oxford). Abbreviation of the Latin name *Collegium Omnium Animarum*. See *Aedes Christi, Aenei Nasi* and *Corpus Christi*.

Colosseum. Name of the ancient stadium (amphitheatre) in Rome, the scene of gladiatorial contests, public executions and countless other barbaric spectacles staged for public entertainment in the heart of the world's most civilised nation. It took ten years to build and was completed in AD 80, the year after the death of the emperor Vespasian. Its inauguration was marked by Titus (son of Vespasian) with one hundred days of games during which appalling numbers of gladiators and wild animals were slain in all manner of permutations of bloody contest. Countless Christians were martyred there, devoured by wild animals: especially in Diocletian's ferocious persecution begun in 303.

St. Ignatius of Antioch was thrown to lions in 107 when Trajan was emperor. The Christians were seen as atheists (they did not worship the deified emperors or the Roman gods) and as a threat to public order. This emperor directed that they were not to be hunted down but, if charges were laid against them and proved, they were to be punished (what charges are unclear). Nero's earlier persecution (before the Colosseum was built) was a diversionary exercise, making them scapegoats for Rome's great fire.

The Colosseum seated up to fifty five thousand (fewer than the *circus maximus*. Chariot racing was the more popular entertainment). A large part of the building is still standing. See *ave Caesar, circus, editor, munera nunc, retiarius, secutor* and *silentium*.

Compos mentis 'having power over mind'. Of sound mind. Having control of mind, sane'. See *mens sana* and *non compos mentis* .*

Commentarii 'commentaries'. Caesar's commentaries on the Gallic war and the civil war (*De Bello Gallico* and *De Bello Civile*). When on campaign both Napoleon Buonaparte and the Duke of Wellington took with them a copy of these works (which are available in translation from

Penguin books as 'Caesar The Conquest of Gaul' and 'Caesar The Civil War'). See *Caesar* and *virtutis fortuna*.

Commune bonum 'the common good'.

Concubina 'concubine or mistress'. In Rome a permanent union short of marriage, in which a man did not wish to accord to the woman even the limited social and legal consequences of marriage, came to be accepted as social fact and was called concubinage. In the early empire legislation forbade marriage between persons of widely differing rank and the only permanent union possible between such persons was concubinage. In other cases concubinage was freely chosen for social reasons. Nor was it always alternative to marriage; a man might not have two wives but there was no reason why he should not have a wife and a concubine or more than one concubine. The emperor Constantine and Christianity brought change.

The concept of concubinage pre-dates Rome.

A child in his scripture lesson once wrote: 'Soloman had two hundred wives and seven hundred porcupines'.

Condimentum 'sauce or seasoning'. The salt and pepper on a meal table are the condiments. See *Liquam*.

Conscia mens recti 'a mind conscious of its own virtue/rectitude'. Ovid. Fasti iv. 311. Not the mind of a smug prig. Ovid tells of a beautiful patrician Roman woman who is able to shrug off false gossip directed against her virtue. See *mens sibi conscia recti*.

Consensus 'agreement'. A general agreement of opinion or testimony. A collective opinion. There is more or less generalised consensus that Hitler was a bad man. See *constat*.*

Consilio et prudentia 'by wisdom and prudence'. Motto.

Consolamini consolamini populus meus dicit Deus vester 'comfort ye, comfort ye my people, saith your God'. Vulgate. Isaiah 40.1. Set to music by Handel in the Messiah; but what exactly does it mean? There is no punctuation in the Latin of the Vulgate. 'Comfort ye my people' means 'give comfort to my people'. Differently punctuated, 'Comfort ye, my people' it might mean 'cheer up, it may never happen'. In 'Eats Shoots and Leaves' (2003 Profile Books Ltd.) at pages 74-75 Lynne Truss points to some interesting biblical punctuation (including this). See *scriptio continua*.

Consortium 'a community or fellowship'. The same word is used in English but tends to be used in reference to those in association for a business purpose or venture, often to take over a company. The Latin plural, *consortia* (consortiums) is optional in English; likewise with *ultimatum*. On 29th June 2001, while giving evidence at the Old Bailey in the trial of Lord Archer for perverting the course of justice and for perjury, Lady Archer said that she did not deliver *ultimata*. See note to appendix 4.*

Constat 'it is agreed'. *Constat inter omnes* . . . 'it is agreed among all'. *Non constat:* 'it is not agreed or is unclear'. See *ad idem, consensus, nemine contradicente* and *una voce*.

Consul. Name given during the Roman Republic to the supreme civil and military magistrates. Two were elected annually by the people from senators. In time of war they held joint command of the army (but see *cunctator*). In Imperial Rome (ie., from circa 42 BC) the office of consul became progressively honorary. See *ab urbe condita, consule Planco, cursus honorum, plebs* and *veto*.

Consule Planco 'when Plancus was consul'. Horace Odes III. xiv. 28. Horace's way of saying 'in my younger days'. In 42 BC Lucius Munatius Planco was consul. This was the year of the battle of Philippi when the twenty two year old Horace fought against the victorious Octavian. See *ab urbe condita, Augustus, me consule, occasionem cognosce* and *qui fugiebat*.

Contra 'against'. Before administering a drug with known side effects on certain people, a doctor will look for *contra* indications in his patient.*

Contritionem praecedit superbia et ante ruinam exaltatur spiritus 'pride goes before destruction and an haughty spirit before a fall'. Vulgate. Proverbs Ch 16 v 18. Source of the English proverb pride goes before a fall.

'Every cocke is proude on his own dunghill'.

John Heywood circa 1497-1580. Proverbs Part 1 Ch X.
See *cave ne cadas*.

Cor cordium 'heart of hearts'. One inscription (chosen by Leigh Hunt) on the tomb containing the ashes of the poet Percy Bysshe Shelley in the Protestant Cemetery at Rome. He drowned while sailing in 1822.

Coriolanus. Name of a great legendary Roman character of whom Livy writes (2.33). He is the leading character in Shakespeare's tragedy of that name. Based upon Plutarch the play tells of the fall of a successful but proud and aloof Roman general. This inspired Beethoven's Overture Coriolan. Opus 62. His real name was Gnaeus Marcius, but he became known as Coriolanus after his feats in capturing the Volscian town of Corioli in 493 BC. See *Titus Andronicus*.

Corona civica 'the civic crown or garland'. The Roman Victoria Cross awarded for personal courage. 'For Valour'. The VC.

Corpora lente augescunt, cito extinguuntur 'bodies grow slowly but decay rapidly'. Tacitus. Agricola 3. Realisation of those past a certain age. See *non sum qualis, senex* and *volo non valeo*.

Corpus Christi 'Body of Christ'. Festival in honour of the Holy Eucharist observed on the Thursday after Trinity Sunday.

At Cambridge there is a college named 'Corpus Christi and the Virgin Mary' founded in 1352 by members of two guilds. Corpus Christi College, Oxford was a much later foundation in 1516 by Richard Foxe, Bishop of Winchester, a man who had been much engaged with secular affairs and who in his old age feared that he had given insufficient attention to successive bishoprics. To compensate he decided to endow a foundation at Oxford for the good of the church and the college he founded narrowly missed being a monastry. The college statutes of 1517 made the first provision at Oxford for the learning of Greek and provided for three readers, whose lectures were to be open to the whole university, in theology, Greek and Latin. See *Aedes Christi*, and *Aenei Nasi*.

Corrigendum 'to be corrected'. Plural *corrigenda*. Errors to be corrected; usually spelling or printing. Cf., and see *erratum* and note to appendix 4.*

Credite posteri 'believe me, you who come after'. Horace. Carmina 2.19.1.

What child ever heeded what a parent says? Until its own experience shows it to be good sense.

'We think our fathers fools, so wise we grow;
Our wiser sons, no doubt, will think us so'.
  Alexander Pope (1688-1744). Essay on Criticism 438-439.

See *est adulescentis maiores, experientia docet,* and *longinquo reverentia*.

Credo 'I believe'. Mozart's Mass in C K257, in which the word *credo* appears many times, is in the Austrian tradition of *credo* Masses.

Credo quia absurdum est 'I believe it because it is absurd'. Tertullian. Based probably on *de carne Christi 5*.

Crescit amor nummi quantum ipsa pecunia crevit 'the love of money increases as wealth increases'. Juvenal 14. 139.
Fat cat beware (*caveat felix obesus*). Most like the idea of riches, but there is abundant warning. The emperor Marcus Aurelius acknowledged with apparent gratitude that his mother had bade him to be far removed from the ways of the rich. (Marcus Aurelius Meditations Book I iii). Christ stated it to be: ' . . easier for a camel to go through the eye of a needle than for a rich man to enter into the Kingdom of God'. St. Matthew Ch 19 v 24.
G. K. Chesterton painted a vivid picture in 'The Aristocrat':
' . . . . . but do not go to stay
At the little place in What'sitsname where folks are rich and clever:
The golden and the goodly house, where things grow worse for ever;
There are things you need not know of, though you live and die in vain,
There are souls more sick of pleasure than you are sick of pain;
There is a game of April fool that's played behind its door,
Where the fool remains for ever and April comes no more,
Where the splendour of the daylight grows drearier than the dark,
And life droops like a vulture that once was such a lark
. . . . . '
But . . . 'Young people, nowadays, imagine that money is everything, and when they grow older they know it'. Oscar Wilde.
See *dummodo sit dives, esurientes implevit bonis, inopem me copia fecit, intolerabilius nihil, lucri bonus, nolite thesaurisare, oportet ergo, pecunia non olet, radix malorum* and *si possis rectis*.

Cucullus non facit monachum 'the cowl does not make the monk'.
Do not be taken in by appearances. The point is made too pointedly in modern times with so much child abuse by clergy. The proverb (in the Latin) is used by Shakespeare in Measure for Measure V.i.261 and in Twelth Night I.v.62-2). Cf. *ne fronti crede* 'do not believe in the face'. See *fronti nulla fides* and *quomodo adulator*.

Cui bono? 'To whom good?'. Who profits?
Cicero. Pro Milone 32 (and again in Pro Roscio Amerino). Who stands to gain? . . . who will benefit? Famous expression from Cicero's forensic

rhetoric. *Cui bono fuerit* 'who stood to gain?' If investigating who may or may not be responsible for something, it is usually useful to ask *cui bono?* The words are often wrongly used intending the meaning: 'what's the good of?' See *Cicero*.

Cui licitus est finis, etiam licent media 'where the end is lawful, the means are lawful'. Jesuit maxim. Very dangerous.

Cum grano salis 'with a grain of salt', With a pinch of salt.
Accept cautiously, with reservation, making some allowance. Don't take too seriously.

Cunctator. One who delays or puts off.
After the disastrous Roman defeats in the second Punic war at Ticinus in 218 BC, at Trebia and at Lake Trasimene in 217 BC and finally at Cannae in 216 BC, each at the hands of Hannibal, Quintus Fabius Maximus was chosen as *dictator* (sole commander in chief: in the Republic consuls were usually joint commanders). He bided his time and allowed the Romans to recover by stalking, threatening and harrassing but never fully engaging the Carthaginian army and its allies in Italy. He was accused of cowardice but his strategy of delay succeeded: *unus homo nobis cunctando restituit rem* 'one man by delaying restored the state' (the verdict of Ennius. Annals xii. 363, a verdict quoted by Cicero eg., *De Officiis* 1.84, Seneca and Virgil). His tactics earned him the name *'cunctator'*.
A Fabian policy in British politics is one which urges cautious socialist progress as opposed to speedy reversal risking civil disorder and possibly revolution. See *age dum, bellum maxime omnia, delenda est Carthago, fides Punica, nullus amor populis, puella Carthaginis ridebat,* and *summa sedes non capit duos*.

Curriculum vitae 'the course of life'. Abbreviated to CV this has come to be used to describe a document summarising what a person has done and achieved. Such a document is needed at various stages of life: applying from school to a university, applying to an employer for a job etc.*

Cursus honorum 'the succession of honours'. An expression descriptive of the prescribed succession of offices through which a Roman, ambitious of public distinction, had to pass. Service in the army followed by *Quaestor* (*Curule Aedile* not obligatory*) Praetor, Consul* and *Censor*.

D

Da mihi castitatem et continentiam, sed noli modo 'give me chastity and constancy but not yet'. St. Augustine of Hippo AD 350–430. Confessions, Book viii, ch. 7.

St. Augustine converted and was baptised in 386. Prior to that he had lived with a woman by whom he had a son, Adeodatus.

Damnatio memoriae 'damnation (condemnation or desecration) of memorials'. Destroying and defacing statues and memorials of a fallen or past régime is a recurring historical phenomenon. Crowd behaviour in Rome after the fall in AD 31of Sejanus, a man who as prefect of the praetorians administered Rome (after the emperor Tiberius had retired to live in Capri) and whose ambition augmented as his scruples deteriorated, is described by the poet Juvenal (10. 58–60):

> 'The ropes are heaved; down come the statues: axes destroyed the chariot wheels and the unobjectionable legs of their horses are broken'.

Denounced by the emperor to the senate for plotting overthrow, Sejanus was executed and his body torn to pieces by the people whose hatred he had incurred.

The expression *damnatio memoriae* was used in an article in the Times by Alan Hamilton on 1st April 2003, a time when effigies and portraits of Saddam Hussein (reminiscent of George Orwell's 'Big Brother') began to be defaced by dissident and brave Iraqis during the US/British coalition war with Iraq. See *merobibus, praetor, rescripsit boni* and *verbosa et grandis*.

Data 'things granted or given'. The word is used in English to denote things or facts which are to be accepted and from which inferences can be drawn or upon the basis of which plans, policies or calculations may be made.*

D.d., See *dono dedit*.

Deciens repetita placebit 'ten times repeated it will still please'. Horace Ars Poetica 365. What might the poet be talking about?! He was in fact comparing poetry with painting.

Decimare 'to kill one in ten by way of punishment *in terrorem*' (see below). Decimate. If Roman legionaries fled the battlefield, they were liable to be rounded up and subjected to this military discipline, *pour encourager les autres*. The procedure meant beating to death with rods.

It must have been difficult in the heat of battle to assess one's chances: better to fight on? . . . or to run with a nine tenths chance of survival if rounded up? Virgil tendered advice: *una salus victis nullam sperare salutem* Aeneid ii. 354 'the only safe course for the vanquished is to expect no safety (mercy)'. In combination with honour this accounted for the defeated Roman's practice of falling on his sword.

In English the derivative decimate is too often erroneously used when annihilate conveys the meaning intended. See *fasces, qui fugiebat, tempori cedere* and *vae victis*.

Decus et tutamen 'an ornament and means of protection'. From Virgil's Aeneid V 262 where Aeneas presents a warrior with a gift, an ornate armoured garment, exquisitely crafted, taken from the vanquished body of Demoleos (an ornament and a protection) described also variously in translation as: 'a handsome thing and a safe-guard in battle' (C. Day Lewis. OUP World Classics): 'his pride and protection in battle' (W.F. Jackson Knight. Penguin Classics).

Decus et tutamen appears as an inscription in lettering cut into the milled edge of current English and Northern Ireland one pound coins. The Scottish versions of this coin bear the inscription *nemo me impune lacessit* 'no one attacks me with impunity'. The Welsh version spurns Latin and favours Welsh: '*Pleidiol wyf I'm Gwlad*' . . . true am I to my country, from the Welsh National Anthem.

In its relation to coinage *decus et tutamen* is better translated as 'an ornament and a <u>safeguard'.</u> When English coins were hand hammered and made from gold and silver a criminal practice grew up of debasing the coinage by clipping or filing metal from the edges.

In 1662 hand hammering was abandoned in favour of manufacture by improved mill and screw presses. To thwart would-be clippers, larger coins were made with the inscription *decus et tutamen* and the regal year cut into the rim: medium sized coins were given a milled edge. Though present day pound pieces are not made from valuable metals, they enjoy still the double protection of milling and rim inscription. The inscription remains because its presence makes forgery more difficult.

During the Commonwealth coins were not generally inscribed with Latin. To the Puritans this smacked of Popery. During the Protectorate on the edge of a rare fifty shilling piece of Oliver Cromwell appear however the words *protector literis literae nummis corona et salus* 'a protection to the letters [on the face of the coin] the letters [on the the rim or edge] are a garland and a safeguard to the coinage'. See too *has nisi periturus* and *pax quaeritur bello*.

De die in diem 'from day to day'.

De Excidio et Conquestu Britanniae 'about the Ruin and Conquest of Britain'. Name of a treatise written by St. Gildas (monk and historian c.493 – 570) about the Celts in Britain from the arrival of the Romans until his time. It is the only contemporary British version of events in this period. It paints a gloomy picture of decadence and corruption in the secular rulers and clergy of the time and is cited by Bede.

De facto . . . de jure 'from or by the fact . . . from or by the law'. A government may rule in reality and fact, even though it has no legal or constitutional right to do so. It is a *de facto* not a *de jure* government.

In Australia there is law governing the rights as between unmarried couples living together, *de facto* spouses. In 2003 an Australian might introduce his lady companion as 'my *de facto* Shiela'.

Defixio 'a curse or spell'. A word rare in Roman usage but see *circus* and *qui mihi.*

De gustibus non est disputandum 'there is no disputing tastes'. Since everyone has his own tastes there is no scope for dispute. Chacun à son gout.

De Heretico Comburendo 'concerning the burning of a heretic'. The name of an English Statute of 1401 (the reign of Henry IV). Probably the most terrible enactment of English history it compelled the burning of heretics at the stake. It was repealed in 1547 after the death of Henry VIII. Historically most notorious in determining the status and hence the fate of heretics was Tomas de Torquemada (1420-98) the inquisotor general of Spain out of whose Holy Office emanated so many adjudications from which followed appalling death. It is however thought that more heretics (in particular Cathars) were burned in France (at the instance of the Dominican Inquisitors) than in Spain. The church burned nobody. The inquisition determined heretic status and the secular authorities then did what was expected. For a tale giving insight into the Spanish Inquisition read W. Somerset Maugham's 'Catalina'. See *tantum religio* and *Te Deum.*

Dei gratia 'by the grace of God'. To be seen on British coinage. *Regina* (queen) *Dei gratia*. Abbreviated usually to *D.G.* eg., *Elizabeth D.G. Regina*. The florins of Queen Victoria (silver two-shilling pieces: twenty pence in decimal coinage) minted in 1849 omitted the words *Dei Gratia* (or *DG*). They carried only the legend *Victoria Regina* and are known as the 'Godless' florins.

In 1948 a penny of King George VI bore the inscription: D:G:BR:OMN:REX:F:D:IND:IMP. An abbreviation of *Dei Gratia Britanniarum Omnium Rex Fidei Defensor Indiae Imperator. . .* 'by the grace of God King of all the Britains (i.e., Britain and all the British Territories overseas) Defender of the Faith, Emperor of India'. When India attained independence in 1949, 'IND:IMP' was removed but what remains (with the later substitution of Regina for Rex) persisted until 1953 when, in the reign of H M Queen Elizabeth II, on account of the changing status of many overseas territories, BR: OMN was removed. See *fidei defensor*.

De jure. See *de facto* above.

De Jure Belli et (ac) Pacis 'concerning the law of war and Peace'. The name of a work written by Huig Van Groot, better known as Grotius, and published in 1625, which earned him the name 'founder of international law': a title which perhaps exaggerated its originality and did less than justice to writers who had preceded him. See The Law of Nations. J.L.Brierly. Oxford University Press. 5th edition at p.28 and *inter arma*.

Delenda est Carthago 'Carthage must be destroyed'. A regular exhortation of Cato the elder (234 –149 BC) in his speeches to the Roman Senate. After a fearsome and protracted struggle Carthage was indeed destroyed in 146 BC. The phrase has come to be used in relation to anything that has to be done whatever the cost. *Delenda est* is an expression particularly appropriate for use by President George W. Bush in relation to terrorism or those producing weapons of mass destruction since the events of September 11th 2001. See *bellum maxime omnium, cunctator, fides Punica, Hannibal ante portas, nullus amor populus, puella Carthaginis ridebat, rem tene* and *summa sedes non capit duos*.

Delirium tremens 'trembling derangement'. Disorder involving one, or more in combination, of delirium, excitement, frenzy, incoherent speech and hallucination, which often involves seeing strange imaginary objects such as coloured spiders and pink elephants, floating or crawling up walls. Usually associated with excess drinking of alcohol and referred to as the 'DTs'.

Also the name given to a Belgian beer, traditionally produced at a family brewery since 1654. Three times fermented, it is very potent. The label depicts the kind of imaginary beasts seen in hallucination by those who have drunk to the point of *delirium tremens.*

Belgium boasts some six hundred different beers.*

De mortuis nil (nihil) nisi bonum (bene) 'Concerning the dead nothing unless it be good'. Don't speak ill of the dead. Derived from a Greek saying but also perhaps in deference to the legal maxim *audi alteram partem* ('let the other party be heard': a canon of natural justice); the dead are not here to be heard in defence of themselves. There is anyway usually no need, for:

'The evil that men do lives after them;
The good is oft interred with their bones;
So let it be with Caesar'.
    William Shakespeare. Julius Caesar. Act III Sc.2 ll 80-81.

Denarius. The name of a Roman silver coin. In 23BC the emperor Augustus reformed the Roman currency. Thenceforth the *aureus* was struck in gold and was the highest denomination. Next was the silver *denarius* of which there were twenty five *(denarii)* to the *aureus.* Thereafter four brass *sestertii* (singular *sestertius*) equalled one *denarius*: two brass *dupondii* (singular *dupondius*) equalled one *sestertius*: two copper *asses* equalled one brass *dupondius*: two brass *semises* (singular *semis*) equalled one copper *as* and two copper *quadrantes* equalled one brass *semis.* One gold *aureus* therefore equalled 1,600 copper *quadrantes.* The departure of the Romans from Britain in 410 was the last time Europe had a single currency.

The LSD of British pre-decimal coinage is Latin related, but not entirely Roman coinage based. The "L" is from *libra* a pound, the "S" from *solidum* (solid, dense, real) shilling and the "D", representing a penny, from *denarius.* See *aureus.*

Note *reddite quae sunt Caesaris* below, where the Vulgate refers to the coin in question as a *denarius.* The authorised King James Bible refers to this in translation as a penny.

In the late empire other Roman coins not mentioned here were introduced: for some see *follis.* See *Aureus, Britannia, reddite quae sunt Caesari, sum tua* and *Vulgate.*

De novo 'anew'. To start all over again may be expressed shortly by use of this expression. Start *de novo.*

De Officiis 'on or concerning duties'. Name of one of Cicero's many works, a copy of which was kept always to hand by Sir William Cecil secretary to Queen Elizabeth I from her accession until his death forty years after. He was a reliable, efficient and intuitive servant of the Queen. See *semper eadem.*

Deo gratias 'thanks be to God'.

Deo volente 'by the wish of God', God willing. Abbreviated to DV. I will see you next year *deo volente* i.e., all being well or provided I am still alive.

De profundis 'out of the depths'. The first two words of the Latin version of Psalm 130 (129 in the Vulgate, below) where the full context is:
De profundis clamavi ad te, Domine. Domine, exaude vocem meam 'From the depths I have cried to thee O Lord. O Lord hear my voice'. These words are sung by Roman Catholics in the burial service at the interment. How many, whatever their denomination, have not, in the hour of real trouble, felt what is expressed in the moving pathos and desperation of these words? Cf., *auditque vocatus.*

Words used by Oscar Wilde as title to a written record and lament concerning the circumstances which led to his imprisonment, during which he wrote so movingly of the human condition in the 'Ballad of Reading Gaol'.

Desine de quoquam quicquam bene velle merere, Aut aliquem fieri posse putare pium 'give up wishing to deserve anything well from anyone or thinking that anyone can be dutiful/grateful'. Catullus lxxiii.

Never expect gratitude. It is a rare commodity. If it comes your way, rate it a bonus of life. 'The still small voice of gratitude'. Thomas Gray. Installation. Ode V. 'How sharper than a serpent's tooth to have a thankless child' observed Shakespeare in King Lear 1.iv.294.

De Titini et Miluli facinoribus 'the adventures of Tintin and Milou' (his dog). A comic pictorial series with bubble dialogue published in France in French *(Gallice)* and Latin *(Latine).*

Detritus 'rubbed off or worn'. A pile or mass that has been rubbed or worn off a solid mass. The same word in English (derived) means matter produced by erosion. Silt or debris. A Crown Court judge will see much of humanity's *detritus.**

Deus dat incrementum 'God gives increase'. One motto of Tonbridge School. The other is: *In Christo Fratres* 'brothers in Christ'. In the 1950s to be learned by new boys *(novi)* upon pain of something akin to death.

Deus deorum Dominus locutus est et vocavit terram a solis ortu usque ad occasum 'the mighty God, even the Lord, hath spoken and called the earth from the rising of the sun unto the going down thereof' (Psalm 49 v. vi in the Vulgate . . . 50 in the authorised Bible). A passage immortalised for its part inclusion in Laurence Binyon's (1869-1943) moving verse 'For the Fallen (September 1914)': read on Remembrance Day.

> 'They went with songs to the battle, they were young . . . .
> They fell with their faces to the foe.
> They shall grow not old, as we that are left grow old:
> Age shall not weary them, nor the years condemn.
> At the going down of the sun and in the morning
> We shall remember them'.

See *dulce et decorum est.*

Deus ex machina 'God from a machine'. A providential intervention or solution, just in time. The explanation of this meaning, apparently unrelated to the Latin, is that in the Greek theatre it was not unusual for a god to be introduced to 'sort things out'. His arrival on the scene was from above and was effected by mechanical means, with machinery.*

Deus misereatur 'may God have mercy', God be merciful. The title to psalm 67. To be said or sung (alternative to *Nunc Dimittis* see below) in English after a lesson from the New Testament at Evening Prayer in accordance with the Church of England Book of Common Prayer. "God be merciful unto us, and bless us: and shew us the light of his countenance . . ." See *miserere.*

De Vita Caesarum 'about the lives of the Caesars'. Suetonius' biography of the Caesars beginning with Julius Caesar. Available in translation. Penguin Classics *sub nom.*, 'Suetonius The Twelve Caesars'.

Deus vobiscum; sometimes *Dominus vobiscum* see below. 'God or the Lord be with you'.

Deus vult 'God wills it'.

Dictum factum 'said, done', no sooner said than done.

In his famous poem *Willkommen und Abschied,* Goethe took this just a little further. *Es war getan fast eh' gedacht* 'it was scarcely thought of than done'.

Dies annorum nostrorum in ipsis septuaginta anni 'the days of our years are three score years and ten'. Vulgate Psalm 89 v.10.

Dies irae 'day of wrath', or anger. The first words of a medieval hymn concerning judgement day. Sung in the requiem Mass. See *Agnus Dei* and *requiem aeterna.*

Digitalis. Literally 'of the finger'. Classificatory name for the foxglove. Extract from this plant is used for treating heart conditions and used to be called plain *digitalis;* but refined variants with differing brand names are now available.

Digito monstrari. Et dicier 'hic est' 'to be pointed out with the finger and to have it said 'it's him.' Persius i.28. To be famous; or notorious.

By successive Home Office Circulars the conduct of police identification parades has become increasingly sophisticated. While circular 9/1969 was in force the witness had to touch the person who he identified on the parade as the perpetrator of a crime in question. Where a witness was nervous or afraid (as when violent or vicious crime was involved) it was however permissible for such a person to be pointed out with a finger.

As to being famous: 'The fame of great men ought always to be estimated by the means used to acquire it'. Francois Duc de la Rochefoucauld 1613 – 1680. Much the same perhaps goes for wealth. 'Fame is no plant that grows on mortal soil'. Lycidas. John Milton. See *exegi monumentum, dummodo sit* and *si monumentum.*

Dimidium facti qui coepit habet: sapere aude 'to have begun is half the battle: be sensible and bold'. Horace Ars Poetica 40. We all put off disagreeable tasks with escapist mental excuse. The thing is to be strong minded and sensible and to get them started. Usually they turn out not to be so bad as we had thought. The old adage, that 'the road to hell is paved with good intentions', is surely well founded. See *non omnia possumus.*

Dis aliter visum 'it seemed otherwise to the Gods'. Virgil. Aeneid (ii) 428. He was such a decent chap that he didn't deserve such bad luck but *dis aliter visum.*

John Dryden translated these words loosely as: 'Heav'n thought not so'.

Discite justitiam moniti 'be warned and learn justice'. Virgil Aeneid 6.620. Inscription written above the entrance to the old courts in the Town Hall of Oxford.

Ditior in toto non alter circulus orbe 'no other circle in the whole world is richer'. In about 1590 a medal of Queen Elizabeth I was cast in gold by Nicholas Hilliard the court goldsmith and painter of miniatures. It was to mark the relief and security felt in England following the destruction of the Spanish Armada in 1588. The Queen is shown crowned, with orb and sceptre, surrounded by the above Latin inscription.

On the reverse is portrayed a small town on an island from which grows a bay tree (a symbol of security because it was thought then that it was not susceptible to damage from lightning) and the Latin inscription: *Non ipsa pericula tangunt* 'not even dangers touch it': symbolic of post Armada England. One of these medals is in the Fitzwilliam Museum, Cambridge and gilt reproductions used to be, but are no longer, obtainable there. This medal is however reproduced on the cover of "Tudor England" by S.T.Bindoff. Pelican History of England series. See *afflavit Deus et dissipantur* and *semper eadem*.

Domine dirige nos 'Lord guide us'. The City of London's motto. Prominent on the City's coat of arms heading the menu of the Guildhall luncheon given for Her Majesty the Queen on 4th June 2002 in her Golden Jubilee year. The wine with each of the three courses was: Sancerre Domaine de la Moussiere Mellot 2000, Chateau Leoville Barton 1989 and Delwhinnie 15 years old. See *annus horribilis*.

Domine labia nostra aperis et os mea annuntiabit laudem tuam 'O Lord open thou our lips and my (our) mouth shall proclaim (show forth) thy praise'. Words sung in English as an antiphon by priest and congregation as part of the liturgy for Morning and Evening Prayer in the Church of England Book of Common Prayer.

The words feature in C.S.Forester's epic novel 'The Gun' which portrays the struggle of Spanish resistance to Napoleon's occupying armies with the aid of a massive eighteen pounder gun. Inscribed round the muzzle in metallic relief were the last five words of the above expression suggesting that it was one of a pair of such guns. The Latin was translated for the peasant partisans by the Roman Catholic priest, Father Prieto.

Dominus custodiat introitum tuum et exitum tuum 'may the Lord preserve thy going in and thy coming out'. From the Vulgate Psalm 121.8. Words cut into the face of stone steps in front of the entrance to the University Church of St. Mary the Virgin in Radcliffe Square, Oxford. Placed with laudable strategic skill they are visible only to those exiting the church who are about to step over them for the second time.

Dominus illuminatio mea 'the Lord is my light'. Motto of Oxford University. Less well known are the words (from Psalm 26.1) which follow in the Vulgate: *Dominus illuminatio mea, et salus mea, quem timebo?* 'the Lord is my light and my safety, whom then shall I fear?' The mottos of both Oxford and Cambridge look to the Deity. 'Educate without religion and you get clever devils' said the Duke of Wellington. *Nihil sine Deo* or *sine Deo nihil* (without God there is nothing) are not uncommon mottos. See *hinc lucem, in principio* and *lux mundi*.

Dominus vobiscum 'the Lord be with you'. Words used *(inter alia)* as a refrain in Gregorian chants usually with the response *et cum spiritu suo* 'and with thy spirit'. See *Deus vobiscum* and *Missa in Dominica Resurrectionis*.

Domitianus. Name of a forgotten Roman emperor. His head, featuring on a coin found near Oxford, made a big splash on the front page of The Times for 25th February 2004 and caused great excitement among historians and archaeologists. He fits into a troubled period of the Roman Empire. The emperor Valerian struggled for years to contain Persian advances in the east. In AD 260 however his army was beset by plague and he was forced to seek terms. With an imprudently small retinue he sought to parley, only to be seized by the dishonourable Shapur. Thereafter he was humiliated (made *inter alia* to serve as a human footstool for the Persian king to mount his horse), brutalised and eventually put to death and his preserved body publicly displayed *in terrorem*. Christians, who he had resolutely persecuted, thought this the wrath of God and a deserved come-uppance. His son, Gallienus, continued with an on-going separate struggle to contain Germans on the Rhine and the Danube, but was outshone by the military success of one M. Cassianius Latinius Postumus, a Roman governor of southern Germany whose soldiers proclaimed him emperor.

Postumus re-established the Rhine frontier and cleared the western provinces of foreign invaders. By 262 he was recognised as emperor of

Gaul, Britain and Spain and Gallienus, left in the west only with Italy, failed to dislodge him. The provinces comprising this area became known as The Gallic Empire. It lasted nearly fifteen years and was presided over by what used to be thought to be five emperors in succession: Postumus, Laelianus and Marius, all murdered in 269. Victorinus followed (not recognised in Spain, which returned its allegiance to Rome) but indulged a disagreeable habit of molesting and sometimes raping his courtier's wives. This he overdid, was killed and succeeded by one Tetricus, for whom a wealthy benefactor bought support from the legions.

Defeat of Tetricus by Aurelian in 274 brought an end to the Gallic Empire. Domitianus probably ruled this empire at some stage during the period 271-274 possibly for a very short time. The coin evidencing his existence (beautifully struck and preserved) uses the imperial title (*IMP.C. Domitianus P.F.AVG imperator* 'emperor, Caesar' . . . *pius, felix, augustus* 'dutiful, happy, Augustus') and was displayed in the British Museum during early March 2004 when acquisition by Oxford's Ashmolean Museum was anticipated.

Domitianus is not here described as Domitian II since he is associated only with the breakaway Gallic Empire. There was of course a previous Domitian, emperor AD 81-96. See *Carausius.*

Domus Anguli Puensis 'The House at Pooh Corner'. Latin translation of A.A. Milne's English text of October 1928 first published in Latin by Methuen Children's books 1980. See *Winnie ille Pooh.*

Domus Dei 'house of God'. The Domesday Book was drawn up by 1086 on the orders of William I (of Normandy, the Conqueror) and written the following year in Latin and in a semi-cursive script (remarkably by one scribe). A register of all land in England, its ownership, value etc., intended for taxation assessment purposes, it is a unique record of the times. 'Domesday' may owe its name to the authoritative finality of its content (it was for long the final proof of legal title to land) or to where it was initially kept, in Winchester Cathedral (*Domus Dei*).

It is now kept at the Public Record Office in Kew.

Domus et placens uxor a home and a pleasing wife. Horace Odes 11.xiv.21-22. On the whole humans are little different from birds. They look for a mate with whom to make and share a nest. Horace's observation is not sexist for the converse is true. Most look for an agreeable and supportive companion with whom to face life's vicissitudes. Horace was in fact talking of what he must leave when death came. Kathleen Ferrier's 'What is life' from Gluck's Orfeo ed Euridice comes to mind: the distressed anguish of separation conveyed on a recording which, in the 1950s, outsold all contemporary popular music and, preceding by only a short time the tragedy of her own premature death in 1953, mirrored the feelings of her adoring audiences.

Dona clandestina sunt semper suspiciosa 'secret gifts are always suspicious'. In modern times such gifts seem usually to involve brown envelopes. See *lucri bonus, nec prece, omnia Romae, pecunia non olet* and *si possis recte*.

Donec eris sospes, multos numerabis amicos 'While all goes well (you will be fortunate) you will have (count) many friends'. Ovid. Tristia 1.IX.5.

A friend in need is a friend indeed. See *felicitas multos, dummodo sit* and *tempora si fuerint nubila*.

Dono dedit 'given as a gift'. Often written in the front of a book given as a present. Usually abbreviated to 'd.d.' See *e libris* and *hic liber*.

Draco dormiens nunquam titillandus 'never tickle a sleeping dragon'. Essential Latin for every child; to be learned by heart from the earliest age. More than the motto of Hogwarts, the school for wizards in J.K.Rowling's Harry Potter and the Philosopher's Stone' (a school not for Muggles and accessible by steam train from platform nine and three quarters at London's King's Cross Station) it may spark youthful inter-est in learning Latin and is a more compelling caution than the dull Latin quasi-equivalent *quieta non movere* 'not to move things that are settled'; or even the English, let sleeping dogs lie; leave well alone.

St. George may have to be called upon if the warning be not heeded. Since 1817 his struggle with a dragon has been depicted on the reverse of English gold and silver coinage. The famous design is by Benedetto Pistrucci. It was in 1817 also that the twenty shilling (one pound) gold piece (the sovereign) replaced the golden guinea (twenty one shillings or 110p decimal): though barristers continued to charge their fees in guineas (multiples of twenty one shillings, not gold coins!) until the advent of decimal coinage on 15th February 1971. The only departure from Pistrucci's design is on the five shillings piece issued by the Royal Mint in 1935 to commemorate twenty five years of King George V's reign. This was Britain's first commemorative coin, known as the Rocking Horse Crown because a solid almost Teutonic St. George is seen riding over a dragon which lies with the curve of the rim beneath him. If today's one pound pieces were minted in gold, they would be worth very approximately £75.

Harry Potter and the Philosopher's Stone (Bloomsbury Publishing PLC 1997) is published also in Latin. See *amor populi*, *Anno regni*, *apud Lapidomurenses*, *Caput Draconis* and *quieta non movere*.

Draco Malfoy 'dragon Malfoy'. Name of Harry Potter's arch rival in J.K. Rowling's Harry Potter and the Philosopher's Stone.

Dramatis personae 'persons of the drama'. Usually applied to a play but may apply to a book, poem, film etc. The expression is generally applied to a list identifying such persons.*

Duas tantum res. See *circus*.

Dubitante 'doubting'.

Dulce et decorum est pro patria mori 'it is sweet and honourable to die for one's country'. Horace Odes III.ii.13. The very different reality is powerfully put in Wilfred Owen's 1917 poem *'Dulce et decorum'* and A.P.Herbert's 'Beaucourt Revisited'.

'If in some smothering dream, you too could pace
Behind the wagon that they flung him in . . . .
If you could hear at every jolt, the blood
 Come gurgling from the froth corrupted lungs
. . . My friend you would not tell with such high zest
To children ardent for some desperate glory,
The old Lie: *dulce et decorum est*
Pro patria mori'.

Wilfred Owen was killed just one week before the armistice, aged twenty five.

'The new troops follow after, and tread the land we won,
To them is so much hillside re-wrested from the Hun;
We only walk with reverence this sullen mile of mud;
The shell holes hold our history, and half of them our blood'.

A shortened form *pro patria mori* is frequently used on the gravestones of those fallen in battle. 'Mort pour la France' is commonly seen on the graves of French soldiers. See *bellaque matribus*, *Deus deorum* and *requiem aeterna*.

Dummodo sit dives, barbarus ipse placet 'if he be only rich even a barbarian pleases us'. Ovid. The most unattractive of men may become acceptable when they become rich or famous.

'They who are of opinion that money will do everything may very well be suspected to do everything for money'. Lord Halifax 1633 – 1695. Every man has his price. 'As a general rule, nobody has money who ought to have it'. Benjamin Disraeli 1804 – 1881. As another general proposition, 'those who have amassed great wealth in one generation have, for the most part, been none too scrupulous in how they went about it'. Anon. See *donec eris* and *felicitas multos*.

Dum spiro spero 'while I breathe I hope'. Inscription on English coinage struck at Pontefract Castle during the Civil War after King Charles I had been captured by the Parliamentarians.

Hope is as essential to life as daily bread.

'Hope springs eternal in the human breast;
Man never Is, but always To be blest'.
   Alexander Pope 1688-1744.

'While there is life, there's hope he cried;
then why such haste?' so groaned and died'.
   John Gay 1685-1732.

'Hope, like the gleaming taper's light
Adorns and cheers our way,
And still as darker grows the night
Emits a brighter ray'.
   Oliver Goldsmith (see *nullum quod tetigit*).

In William Shakespeare's King Richard III, Richard, then Duke of Gloster, pressed the recently widowed Lady Anne Neville (daughter of Warwick the Kingmaker) for her hand in marriage. Despite his entreaties and denial that he had killed her husband or was the blackguard she thought him, she deferred any decision:

Duke of Gloster. "But shall I live in hope?"
Lady Anne. "All men I hope live so".
   Act I Scene II.

Claire Bloom plays Lady Anne in Sir Laurence (Lord) Olivier's masterpiece of a film Richard III.

'I still retire each night with hope to see the morning'.

The emperor Hadrian as an old man from 'Memoirs of the Emperor Hadrian'. Marguerite Yourcenar. Penguin Books 1959.

BUT:

> 'They are countless, voiceless, <u>hopeless</u> as those fallen or fleeing on,
> Before the High King's horses in the granite of Babylon'.
>   G.K. Chesterton. 'Lepanto'. See *vivat Hispania*.

See too *at spes non fracta*, *nil desperandum*, *nunc demum redit animus*, *post mortem patris* and *spero meliora*.

Dum vivimus, vivamus 'while we live let us live'. Epicurian motto. See *age dum*, *gaudeamus igitur*, *ille potens* and *carpe diem*.

Dux femina facti 'the leader of the enterprise a woman'. Virgil Aeneid, (i), 364.

Venus told Aeneas of Dido's spirited qualities. Shame that Barbara Cassani's burgeoning enterprise ("Go" no frills airline) should have been wrested prematurely from her in May of 2002. She came quickly back however to lead the London 2012 Olympic bid.

E

Ebor. Abbreviation of *eboracensis* (of York) and signature of the Archbishop of York (preceded by his Christian name). The Roman/Latin name for York was *Eboracum*.

Ecce Agnus Dei 'behold the lamb of God'. The English is set to music in Handel's Messiah. The Latin (from St. John's gospel see *Agnus Dei* above) is etched as an inscription, midst elaborate decoration, on the steel breastplate forming part of the armour of Jean Parisot de la Valette, Grand Master of the Knights of the Order of St. John of Jerusalem. He wore the armour during the Sultan Suleiman's great siege of Malta in 1565: possibly the greatest feat of resolute bravery and endurance in history. The armour is to be seen in the armoury, forming part of the Grand Master's Palace, Merchant's Street, Valetta, in Malta. See *Agnus Dei*, *Masada*, *plus quam valor* and *vivat Hispania*.

Ecce cor meum 'behold my heart'. Inscription on Sir Paul McCartney's coat of arms. Also the name of an oratorio written by Sir Paul during the illness of Linda McCartney and first sung by the choir of Magdalen College, Oxford in November of 2002.

Ecce gubernator semi-coronam furcavit 'lo the governor forked out half a crown'. A schoolmaster's reaction in the early 1950s to a pupil who surprisingly topped the three weekly Latin orders and who had announced that it was timely, since his father was to visit at the weekend.

Half a crown was a pre-decimalisation silver coin representing two shillings and six pence or twelve and a half post decimalisation (new) pence. The purchasing power of half a crown then was the equivalent of something well over £2 in 2004.

Ecce homo 'behold the man'. The words spoken by Pontius Pilate as he showed Christ to the mob, wearing a crown of thorns: they are used as the title to a number of paintings depicting Christ so attired. Note the first verse (and triumphant accompanying tune . . . not reproduced here) of hymn number 147 English hymnal. T. Kelly 1769-1854.

'The head that once was crowned with thorns
Is crowned with glory now:
A royal diadem adorns
The mighty victor's brow'.

See *accepta aqua*, *Jesus Nazarenus*, *quid est* and *quod scripsi*.

Editor. One who publishes or exhibits: who produced or organised games, including gladiatorial contests in the Roman amphitheatres. See *Ave Caesar, Colosseum, morituri te salutant, retiarius, secutor* and *silentium*.

Ego ero post principia 'I will keep behind the first rank'. Terence.
I will keep out of harm's way. Not ultimately possible. Our seniors pass away and we move inexorably into the front rank of life.

Ego et Rex meus 'I and my king'. An expression used by Cardinal Wolsey, relating to King Henry VIII. When Wolsey fell from royal favour, this was used against him: he had got above himself and even suggested perhaps that the King might be his subordinate. Note Shakespeare's King Henry the Eighth III. II. 313-316: allegation of the Duke of Norfolk against Wolsey:

"Then, that in all you writ to Rome, or else
To foreign princes, *Ego et Rex meus*
Was still inscribed; in which you brought the King
To be your servant".

See *Laus est facere* and *legatus a latere*.

Egomet mihi ignosco 'I pardon myself', I don't care what I do: I do it my way: I do my own thing. Horace.

Ego sum pastor bonus et cognosco meas 'I am the good shepherd and know my own'. St. John's gospel Ch 10 v.14.

Ego sum via et veritas 'I am the way and truth'.
Inscription written on the painted ceiling of the village church at Ceserano in the Tuscan Hills of Northern Italy. The church was badly damaged by earthquake in October 1995 but has been restored. See *fortis est, lux et, magna est, quid est* and *veritas*.

Eheu fugaces, Postume, Postume labuntur anni 'alas, Postumus, Postumus, the fleeting years slip by'. Horace Odes II xiv. 1-2.
A useful quotation for use by the ageing to greet friends whom they have not seen for a long time. Postumus is one to whom the lament is addressed. Note Ovid's less flamboyant contribution; *labitur aetas* 'time glides away'. 'Man that is born of a woman hath but a short time to live, and is full of misery': a part of the order for the burial of the dead in the Church of England Book of Common Prayer. Note The Book of Job Ch 14 v 1: 'Man that is born of a woman is of few days, and full of trouble'. See *age dum* and *carpe diem*.

Elegantiae arbiter. See *arbiter elegantiae*.

E libris sometimes **ex libris** 'from the books (of)'. Appears usually on book labels followed by the owner's name showing that the volume comes from his library or collection. Lawyers reading in the Inner Temple library will find older books labelled: *Ex libris bibliothecae Interioris Templi* 'from the books of the Inner Temple library': usually followed by the date.
'I hate books; they only teach us to talk about things we know nothing about'. Jean-Jacques Rousseau 1712-1778. See *dono dedit* and *hic liber*.

E mare libertas 'from the sea, freedom'. Inscription on Sealand's coat of arms.
In the North Sea, about seven nautical miles from England's coast (and just north of the Thames estuary), lies a small island. During world war II it was fortified by the British. After the war the admiralty withdrew all personnel. Outside the then three mile limit of UK territorial waters, deserted and abandoned, it became *terra nullius* (land subject to nobody's ownership). In September 1967 one Paddy Roy Bates, a former English Major, and his family occupied the island and settled

there. Shortly after he proclaimed it a sovereign state, 'The Principality of Sealand' presided over by 'Prince Roy of Sealand'.

In 1968, after armed challenge to British naval units entering its territorial waters, Sealand's sovereign status was *de facto* upheld in the English courts, to which Roy had submitted as a UK citizen. It was not part of the UK and no other state claimed it.

In 1975 a constitution was proclaimed and in due course it acquired a flag and a national anthem: stamps, passports and coinage (gold and silver Sealand dollars) followed.

During 1978, in Roy's absence, some Dutchmen with a German company, took the island by force. Roy returned, captured it and took prisoner the usurpers. Governments of the Netherlands and Germany sought their release and appealed to the UK, which declined involvement for want of jurisdiction over an independent state. A diplomat had to be sent to Sealand from Germany to negotiate release.

Despite increases in the range of territorial waters vis-à-vis the UK and *vice-versa* Sealand continues as an independent sovereign state.

Emeritus 'having served his time'. An expression used of one who has served his time and retains his title as an honour. Generally in universities: e.g., *emeritus* professor.

In 2003, for gallantry in Iraq, Christopher Finney received the George Cross. Had this reflected bravery in face of the enemy, instead of friendly American fire, it could have been a Victoria Cross. Is one who attacks even mistakenly not a *de facto, pro tempore* enemy? Not much ingenuity or legal fiction was needed to award a VC. In any event, as suggested by Mr. Graham Housam (letter to the Daily Telegraph 3rd November 03), by that stage of the Iraq conflict the American arm of the US/British coalition's practices might properly have warranted the designation 'honorary enemy' or 'enemy *emeritus*'. See *praemonitus praemunitus.*

Eo nomine 'in that name or character'.

E pluribus unum 'out of many one'. Motto of the United States of America. A single nation emerged from the unification of many states. But how many want to see its application to a federal Europe?

Ergo 'therefore'. See *cogito ergo sum.**

Ergo bibamus 'therefore let us drink'. See *in vino veritas, nunc est bibendum, nunc scripsi totum pro . . .* and *nunc vino pellite curas.*

Erratum 'an error'. An error in writing or printing. The plural, *errata*, is often used in a list of corrected errors attached to a book etc. Cf., *addendum* and *corrigendum*.*

Esox lucius. Classificatory Latin name for the pike, a predatory fresh-water fish.

Esse quam videri bonus malebat 'he preferred to be good rather than to seem good'. Sallust Catiline 54. Of Cato.

Est adulescentis majores natu vereri 'it is for a young man to rever-ence his elders'. Cicero. From pre-christian Rome. Compare:
> 'Honour thy father and thy mother: that thy days may be long upon the land which the Lord thy God giveth thee'.

One of the ten commandments at Exodus 20 v.12: and at Christmas:
> '. . . And through all his wondrous childhood
> He would honour and obey
> Love and watch the lowly maiden
> In whose gentle arms he lay'.
>> From Hymn number 605 in the English Hymnal. Once in Royal David's City. Mrs. C.F. Alexander 1818 – 95.

But see *credite posteri* and *maior e longinquo reverentia*.

Est egentissimus in sua re 'he is in dire financial straits'. He has a pension with Equitable Life! (in 2001-2004). Cf., *res angusta domi* hard times at home. Juvenal iii.165.

Est in Britannia flumen quod appellatur Tamesis 'there is in Britain a river which is called the Thames'. Caesar. See *Britannia*.

Est modus in rebus 'there is a right proportion in things'. Horace Satires I.i.106.

Moderation in all things. There is a delightful example in Sir Gawain and the Green Knight. After Sir Gawain had struck off the head of the mystical and splendid Green Knight, visitor to King Arthur's court (with the latter's own great axe and at his challenging request) and after this visitor had gathered up and walked off with his own severed head, the assembled company was quite traumatised until the King directed Sir Gawain (gracefully!):

> 'Now Sir, hang up your axe: you have hewn enough'.

The intriguing fourteenth century tale is available in Penguin Classics translated engagingly by Brian Stone. See *ne quid nimis*.

Esurientes implevit bonis, et divites dimisit inanes 'he hath filled the hungry with good things and the rich he hath sent empty away'. From the Vulgate: Book of Common Prayer translation. Part of the Magnificat. See *crescit amor nummi, inopem me copia fecit, intolerabilius* and *Magnificat*.

Et al 'and others'. Abbreviation of *et alii, et aliae, et alia* the masculine, feminine and neuter forms respectively.

Et cetera 'and other things', the rest. Abbreviated to *etc*.

Etiamsi tacent, satis dicunt 'even if they are silent, they say enough'. Cicero.

To be punished for dumb insolence was permissible in the army if a displeased senior (usually a sergeant major), in his absolute discretion, chose to think silence to be impudent or challenging. Note legal maxims relating to silence of an accused in court (eg, *qui tacet consentit* and *qui non negat confitetur*) are in John Gray's Lawyers' Latin. Robert Hale 2002.

Et in Arcadia ego 'and in Arcadia I'. Translation is debated. Goethe and others have taken these words to mean: 'I too was in Arcadia'. In a letter to The Times of 27th Jan 1982 L.A. Moritz of University College, Cardiff asserted that the only possible translation is 'Even in Arcadia am I'. (Arcadia is the Greek name for a place of rural peace and tranquillity in the Peloponnese). It is a colourful phrase, mysterious and a source of fascination to many, which has become associated with tombs, skulls and Arcadian shepherds. In two of Poussin's paintings shepherds are depicted reading the words carved on a tomb. (One painted in 1626–8 hangs in Chatsworth House, Derbyshire. The other, 'The shepherds of Arcady' is in Paris, in the Louvre).

The association with death may go back to Virgil's tenth Eclogue, which placed Arcadian shepherds in an Arcadian landscape. A painting by Guercino in the Galleria Corsino in Rome bears the title *'In Arcadia ego'*.

In 1816 Goethe used the phrase as the motto for his 'Travels in Italy'. Book one of Evelyn Waugh's 'Brideshead Revisited' is titled *'Et in Arcadia ego'* and contains a skull related episode.

In the early days of the the the law's *'Mareva Injunction'* (now to be called a 'freezing order') Lord Hailsham asserted that such injunctions 'could not be allowed to flourish independently in the *Arcadia* of the commercial list without being applied in the High Court generally'. See The

Siskina [1979] AC 210 at 262. Did he mean Arcadia? Utopia? It is hard to see a connection between the Commercial List and either death or the peace of Arcadian rural landscape.

P&O in 2001 advertised cruises to 97 inferentially Arcadian destinations if you join their cruises on Arcadia.

The association with death may be based on the thought that Arcadia would be a nice place in which to die: equally the point may be made that death cannot be escaped even in Arcadia.

Et regat illas in virga ferrea quam vas figuli confringentur 'and he shall rule them with a rod of iron; as the vessel of a potter shall they be broken to shivers' (small pieces or smithereens). Vulgate Revelations 2.27. Source of the expression 'rule with a rod of iron'.

Et semel emissum volat irrevocabile verbum 'and once uttered a word flies, never to be recalled'. Horace. A word spoken in anger may be regretted and not meant, but it is seldom forgotten by the recipient of the venom. Horace was very aware: *nescit vox missa reverti* 'a word once uttered cannot be recalled', he wrote also (Ars Poetica 390). A writer should edit many times before offering for publication. Nine years was the period he suggested for mulling over and revision! See *cave quid dicis*.

Et seq. Abbreviation of *et sequentia*. And the following things. And what follows.

Et tu Brute 'And you, Brutus!' From Shakespeare's 'Julius Caesar' reflecting Plutarch's account of Caesar's murder in 44BC. From a source unknown Shakespeare attributes these words to Caesar on seeing Brutus among his assassins. Caesar had regarded Brutus as an honourable man to be trusted. His therefore was 'the unkindest cut of all' (Act III. ii. 188).

According to Suetonius Caesar in fact said 'and you my child (son)': and he said it in Greek. (Suetonius. Julius Caesar 82).

Suetonius states too that Caesar spoke to Marcus Brutus. However Decimus Brutus (a relative of Marcus Brutus) was also among the assassins and was a man in whom Caesar had placed great trust; who had accompanied Caesar to the senate house on the day of his murder. Caesar's third wife, Calpurnia, sensed omens and begged him not to go to the senate that day.

Caesar's first wife Cornelia died. Pompeia, his second, was divorced, since, according to Plutarch 'The wife of Caesar must be above suspicion' (see too Suetonius Julius Caesar 74). Yet Caesar himself was a rampant Lothario from whom nobody's wife was safe (Suetonius Julius Caesar 49 – 52). See Caesar above.

Between Caesar's murder in 44 BC and AD 235 at least fourteen of the Roman emperors were executed, murdered or committed suicide.

The expression '*et tu Brute*' is used to denote betrayal by a trusted friend and in this is loosely comparable with 'thirty pieces of silver' an expression used in relation to one not to be trusted and derived from the price paid to secure betrayal of Christ by Judas Iscariot. See *Anno Domini, Caesar, fide sed cui, occasionem cognosce, ides, Rubicon, triumviri* and *veni, vidi, vici.*

Et vera incessu patuit dea 'and in her walk it showed; she was in truth a goddess'. Virgil Book 1 405. Part of a description of Venus, mother of Aeneas. Perfect words for a young man of romantic disposition. Inspired translation (there are many and varied others) courtesy of the Concise Oxford dictionary of Quotations second edition 1981. OUP. Cf.,

'She walks in beauty, like the night
Of cloudless climes and starry skies;
And all that's best of dark and bright
Meet in her aspect and her eyes'.
Lord Byron 1788 – 1821. 'She walks in Beauty' 1815.

The story of Agnes Bernauer, preserved from the second half of the 15th century in German (especially Bavarian) folk-song and legend and in Friedrich Hebbel's play which bears her name (1851), portrays the tragedy too often inherent in beauty. The prince Albrecht is smitten by Agnes the burgher's daughter. This cannot be and Agnes' awful fate is sealed by powers beyond the control of a temporarily absent and later anguished Albrecht. There is foreboding in the talk of noblemen:

' . . . wunderschön, das ist wahr!
Und der Engel von Augsburg, das ist auch wahr!' 'stunningly beautiful, that is true and the angel of Augsburg, that is true as well'.

And the prince Albrecht's reaction:

' . . wenn auf dem Wege zu dir ein Himmelswagen flammend vor mir niedergefahren wäre, jeder Radnagel ein Stern, ich wäre nicht eingestiegen' 'if on the way to you a heavenly carriage, all aflame, the nail of every wheel a star, were to descend in front of me, I should not get in'.

Did Hebbel borrow from II Kings 2 xi ?

'and . . there appeared a chariot of fire and horses of fire, and parted them both asunder and Elijah went up by a whirlwind into heaven'.

See *plenus et optabilis, quam pulcher es* and *muscosi fontes.*

Exacta diligentia 'with precise diligence', or with appropriate prudence.

Ex abundanti cautela 'from an abundance of care'. One concerned for the safety of his house from burglary might have search lights in the garden, an alarm system, a mobile telephone, five lever locks on all doors, iron grills on the windows, several big fierce dogs and, strategically placed on the bedroom wall, a rapier and a mediaeval mace . . . *ex abundanti cautela!*

Ex cathedra 'from the chair'. If the Pope speaks 'ex cathedra' to the faithful, he may sometimes speak with infallibility; and the chair from which he speaks is the Papal throne. An expert, speaking knowledgeably in his field may be said to speak '*ex cathedra*'. . . with full authority. The expression may however be used sarcastically to question the pretensions of one who is suspected of knowing little of what he is talking about.*

Excelsior 'higher', more exalted. Motto of New York State.

Excelse means loftily. Judges should beware lest they behave *excelse*. It may help to avoid saying: not one jot or tittle: I am much obliged: there is not one *scintilla* (see below) of evidence: it matters not: beyond peradventure: abundantly clear and so be it.

Exceptis excipiendis 'the requisite exceptions being made'.

Exeat 'let him go out or forth'. An expression used originally in relation to a priest's absence from a diocese or monastry. Used in the case of absence from a school or college.

Exegi monumentum aere perennius 'I have erected a monument more lasting than bronze'. Horace. Odes III. xxx.I. Horace refers to the lasting nature of his poetry. See *aere perennius, digito monstrari, non omnis moriar* and *si monumentum.*

Exempli gratia 'by the sake of an example'. To give an example. Abbreviated to *e.g.,* for example. Used in English to introduce an example.

Exeunt 'they go out'. Used as a stage direction in the text of a play to denote that two or more actors leave the stage. The singular is *exit* he goes out. *Exeunt omnes* they all go out. See *exit* below.*

Ex gratia 'from favour'. As a favour and not from obligation. A payment is often made *ex gratia* to conclude a dispute but, at the same time, to make clear that liability is denied and to avoid payment of any litigation costs.*

Ex hypothesi 'from the hypothesis' (proposed).*

Exit 'he goes out'. Used in English to denote a way out or the route by which a building can be left. See *exeunt*.*

Ex libris. See *e libris*.

Ex officio 'from one's office'. By virtue of one's office or status. On account of a person's office or status he may be entitled to sit on a committee or be afforded some other privilege, favour or position.*

Exordium et praefatio 'introduction and preface'.

Experentia docet stultos 'experience teaches fools'. Those who can be told nothing must learn the hard way. But: 'We learn from experience that men never learn anything from experience'. George Bernard Shaw. See *fas est*, *credite posteri* and *senex*.

Ex post facto 'from what is done after'.*

Exsultate Jubilate 'exalt be joyful'. Name of an exhilarating and tuneful motet written by W.A.Mozart (1756-1791) in 1793 (K 165/158a) for the composer and singer Venanzio Rouzzini. Now it is usually sung by a soprano voice: particularly pleasingly by that of Emma Kirkby.

Extant 'they are standing out'. The following matters are '*extant*' outstanding or still to be dealt with. A document still existing or surviving is *extant*.*

Ex tempore 'from or out of time'. Extemporaneously. On the spur of the moment. Unpremeditated. To speak *ex tempore* is to speak off the cuff, without preparation. A judgement given immediately at the end of a court case is given *ex tempore*.*

Exurgat Deus et dissipentur inimici eius 'let God arise and let his enemies be scattered'. Psalm 68. 1. Inscription chosen by King James I and on his early English coins. Words also on the banner of Cl. Ridgeley

69

in the civil war of 1642-1645. Standards and banners of the civil war are on view in the British Museum.

These words (not *eius*) were also inscribed on the reverse of the Oxford Crown Piece struck at the Oxford Mint by Thomas Rawlins in 1644 during the civil war when King Charles I had made Oxford his capital. The King is seen mounted on a charger with the City of Oxford visible between the legs of his horse in the distance. One of these coins is displayed in the Heberden coin room of the Ashmolean Museum, Beaumont Street, Oxford. Bullion for coinage minted during this time was obtained by requisitioning silver plate from the colleges of the university. See *afflavit Deus et dissipantur, amor populi, quae Deus conjunxit* and *ut Rex noster sit Noster Rex*.

F

Faber est quisque fortunae suae 'each man is maker of his own fortune'.
Proverb quoted by Sallust *De Republica*, 1.2. 'God helps them who help themselves'. English proverb: quite often a matter of being sufficiently hard working and industrious. See *per ardua ad astra*.

Fabulae Faciles 'easy fables or stories (myths)'. A first Latin Reading Book remembered by senior citizens. It was written by Mr. F. Ritchie and published in 1880. Since no authentic and easy text suitable as a First Latin Reading Book had come down from the Romans, Mr. Ritchie told the stories of Perseus, Hercules, the Argonauts and Ulysses in 'relatively' simple Latin. His initial version has been revised after some vehement criticism and illustrations were added in the 1951 edition. Published by Longman it was used in conjunction with Kennedy's Shorter Latin Primer to which it refers: another well remembered volume, too often damaged by schoolchildren so as to read: 'Eatin Primer' (and even 'Shortbread Eatin Primer'). Older generations may have memories stirred, happily or otherwise, by names such as *'Paginae Primae'* a first Latin course by F.R.Dale and G.G. Henderson published by Blackie and Son in Dec 1932: Hillard and Botting and North and Hillard. By 1950 there had been many editions of the last identified two, published by Rivingtons. See *Latium, locus classicus, oratio obliqua* and *vivat lingua Latina*.

Facit indignatio versum 'indignation instigates (makes) verse'. Juvenal. I.79. How much literature and how many letters to the newspapers are prompted by indignation or a sense of outrage? *Indignatio* sparked the writing of 'Lawyer's Latin' (see preface) and was thus the *sine qua non* of this book. See *ubi saeva*.

Facito aliquid operis, ut semper te diabolus inveniat occupatum 'keep doing something so that the devil will always find you occupied'. St. Jerome . Two English proverbs along the same lines are: 'The devil tempts all, but the idle man tempts the devil'. And 'The devil finds work for idle hands' (of which latter almost certainly St. Jerome is the source).

St. Jerome is the patron saint of librarians. But remember:

'The devil can cite scripture for his purpose'.
William Shakespeare. Merchant of Venice Act 1 Sc.3. l. 98.

Cf., from the pre-christian era: *res age tute eris* do something and you will be safe. Ovid. See *Biblia sacra vulgata* and Vulgate.

Fac simile 'make or do like'. An exact copy. Facsimile.*

Facta non verba 'deeds not words'. Motto. Cf., *lingua factiosi, inertes opera* 'all talk and no action'. In the vernacular 'all piss and wind'.

"Our England is a garden, and such gardens are not made
By saying 'Oh how beautiful' and sitting in the shade".
Rudyard Kipling.

Kent, with its neatly tended hop fields and orchards, was (?) the Garden of England. See *facito aliquid*.

Fac totum 'do all, everything'. Factotum. An employee, or member of some families, who does everything. Cinderella is a famous factotum.*

Facultas (Iuridica) Polonorum in Universitate Oxoniensi 'the Polish faculty of Law in the University of Oxford'. Inscription on a brass plaque at the rear of the law faculty board room in Oxford. Between 1944-1947 there was such a faculty situated in Oriel College and 266 students were awarded degrees.

After the German invasion of Poland a large number of Poles came to England and, following some political pressure, a number of them were accepted into Oxford University. See F.H.Lawson. The Oxford Law School 1850-1965 OUP.

Faex populi 'the dregs of society'. The scum of the earth.

71

The 'sans culottes'. Humanity's detritus. See *ad captandum vulgus, belua multorum capitum, mobile vulgus, plebs* and *profanum vulgus.*

Fama clamosa 'a noisy rumour, current scandal'.

In 2002 was revealed a practice of shredding damaging documents by large ostensibly reputable institutions and their professional advisers for concealment purposes. In 2003 persistent rumour focused attention on some leading wall Street and London investment banks and on accountants. Charged with investigation of this *fama clamosa,* the New York State attorney-general, Mr. Eliot Spitzer, became their scourge and a household name.

Fama nihil est celerius 'nothing is faster than rumour'. In Virgil's Aeneid (iv.174) rumour is referred to (in different words) as being speedier than any other evil.

Fasces. The name given to the bundle of rods carried in Rome by the *lictor* (see below) as a symbol of his power. A symbol of power generally. More specifically, the rods symbolised beating. The *fasces* included an axe when carried outside Rome or by Roman armies (with *SPQR* see below) on their standards. The axe symbolised execution so that the *fasces* served at once as a warning to enemies and as a perpetual reminder to legionaries that retreat may render them liable to decimation (see *decimare*).

In 73 BC Spartacus, the rebel gladiator from Thrace in the Balkans, escaped with seventy comrades from his gladiatorial school, then, with consummate resource and administrative skill, raised, trained and equipped an army in the dense forests around Vesuvius. A small Roman army (three thousand strong), sent to bring him and his renegades to heel, was routed and the *fasces* taken: that it should be in the hands of rabble caused outrage in Rome. Spartacus inflicted four further defeats on Roman armies before he was finally overwhelmed in 71 BC and killed and the *fasces* restored to Rome. He did well to fall in battle: six thousand of his comrades were captured and crucified on the *Via Appia* (the Appian way) between Capua and Rome. Note Virgil; Aeneid iii 354 *una salus victis nullam sperare salutem* 'the only safe course for the vanquished is to expect no safety (mercy)'.

A victorious Roman general, saluted by his troops as *Imperator* (chief), had his *fasces* crowned with laurel. '*Concessos fasces laureatos tenui*' 'I held the grant of laurelled fasces'. Cicero. Pro Ligario 7.

Mussolini's fascist party in Italy took the *fasces* as its symbol and the word fascist is derived from it. See *Caractacus* and *vae victis*.

Fas est et ab hoste doceri 'it is right to be taught (learn) even by (from) the enemy'. Ovid. Met. Iv, 428. In the adversarial system of the English courts the advocate regularly learns from the enemy; to his and his client's cost but to his long term gain and that of subsequent clients. This is called experience.

'A man cannot be too careful in the choice of his enemies'.
   Oscar Wilde.

See *a bove* and *experentia docet*.

Fecit 'he made'. Followed by a name, this is used to indicate who was the maker of some object e.g., a piece of furniture or pottery. An early example, *Fecit Clementius* 'Clementius made it', appears in cursive script on a Roman flue tile, the last of a kiln load (in the Silchester Collection of Antiquities. Excavation began in 1865 and has been ongoing). Writ large and flamboyant the signature speaks as to the commendable pride of Clementius in his product.

On the moulded stem at the foot of the brass lectern in the chapel of Queen's College, Oxford is inscribed: *Gulielmus Borroges Londini me fecit AD 1662* 'William Burroughs of London made me in 1662'. See *ad unguem, pax possessori, pinxit* and *salus factori*.

Fecundi calices quem non fecere disertum? 'who is not made eloquent by (full cups)'? Horace, Epist.; 1.v.19.

How much more readily does the average Englishman speak his awful French when well plied with wine: and how many likewise fortified hold embarrassingly forth at dinner parties? See *in vino veritas*.

Felicitas multos habet amicos 'good fortune has many friends'. So too has prosperity which frequently goes hand in hand. See *donec eris* and *dummodo sit dive*s.

Felix, heu nimium felix 'happy alas! Too happy'. Virgil. Blissful happiness seldom lasts long; and how many who know it for a moment wonder: can this really be true? The French poet Alphonse De Lamartine 1790-1869 expressed it well:

'Ne pourrons-nous jamais sur l'océan des âges.
Jeter l'ancre un seul jour?' 'can we never cast an anchor into time's ocean for a single day'?

See *militat omnis amans*.

Felix qui nihil debet 'happy is he who owes nothing'. With the UK government's 2004 attitude to undergraduate funding too many graduates will be quite old before they stand any chance of achieving happiness. And with banks lending up to six times earnings by way of mortgage, many may never achieve it. See *quid faciam*.

Felix qui potuit rerum cognoscere causas 'lucky is he who has been able to understand the causes of things'. Virgil: Georgic. ii. 490.

Ask a doctor what causes a cross section of diseases and too often the reply will be 'aetiology unknown' (we don't know).

Felo de se 'felon concerning himself'. One who commits suicide. A suicide.

Felo (onis), 'felon' (ie., one who has committed a felony, broadly a serious crime). *Felo* is French medieval Latin of unknown origin.

Following review of procedures relating to powers of coroners and death certification by the team set up after conviction of Harold Shipman (the serial killer doctor) it was proposed on 30th August 2002 that the expression "death by own actions" should replace the word 'suicide'; so that the stigma attaching to suicide should be removed. Suicide was the intentional killing of oneself and, until the Suicide Act of 1961, was a serious crime: self murder with the awful consequence that a failed attempt meant prosecution. 'Suicide' as a possible verdict for coroner's juries however remained and often involved detailed and protracted investigation of the deceased's intent distressing to relatives. The proposed terminology would include the cri de coeur which went wrong and remove any issue as to a deceased's real intent to kill himself.

Fere libenter homines id quod volent credunt 'men believe willingly that which they want to accept'. Julius Caesar. *De Bello Gallico* III. xviii 7.

Men willingly believe what they want to believe. 'Peace in our time' said Prime Minister Neville Chamberlain after appeasing Hitler at the Munich conference of 1938. Too many believed him: with terrible memories of 1914 – 1918, what they desperately wanted to believe. See *commentarii*.

Fertilior seges est alienis semper in agris 'the corn is always more fruitful (abundant) in the fields of others'. Ovid. The grass is always greener on the other side. See *oratio congratulatoria*.

Festina lente 'hurry slowly'. More haste, less speed. Suetonius tells us that the emperor Augustus was fiercely critical of military commanders who were reckless or hasty and was fond of quoting Greek proverbs including *festina lente*. Suetonius Augustus 25.

Fiat lux 'let there be light'. From Genesis 1:3 in the *Vulgate* see below. Motto of Berkeley, the University of California.

Fiat justitia 'let justice be done'. See *ruat caelum*. Used to be the motto of the General Council of the Bar until (in deference to the politically correct?) superseded in language and meaning by the English, 'justice for all,' in December 1999.

Fidei defensor 'defender of the faith'. Abbreviated to *FD* or *Fid Def* these words are to be found on English coinage, being the Monarch's title as head of the Church of England: this was given by Pope Leo V to Henry VIII while he was still a Roman Catholic. After his breach with Rome, Henry kept it in relation to his breakaway Anglican Church. See *Dei Gratia*.

Fidem qui perdit, nihil pote ultra perdere 'who loses his honour can lose nothing more'. Publilius Syrus. Sententiae F.14. Another aspect of the Roman's tradition of falling on his sword. Cf., *potius mori quam foedari* 'better to die than be disgraced'. Motto.

'I could not love thee, dear, so much,
Loved I not honour more'.
    Richard Lovelace 1618-1641.

See *nemo me*, *non revertar*, *rem tene*, *sit sine* and *una salus*.

Fide, sed cui vide 'trust, but watch (take care) in whom'.
Sir Walter Raleigh's advice to his son was: 'trust no man too much'.

'The man that hath no music in himself,
Nor is not moved with concord of sweet sounds,
Is fit for treasons, stratagems and spoils; . . . .
Let no such man be trusted'.
    William Shakespeare. Merchant of Venice. Act V. Sc.1 ll. 83-88.

'Let me have men about me that are fat;
Sleek headed men, and such as sleep o'nights:
Yond Cassius has a lean and hungry look;
He thinks too much: such men are dangerous'.
    William Shakespeare. Julius Caesar. Act 1. Sc.2 ll 191-194.

Conclusion: trust nobody too much and certainly don't trust thin men who think a lot and have no music in their soul! Rather perhaps trust one's dog. See *homini fidelissime*.See also: *et tu Brute, fronti nulla fides, latet anguis, quis famulus, quomodo adulator, semper fidelis* and *timeo Danaos.*

Fides Punica 'Punic or Carthaginian faith'. Treachery. The feeling was mutual. In 255 BC (first Punic war) Marcus Atilius Regulus, a Roman Consul commanding an invading Roman force in North Africa was defeated and captured by the Carthaginian Xanthippus. Regulus was sent back to Rome to treat for peace on condition that he would return. In Rome he urged more war and did not return. Ten years later he fell into the hands of Hamilcar Barca (father of Hannibal) who asked him what mercy he could expect. His answer (attributed) was *summa sedes non capit duos* (see below; 'the seat of supreme power does not take two or supreme power cannot be shared'). Do with me as you must'. The Carthaginian then personally and publicly cut off his nose before having him tortured to death.

There was much hate, little honour and no quarter given in the Punic wars. For an account of part, which makes the past live, see "Hannibal" by Ross Leckie published by Abacus 1995. See too 'Enemy of Rome' by Leonard Cottrell published 1962 by Pan Books. See *bellum maxime omnium, cunctator, delenda est Carthago, Hannibal ante portas, nullus amor populis, puella Carthaginis ridebat* and *summa sedes.*

Filius nullius 'nobody's son'. See *illegitimi.*

Filius terrae 'son of the soil'. Person of humble birth. See *terrae filius.*
Finem respice (sometimes *respice finem*) 'look to the end'. See *quicquid agas.*

Finis Terrae 'end of the earth'. Name given to what is now Finisterre in Galicia near the north west tip of Spain. Many pilgrims, after reaching Santiago de Compostela, did and do press on (along the Camino Fisterra) to the end of the road, of the world. To the earliest and medieval pilgrims Finisterre was the end of the known world. See *Capitulum hujus* and *Roma semel.*

Flamma fumo est proxima 'flame is very near to smoke'. Plautus. Curculio 53.No smoke without fire.

Florent concordia regna 'through concord kingdoms flourish'. Inscription on the unite and broad, gold coins of Kings Charles I and II.

Floribus Anna tuis faveat sol luci perenni 'Anna may the sun favour your flowers with perpetual light'.

Inscription on the sundial in the gardens of St. Hugh's College, Oxford. A tribute to Annie Rogers 1856-1937 who devoted her life to the improvement of women's position in the university: only in 1920 were women permitted to proceed to a degree. She taught classics and was associated with St. Hugh's, showing a keen interest in its gardens and being given the title *custos hortulorum* 'keeper of the gardens' in 1927.

Sundials have a habit of attracting Latin inscription. A pertinent one is *horas non numero nisi serenas* 'I do not number the hours unless they be bright (sunshine)'.

Fluctus in simpulo exitare 'to raise a tempest in a ladle'. Cicero. Cause a storm in a teacup.

Foenum habet in cornu 'he has hay on his horns'. He is dangerous.

Follis. Name of a Roman coin. The Roman empire suffered inflation and over time the relative and real value of gold and silver fluctuated. Other coins not mentioned under *denarius* above were introduced: *inter alia* the *miliarense* and the *follis*. Smaller dictionaries of classical Latin show *follis* as meaning purse, pouch, bag or sack but make no mention of coins. Visitors to the Museum of London may notice reference to the *follis* but, for valuation purposes, will not find it related to other coins the names of which are familiar (eg., *denarius, sestertius*). This is for good reason. Historical information is scant and, from what is available, all depends upon the date of valuation. The *follis* was probably introduced c.AD 300 around the time of the emperor Diocletian's reform of the coinage. Inflation had so eroded the value of the existing coinage that a new denomination was needed (just as France moved to a nouveau franc, representative of ten old francs in 1958). The *follis* (plural *folles*) was valued in relation to the silver *denarii* which were notionally seen as being contained in a pouch, purse, bag or sack (just as today we value the £ sterling against a 'basket' of other currencies). The number of *denarii* notionally in the bag etc., was increased progressively as inflation and/or the price of silver devalued the *denarius* in real terms. The *follis* however thereby acquired a more or less constant real value.

Fons et origo 'source (fountain or spring) and origin'. The monarch is the *fons justitiae* 'the fountain or source of justice'.

Forsan et haec olim meminisse juvabit 'perhaps some day we will enjoy memory even of these things'. Virgil Aeneid. 1.203.

Time and an insulation of the mind blot out awful episodes, so that they are not remembered as they really were. Winston Churchill remembered one of the most exhilarating experiences of his life as being 'shot at without result'. Others remember with gentle amusement the awfulness of their early days at an English public school. See *quae fuit*.

Fortis est veritas 'truth is good'. Historic motto of the city of Oxford inscribed beneath the clock at Carfax Tower. See *ego sum via, lux et, magna est, quid est* and *veritas*.

Fortiter in re suaviter in modo 'strong in deed gentle in manner'. How a judge should be. Used (the other way round . . . *suaviter in modo fortiter in re*) to describe the Law Lord, Lord Salmon of Sandwich, in his obituary as published by The Daily Telegraph on 9th November 1991.

Lord Chesterfield (1694–1773) said of these words: 'I do not know any one rule so unexceptionally useful and necessary in any part of life'.

Fortunae filius 'child (son) of fortune'.

Fortuna favet fortibus 'fortune favours the strong (brave)'. Cf., *Deos fortioribus adesse* 'the gods are on the side of the strong'. Tacitus after 117: histories. See *audaces fortuna iuvat* and *audentes fortuna iuvat* and *macte nova virtute*.

Forum. Public square in Roman city used for judicial or other business. Place of meeting for public discussion. Court or tribunal.

Even the mighty emperor Augustus found himself subject to the rule of law: the Forum in Rome is assymetrical at its eastern corner because landowners would not sell all the ground he wanted. *

Fronti nulla fides 'no faith in the face'. Juvenal II, 8. No reliance on the face. Don't trust appearances. Things may not be what they seem. All that glisters is not gold. The face is no index to the heart. Fair without, false within. Cf., *ne fronti crede* do not believe in the face. Faceless bureaucrats may turn out to be two faced!

'Is she kind as she is fair?
For beauty lives with kindness'.
William Shakespeare. Song of Host in The Two Gentlemen of Verona. IV. Ii:44-45.

'A cherub's face, a reptile all the rest'.
Alexander Pope (1688-1744) Lord Hervey 1.331.

'Honest in face, shameless at heart': how Sallust described Pompey. See *cucullus non, fide, sed cui vide* and *quomodo adulator*.

Fullones ululamque cano, non arma virumque 'I sing of fullers and an owl, not of arms and the man'. Graffiti at Pompeii. Fabius Ululitremulus' fuller's shop; a fuller being one who finishes, beats and/or folds cloth. See and note *arma virumque cano*.

G

Gaius. Roman jurist (thought to have been a teacher of law) writing in the reign of Antoninus Pius (AD 138-161) and source of much of our modern knowledge of Roman law. Nothing is known of his life or personality save that which can be gleaned from his legal works. His institutes, written circa AD 161, form the basis of Justinian's Institutes. The text of Gaius' Institutes is published in two volumes with critical notes and translation by F.de Zulueta. Oxford Clarendon Press 1946 and 1958 and will be familiar to those who read jurisprudence at Oxford in the 1950s and 1960s. See *Justinianus* and *Justitia est*.

Gallia est omnis divisa in partes tres 'the whole of Gaul is divided into three parts', 'Gaul is made up of three areas'.
  The opening words of Caesar's *Commentarii De Bello Gallico I.i.I* 'concerning the Gallic war' (ie., his campaigns in Gaul 58-52 BC). How many remember schooldays and having to translate these words? Caesar goes on to name and to describe the qualities of those inhabiting each part or area. Available in translation: Penguin Classics: 'Caesar .. The Conquest of Gaul' first published 1951. See *Caesar, commentarii*.

Gallice 'in French'. See *Anglice* and *Latine dictum*.

Gasterosteus aculeatus. Classificatory Latin name for the three spined stickleback. The red throated male is a very fierce protector of his territory.

Gaudeamus igitur 'let us therefore rejoice'. Used by Brahms at the end of his Academic Festival Overture. '*Gaudeamus igitur iuvenes dum sumus* . . .while we are young'. Words from a revised medieval student's drinking song.

'Time the subtle thief of youth'.
>   John Milton 1608-1674. Sonnet 7.

All is transient:

>   'Gather ye rosebuds, while ye may.
>   Old Time is still a-flying:
>   And this same flower that smiles today
>   Tomorrow will be dying'.
>   Robert Herrick 1591- 1674.

>   'Fair daffodils we weep to see
>   You haste away so soon . . . .'
>   Robert Herrick 1591- 1674.

>   'Address yourself to young people. They know everything'.
>   Joseph Joubert 1750 – 1824.

>   'To get back one's youth one has merely to repeat one's follies'.
>   Oscar Wilde.

See *dum vivimus*.

Generalia 'general matters or principles'.

Genus a kind or class having common characteristics.*

Gloria in excelsis Deo 'glory to God in the highest'. Followed by *et in terra pax* 'and on earth peace'. See *Deus irae*.

Graecum est: non legitur 'it is Greek: it is not read'. Placed against a Greek word in medieval manuscripts indicating that it need not be read.

Gratis 'by favour' (contraction of *gratiis*). For nothing, without payment.*

Graviora quaedam sunt remedia periculis 'some remedies are more serious than the dangers/diseases'. Publilius Syrus.

A thought supportive of conservative medicine. There are those doctors who think that more patients die from therapy than ever died from disease! See *medici*.

Grex 'a flock' (as of sheep). Call up: "grex @ topica. com" and you will be able to correspond by e-mail in Latin with enthusiasts all over the world. Send e-mail to this address and in the title write 'subscribe'. E-mails in Latin on diverse topics will then be received and can be responded to (but only in Latin). To end participation write 'unsubscribe' in 'title' of an e-mail directed to the same destination.

H

Habendum et tenendum 'to have and to hold'. Words from the Form of Solemnisation of Matrimony in the book of Common Prayer.

'I take thee (name) to be my wedded husband/wife, to have and to hold from this day forward, for better for worse, for richer for poorer, in sickness and in health, to love and to cherish, till death us do part . . . . and thereto I plight thee my troth'. See *perfecto in* and *ut amem*.

Haec studia adulescentiam alunt, senectutem oblectant, secundas res ornant, adversis perfugium ac solacium praebent, delectant domi, non impediunt foris, pernoctant nobiscum, peregrinantur, rusticantur 'these studies nurture youth and delight old age: they adorn good things, provide refuge and solace in adversity; they enrich home life and do not interfere abroad; they stay with us through the night, as we journey and they accompany us in the countryside'. Cicero *Pro Archia 7.16*.

In this famous passage (to which it is hard to do justice in translation), much loved by those learned in the Latin language, Cicero defended the doubted claim to Roman citizenship of the Greek poet Archia. The studies referred to are studies of literature. In Cicero's rhetoric is a blatant laudatory appeal to sentiment. See *homines enim*.

Hannibal. Name of a Carthaginian soldier 247-182 BC. At the age of nine his father, Hamilcar Barca, made him swear eternal enmity to Rome. He inflicted three devastating defeats upon the Romans. It is not possible to do justice to the man in a short entry here but see *fides Punica*. See too: *cunctator, delenda est Carthago, bellum maxime omnium, Hannibal ante portas, nullus amor populus, puella Carthaginis ridebat* and *summa sedes non capit duos*.

Hannibal ante portas 'Hannibal at the gates'. The enemy is at hand. The expression has connotations of imminent panic as well as peril conjuring up a picture of noisy and hostile besieging hordes. Another English expression is 'the barbarians are at the gates'. See *cunctator, delenda est Carthago, Fides Punica, bellum maxime omnium, nullus amor populus, puella Carthaginis ridebat* and *summa sedes non capit duos*.

Harold Rex interfectus est 'King Harold is slain'. The most significant part of the Latin narrative woven into the Bayeux Tapestries. With this background inscription King Harold is depicted at the battle of Hastings in 1066 standing on Senlac Hill (on which Battle Abbey now stands) pierced in the face by an arrow, which he is holding. There is some doubt as to whether another nearby figure with an axe shown on the tapestry as struck down by the sword of a mounted soldier might be King Harold. Since the arrow stricken figure is directly under the words *Harold Rex,* it is generally accepted that he is the King. The battle was long and bloody and the name of the hill is from the French: Senlac, *sang lac*, lake of blood. Reference is to King Harold II (Harold Godwinson). Medieval chroniclers had it that he survived Hastings and lived to a great age as a hermit near Chester. See *portant armas.*

Has nisi periturus mihi adimat nemo 'under pain of death let no one remove these [letters/words] from me'. Words inscribed on the rim of crowns and half-crowns (silver coinage) of Oliver Cromwell during the Commonwealth [in the period 1656 – 1658]. A dire warning to would-be clippers who could lose their lives for a lot less than half a crown (two shillings and six pence or twelve and a half post decimalisation [new] pence). See *decus et tutamen.*

Hegira. Latin and English word for the Arabic Hijrah meaning flight. The word is used to refer to the flight of Mohammed from Mecca to Medina on 16th July AD 622 and is the starting point for Moslem dating. AH is an abbreviation of *anno Hegirae*, the year of the flight. Moslem dating is not easy to relate to Christian dating because the former follows a 355-day lunar cycle so that e.g., the Moslem equivalent of AD 2000 is AH 1421 (not AH 1378 i.e., 2000 minus 622). See *ab urbe condita, AD* and *anno Domini.*

Hic es 'you are here'. Roman exhibits and remains are exhibited in the basement of the Castle Museum at Boulogne-sur-Mer in northern France. It is labyrinthine and sparsely attended by staff. A series of diagramatic plans of the basement in each room show exactly where the visitor is: by an arrow and the words *hic es.*

Hic et ubique terrarum 'here and everywhere throughout the world'. Motto of the university of Paris.

Hic jacet 'here lies'. Seen on grave and tomb stones. See *hic sepultus, natus* and *obit.*

Hic liber est meus
  Testis est Deus

Si quis furetur
Per collum pendetur
'this book is mine, God is witness. Should anyone steal it he is to be hanged by the neck'.

Doggerel rhyming Latin. In the past often written by children in their schoolbooks. Quoted by Arthur Ransome in Missee Lee.

Long gone are the days when even minor theft was a felony and felony generally meant the death penalty. See *e libris*.

Hic sepultus 'here buried'. Seen on gravestones. See *hic jacet, natus* and *obit*.

Hinc lucem et pocula sacra 'from this source (springs) light and sacred draughts (of learning)'. Motto of Cambridge university. First used by the university printer in 1603. See *Dominus illuminatio mea* and *lux mundi*.

His non obstantibus 'notwithstanding these things'.

Hispania 'Spain'. (Iberia was the Greek). Name given by the Romans to what is now Spain when it became the Roman province of *Hispania*. The word has become associated with pirate and other tales of the Spanish Main. The Hispaniola was the name given to the ship in which John Hawkins, Dr. Livesey and Squire Trelawny set out (with Long John Silver on board) to find treasure in Robert Louis Stevenson's 'Treasure Island'. Santo Domingo was a Spanish colony on the Caribbean Island of Hispaniola raided by Drake in 1585.

One living in the US who is Spanish speaking used to be called an Hispanic: particularly if he was of Latin-American descent. This has fallen into desuetude, the abbreviation 'Spic' having become an offensive term of abuse. 'Chicano' succeeded it and in turn has been succeeded by 'Latino'.

Hoc sensu 'in this sense'.

Hoc volo. See *sic volo*.

Hodie mihi, cras tibi 'to me today, to you tomorrow'. Life tends to balance the scales. If one suffers a setback and others seem to crow or manifest schadenfreude, just think: *hodie mihi, cras tibi* 'my turn today, yours tomorrow'. Expression also used on old epitaphs. *See nihil illegitimis carborundum est.*

Hominem ego iracundiorem quam te novi neminem 'never have

I met a grumpier man than you'. Plautus. Mercator.

Homines enim ad deos nulla re propius accedunt quam salutem hominibus dando 'for in nothing do men come closer to divinity than in granting deliverance to their fellow men'. Cicero Pro Ligario 38.

Quintus Ligarius was prosecuted for bearing arms against Caesar and Cicero had undertaken his defence. Caesar (breaching a fundamental of natural justice, that no man should be judge in his own cause: *nemo judex in causa sua*) appointed himself judge. Worse still, Plutarch tells us, in advance of trial Caesar had declared: 'why may we not give ourselves a pleasure which we have not now enjoyed for so long, that of hearing Cicero speak; since I have already decided about Ligarius, who is plainly a bad man as well as being my enemy'.

Cicero's speech at trial before Caesar in the Forum was a masterpiece of forensic advocacy, perfection in construction, delivery and content. Towards the end he leaned on Caesar with the above quoted words. Caesar was overwhelmed. He became agitated and was seen to be visibly moved before letting some papers fall from his hand and acquitting Ligarius.

Few lawyers can have taken on such an unpromising case and emerged with such dazzling success.

Ligarius repaid the compliment by joining Caesar's assassins. Did Shakespeare borrow from Cicero? . . . . when he wrote:

'And earthly power doth then show likest God's
When mercy seasons justice'.
        The Merchant of Venice Act iv scene 1 195-196.

Mercy seasoned justice for Caractacus but not for the admirable Vercingetorix. See Caractacus above.

Perhaps complementary here is a fragment of the emperor Marcus Aurelius' (121-180) wisdom: 'as it is more human, so it is more manly'. The full passage, from Meditations 11:18:10 is: 'in fits of rage bear in mind that anger is not macho but that what is calm and gentle, as it is more human, so it is more manly'. See *blandae mendacia, Caesar, Cicero, haec studia* and *iniquum est.*

Homini fidelissimi sunt equus et canis 'the horse and the dog are the most faithful to man'. Pliny. The combined wisdom of this and *domus sua cuique est tutissimum refugium* (to each person his home is the safest refuge. Sir Edward Coke) is that a great deal may be said for retreat from the world home to one's horse and one's dog.

84

'Histories are more full of examples of the fidelities of dogs than of friends.' Alexander Pope (1688-1744) in a letter of 1707. See *fide, canis ingens, semper fidelis, quasi* and *quis famulus.*

Hominis vis 'the strength of man'. A household name in British brown bread originated from wheat germ-rich flour registered in 1887 (by a Macclesfield milling company called Fitton and Son) as Smith's patent germ flour. The company launched a competition to find a more catchy brand name. A student won the prize with *hominis vis.* Abbreviation to Hovis produced a name used ever since, currently by Rank, Hovis McDougall.

Homo 'a man'. Man as a species, a human being as opposed to *vir*, man as male, husband, man of honour or courage. Homo is colloquially used sometimes (dated?) to mean homosexual.

Homo cui vivere est cogitare 'man to whom to live is to think'. Cicero. *Tusculanae Disputationes 5.111.* See *Cicero, cogito ergo sum* and *homo sapiens.*

Homo erectus 'erect or upright man'. The name given to man when, as he advanced from ape to *homo sapiens* (see below) in the evolutionary process, he stood upright. This does not mean anything else.

Homo sapiens 'discerning man'. Man as a species in the current state of the evolutionary process.

Honores mutant mores 'honours change manners'. How often do those who become rich or important become arrogant and disdainful: less courteous to those who they no longer need: to men who have become of no consequence? See *quae fuerant* and *tempora mutantur*

Horatius 'Horatio' (*Publius Horatius Cocles*) legendary (7th century BC?) Roman hero written of by Thomas Macaulay in his Lays of Ancient Rome (1842). Horatius, with two companions, held the wooden bridge (across the Tiber into Rome) against Lars Porsenna's Etruscan army while it was cut down behind him. Just before its collapse he sent back his two companions and alone held the bridge before jumping into the Tiber and swimming to safety. The expression 'Horatio held the bridge' has come to refer to any single handed feat of resistance successfully achieved against the odds.

Hostis honori invidia 'envy (is) the enemy of honour'. Motto.

Humanae vitae 'of human life'. Name of encyclical on contraception of Pope Paul VI 1968.

Hyacinthoides non scripta. Latin classificatory name for the bluebell which in early to mid May still carpets in deep blue so much of the ever diminishing woodland in England's green and pleasant land. See frontispiece.

I

Ibid. Abbreviation of *ibidem* 'in the same place'. Used by reference and text books in foot notes referring to an identical source cited in a preceding footnote.

Idcirco ipse me reprehendo et ego in paenitentiam in favilla et cinere 'wherefore I abhor myself and repent in dust and ashes'. Vulgate. Book of Job. Ch. 42.v.16.

Idem the same. See *ad idem* above.

Ides. In the Roman calendar the *ides* fell on what is now 15th March, May, July, October and 13th of all other months. The *ides* was always the eighth day after the *nones* (see below).

For those who may need to remember there is a well known little rhyme:

'March, May, July, October; These are they
Make nones the seventh, ides the fifteenth day'.

The *ides* features in Shakespeare's Julius Caesar.

Caesar 'I hear a tongue, shriller than all the music, Cry 'Caesar'.
Speak; Caesar is turned to hear'.
Soothsayer 'Beware the *ides* of March'.

After Caesar had been stabbed to death on the *Ides* of March in 44 BC, a coin inscribed with *Brut Imp.*, 'Brutus commander' and bearing the head of Marcus Brutus was struck (in 43 or 44 BC) by the army headed by Caesar's assassins. On the reverse appears a *pileus* (a hat-like token of freedom) between two daggers above the inscription 'EID.MAR' (*Eidus Martiae*, 'the Ides of March') symbolising liberty restored by the death of the tyrant, Caesar. All that is missing is blood dripping from the daggers! See *et tu Brute* above. See too *Caesar, ad calends Graecas* and *nones.**

Id est 'that is (to say)'. Abbreviated to i.e. Explanation follows. If example is to follow, e.g. is appropriate. In England and Wales Latin is being driven out of the law. If use of i.e. (*id est*) is not to be permitted, abbreviation of the replacement 'that is to say' will be t.i.t.s!

I.e. See *id est*.

Ignoramus 'we do not know'. Used in English as a noun to denote an ignorant person. Perhaps, according to the Modern Oxford Dictionary, from 'Ruggle's Ignoramus' 1615, exposing lawyers' ignorance.*

Ignotus 'unknown'. Abbreviated to ign. This indicates that a source is unknown. Abbreviated it does not mean ignition!

Illegitimi 'illegitimate ones'. Bastards. See *filius nullius* and *nihil illegitimis carborundum est*.

Ille potens sui laetusque deget. Cui licet in diem dixisse vixi cras vel atra nube polum pater occupato vel sole puro

> 'Happy the man, and happy he alone,
> He, who can call today his own:
> He, who secure within, can say
> Tomorrow do thy worst, for I have lived today'.
> Horace, Odes 3.29 lines 41-45. Translation John Dryden 1631-1700.

As life draws to a close how many could say (underlined words below) with Egmont's calm assurance, in the adept words of Goethe at his best (diminished in translation):

> 'Nun endigt sich das Leben, wie es sich früher, früher, schon auf dem Sande von Gravelingen hätte endigen können. <u>Ich höre auf, zu leben; aber ich habe gelebt.</u> So leb' auch mein Freund, gern und mit Lust und scheu den Tod nicht' 'Now life comes to an end, as it might earlier have done, before now on the sands of Gravelines. <u>I cease to live; but oh how I have lived!</u> And so you too my friend, live your life, to the full, and shy not away from death'.

Count Egmont, the romantic, the impetuous, the victor of Gravelines and hero of the struggle for freedom from brutal oppression in the 16th century Spanish occupied low country, as portrayed in Goethe's tragedy 'Egmont' was the inspiration for Beethoven's overture and incidental music (opus 84). Egmont failed to heed warning from the wily Count of Orange and was lured to parley with the Spanish Duke of

Alva, only to be seized and put to death. Spoken by him the night before execution to a trusted good friend were Goethe's above words. *Die Trommel gerühret* (sung by a woman, 'Klärchen,' a soprano voice and Goethe's creation: he strayed from historical fact) follows the overture and is as stirring and rousing a freedom fighter's call to arms as any man could ever hope to hear.

A memorial statue of Count Egmont stands in the 'Place du Petit Sablon' in Brussels. See *age dum, carpe diem, dum vivimus, omnem crede, vive hodie* and *quid sit futurus.*

Illiterati. Those who are illiterate or unlearned in a particular discipline or subject. Used sometimes derogatorily to denigrate those from a rival educational establishment, professional body etc. The opposite is *literati,* those who are learned. Cf., and see *cognoscenti.*

Immo id, quod aiunt, auribus teneo lupum nam neque quomodo a me, invenio: neque uti retineam scio 'it is true they say I have caught a wolf by the ears and I don't know either how to get rid of him or keep him restrained'. Terence Phormio III. II. 21.

To hold a wolf by the ears as an expression seems to have more to do with having got into an impossible position and not knowing what to do, than 'taking the bull by the horns'. See *tenere lupum auribus.*

Immortalia ne speres 'lest you hope that you be immortal'. Horace Odes IV.vii.7. Horace says that the year's cycle tells him that his own life is not eternal.

'Such,' he said, 'O King, seems to me to be the present life on earth, as if . . . on a winter's night a sparrow should fly into the hall and, coming in one door, instantly fly out through another . . Somewhat like this appears the life of man. But of what follows or what went before we are wholly ignorant'.

Bede. Ecclesiastical History, 11.

See *aere perennius, domus et, non omnis moriar* and *qui fugiebat.*

Impedimenta 'baggage, encumbrance, travelling gear'.*

Imperium. An untranslatable word signifying the right to supreme command in war, to administer the laws and to impose the death penalty subject to a Roman citizen's right of appeal: originally to the people (through the *tribuni plebis* the tribunes of the people, magistrates elected to defend the people's rights. See *veto* below) and later to the emperor. Adopted by English it refers broadly to the extent of absolute sovereignty.

Cum imperio esse 'to be vested with *imperium*' is to have unlimited power. *Imperium in imperio,* translated as an empire within an empire, is the motto of Ohio.*
See arcana imperii.

Imprimatur 'let it be printed'. Used in English as a noun, it is a licence to print material; originally most often an ecclesiastical or a religious book. A word aspiring writers hope to hear. In the appeal courts, where more than one judge constitutes the tribunal, the familiar words after at least one judgement has been delivered 'I agree and have nothing to add' are in the nature of an *imprimatur.* *

Imprimis 'in the first place, principally, chiefly'.

In absentia 'in (one's) absence'. One can usually have one's fine for speeding imposed *in absentia,* without having to attend court. The same may go for taking a degree.

In aeternum 'for eternity'. For ever. See *in perpetuum* and *per omnia saecula.*

In articulo mortis 'at the moment of death'. The French revolutionary leader, Georges Jacques Danton is to be admired for resolute defiance *in articulo mortis.* When on 5th April 1794 the political wheel had turned full circle and he faced the guillotine himself, he urged: 'Be sure you show the mob my head. It will be a long time ere they see its like'. See *in extremis.*

In cauda venenum 'the poison (is) in the tail'. The expression in English, 'the sting in the tail' refers to an apparently innocuous situation which turns out not to be so. Note Revelation Ch. 9 vs. 10 and 11:

> 'And they had tails like scorpions, and there were stings in their tails; and they had a king over them which is the angel of the bottomless pit'.

Incipit 'it begins'. Here begins. Often the first word in some medieval manuscripts. Eg., *Incipit evangelium secundum Mattheum* 'Here begins the Gospel according to (St) Matthew'. From the Vulgate.

In consimili casu 'in a like case'. A phrase of great significance in English legal history. By the 13th century the Royal Writ, sealed by the Chancellor, was fundamental in the provision of civil justice. Such a document was issued with Royal authority and, in recited factual situations, provided the law and the remedy available. Despite rapid expansion of the new writs, the law became very rigid and in many instances wrought injustice and was wanting. The Statute of Westminster II (1285) enacted that the clerks in Chancery might agree to production of a new writ whenever there was a writ but 'in a like case (*in consimili casu*) falling under like law and requiring like remedy is found none'. This gave rise to a crop of new forms of action known as actions on the case. An accurate knowledge of the Register of Writs and the form of action originated by each writ was basic to the professional knowledge of the medieval lawyer. If a client's case could not be fitted factually into an existing writ and if it was not factually sufficiently close (*in consimili casu*) for the Chancery to be willing to frame a new writ, the only remedy was a humble petition to the King's Council. Such petitions were framed in grovelling language 'humbly craving' the relief sought.

Index 'a catalogue or index'. Plural *indices*. See *index librorum prohibitorum*. *

Index expurgatorius. A list of forbidden books which are permitted after expurgation by the deletion and/or alteration of passages. See *index librorum prohibitorum.*

Index librorum prohibitorum 'list of prohibited books'. Books which the Roman Catholic Church forbids its adherents to read. By 1549 the works of Erasmus were on the Spanish index of prohibited books. See *index expurgatorius.*

Indiae Imperator 'emperor of India'. Seen on coinage. See *Dei Gratia.*

Indices plural of *index*. See *index.*

Indulgentia 'indulgence'. In the early 16th century the Roman Catholic Church sold indulgences for the remission of temporal punishment in purgatory, due still for sins even after absolution. Martin Luther protested against the cynical and immoral fund raising nature of these in 1517.

His Honour Judge John Weeks QC was moved on July 10th 2000 to write to the Times:

> 'Sir, I see the Lord Chancellor is to sell key-rings and mouse-mats in the Royal Courts of Justice (report and leading article July 10th). How long before he sells pardons and indulgences?'

In eadem hora apparuerant digiti quasi manus hominis

scribentes contra candelabrum in superficie parietes aulae regiae 'in the same hour came forth fingers of a man's hand and wrote upon the plaster of the wall of the king's palace': *haec est autem scriptura quae digesta est mane mane thecel fares et haec interpretatio sermonis mane numeravit Deus regnum tuum et complevit illud thecel adpensum est in statera et inventus es minus habens* 'and this is the writing that was written, mene thacel and this interpretation of the thing means: God has numbered thy kingdom and finished it'. Mene Mene Tekel Upharsim: 'thou art weighed in the balance and found wanting'. Vulgate *Liber Danihelis Prophetae* (book of the prophet Daniel) Ch 5 v.4 and v. 25-27). The eerie judgment, delivered at Belshazzar's feast, is terrifyingly portrayed in Rembrandt's famous painting which hangs in London's National Gallery. Source of the expression 'the writing's on the wall' meaning the game's up; justice and retribution are imminent.

In esse. Literally 'in to be', 'in being.' Cf., *in posse*.

In extenso 'in full or at full length'. Words usually abbreviated may be said to be set out *in extenso* if they are all reproduced in their entirety.

In extremis 'in the extremity or at the very end'. At the point of death. Used colloquially this may mean 'in a bad way'. Attributed to Voltaire (1694-1778) on his deathbed, when invited to renounce the devil, is the answer: 'This is no time to make new enemies'.

> 'If you do not know how to die, don't worry: nature herself will teach you in the proper time'.
> Michel Eyquem de Montaigne 1533-1592.

See *in articulo mortis* and *omnem crede.* *

In flagrante delicto 'in the blazing crime'. Expression used to refer to wrongdoing where the perpetrator is caught in the act; red handed. It has come to be associated with sexual misconduct: adultery and fornication and used to be used (and perhaps sometimes still is) in the law (particularly in court) to soften the blow of stark and indelicate English words. For detail see 'Lawyers' Latin' by John Gray.

Infra 'below'. In literary usage denoting something that follows 'below' in a text. Often preceded by '*vide*' (see). The opposite is '*vide supra*' 'see above'. *

Infra dignitatem 'beneath (one's) dignity'. Inconsistent with the dignity of one's position. Abbreviated to *infra dig*. It might be *infra dig* for the Lord Chief Justice to clean lavatories. But when Lord Taylor of Gosforth was appointed Lord Chief Justice of England in April of 1992, he was reported as saying to Lady Taylor 'where do I go from here'? 'Into the kitchen to help with the washing up' she replied. Not *infra dig*. But when Lord Goddard was Lord Chief Justice, he told (apocryphally perhaps) of a reluctant witness who pleaded (only after much alternate menace and cajolery) that she had received a threatening note. 'Madam fear not' his Lordship had declared. 'I too received such a note this very morning and, sitting where I am now, ought not to tell you what I did with it sitting in another place'. *Infra dig?* See *aquila non capit*.

In futuro 'in the future'.

In hoc (signo) vinces 'in this (sign, the Cross) you shall conquer'.

The emperor Constantine the Great (AD 272-337) was declared emperor by the army on the death of his father Constantius at York (England) in 306. A complicated power struggle ensued. In 312 Constantine marched on Rome and against the usurper Maxentius. On the way he saw in a vision the cross of Christ in the heavens against the sun with the words *in hoc signo vinces*. He entered battle under Christian banners ('onward Christian soldiers' for the first time?) and engaged the enemy in the west of Rome near where the Milvian Bridge crossed the river Tiber. Maxentius' troops retreated across the bridge, the structure of which collapsed. Maxentius was thrown into the river and died trying to swim to safety.

Constantine was a committed Christian thereafter and made Christianity the official religion of the empire. He was however responsible for a number of less than Christian acts (including the execution of his eldest and illustrious son Crispus for questionable adultery) and passed some barbaric laws (rapists were to be burned alive as was any girl who eloped with her lover) and was baptised only on his deathbed.

Iniqua nunquam regna perpetuo manent 'unjust tyrannies never last for ever'. Seneca. The régimes of Adolph Hitler and more recently of Slobodan Milosevic each came to an end. But an awful lot of people suffered and died before that happened. See *sic semper tyrannis*.

Iniquum est aliquem rei sui esse judicem 'it is unjust that anyone should be judge in his own cause'. Sir Edward Coke 1552-1634.

A judge ought not to try a case which touches upon his own interests or might be seen to do so. A question sometimes of degree. What if he holds one share in a massive company with millions of shares which is involved in the litigation before him? Or an interest in a unit-trust whose portfolio contains shares in a company likewise involved (of which usually he will be unaware)? The problem has been considered by the Court of Appeal in England in Locabail (UK) Ltd. v Bayfield Properties Ltd. Reported at 2000 QB 451. See *homines enim, nemo iudex in causa sua.*

In loco parentis 'in the place of a parent'. An expression used, particularly in English law (until recently) to describe one who is placed in a position of trust to supervise or look after the welfare of a child, young, immature or otherwise vulnerable person. It may <u>not</u> be translated as 'my father was a train driver': equally 'my parents have gone mad' won't do.*

In memoriam 'in memory (of)'. To the memory of a dead person. An expression used widely in epitaphs, books, inscriptions etc.; e.g., an *'in memoriam'* book may contain a list of children, who died young, lest their very existence be forgotten.*

In nomine Patris et Filii et Spiritus Sancti 'in the name of the Father and of the Son and of the Holy Ghost'.

In nomine Dei: 'in the name of God'.

In nuce 'in a nutshell'. From *nux,* 'a nut'.

Inopem me copia fecit 'plenty has made me poor'. Ovid. Metamorphoses iii. 466. The poet referred to Narcissus loving his own reflection and feeling that he has nothing because he cannot have it even though he has everything else. But one who has plenty will have many intimate acquaintances.

'Tis the mind that makes the body rich'.
William Shakespeare. Henry VI part iii Act iv sc.3 line 174.

'Acquaintance is a degree of friendship called slight when its object is poor and obscure and intimate when he is rich and famous'.
Ambrose Bierce 1842-1914?

See *crescit amor nummi, barbarus ipse, donec eris sospes, dummodo sit, esurientes implevit bonis, felicitas multos, intolerabilius nihil* and *oportet ergo.*

In pace 'in peace'. See *vade in pace.*

In Paradisum deducant te angeli 'may the angels lead thee into paradise'. Opening words of Reqiem Mass. Set to music as a choral anthem by G. Fauré.

In pari materia 'in like material or substance'.Comparable. Of equal relevance, in an analogous case.

In perpetuum 'in perpetuity . . . for ever'. See *in aeternum* and *per omnia saecula*.

In posse 'potential'. Children *in posse* are children who may come into existence. An important consideration in wills and settlements.

In principio erat verbum et verbum erat apud Deum 'in the beginning was the word and the word was with God'. Opening words of St. John's Gospel in the Vulgate. Once used as a motto of Oxford University.

In principio came to be used by medieval friars as an expression of reverence, particularly to introduce themselves.

'He was the beste beggar in his hous
For though a widow hadde not a shoe,
So plesant was his *in principio*
Yet wold he have a ferthing er he wente'.
General prologue to Geoffrey Chaucer's Canterbury Tales at 251–255.

See *Dominus illuminatio* and *sicut erat*.

In rerum natura 'in the nature of things'.

Insanus omnis furere credit caeteros 'every madman believes others to be mad'. See William Shakespeare's King John. Act III Scene IV.

Cardinal Pandulph. 'Lady you utter madness and not sorrow'.
Constance. 'Thou art not holy to belie me so;
    I am not mad: this hair I tear is mine;'
But then:

'Great wits are sure to madness near allied
And thin partitions do their bounds divide'.
John Dryden. Absalom and Achitophel.

In silvam ligna ferre 'to carry wood to the forest'. To take coal to Newcastle.

In se 'in itself or themselves'.

In situ 'in its place'. In its original place.*

In specie 'in shape or form'. If I pay in gold coins and then am entitled to repayment, I may be anxious not to receive the paper money of an inflationary currency. I want repayment *in specie*; with coins of the same kind.

In statu pupillari 'in a state of pupillage'. Undergraduate or barrister's pupil.

Integer vitae scelerisque purus 'clean living (blameless in life) and free of vice'. The opening lines of Horace's ode 22 in book 1. The words are quoted in part one chapter six of E. M. Forster's 'The Longest Journey' Penguin Books 1960.

How many politicians (or any of us), hand on heart, could use this phrase of themselves? John Major's personal antics (as revealed in 2002) in the context of his promotion as Prime Minister of a 'back to basics' morality must be *simulatio maxima*, 'greatest hypocrisy'.

'And God shall make thy body pure,and give thee knowledge to endure
This ghost life's piercing phantom pain, and bring thee out to Life again'.
　　The Gates of Damascus. James Elroy Flecker.

See *beati Immaculati*.

Inter alia 'among other things'. *Inter alios* 'among other men' and *inter alias* 'among other women'.*

Inter arma silent leges 'laws are silent in times of war'. Cicero Pro Milone 11. Might is right. History shows that in time of war laws protective of the individual's liberty tend to be arbitrarily suspended in the case of those who are no more than enemy suspects: and nationals of a foreign hostile power are too often interned for that reason without more. Guantanamo Bay and in the U.K. the Anti-Terrorism, Crime and Security Act 2001 are recent examples of knee jerk over-reaction in deprivation of rights basic to justice and liberty in any civilised society. How long before a 'Gestapo' looks after British security and people, denied *habeas corpus*, disappear to languish in a 'Bastille' never to be seen again?

The above is the common understanding and use of this expression. In his speech on behalf of Titus Milo (the source) however, Cicero used it quite differently. In the years 57-52 BC Rome, without a police force, dissolved into anarchy. Armed gangs roamed the streets. Thugs of the arch gangster, an ambitious P. Clodius, intimidated and disrupted the administration. Milo, a close friend of Cicero (but no angel notwithstanding) responded by forming his own armed gang (as did many wealthy Romans) comprised substantially of gladiators. Caught with an insufficient armed escort, Clodius was killed in a clash with Milo's men. Milo ran off into exile and Cicero's speech in his defence to a special court of inquiry was never delivered. Cicero used the above expression in the context of the law of self defence. As between armed persons the one who carries a weapon with a view to homicide, does not necessarily commit a crime when he kills someone. The prima facie presumption is rebutted if the facts show the killing to have been justified as by self defence or otherwise. See *Caesar, Cicero, De Jure Belli* and *quid faciant leges*.

Interdum stultus bene loquitur 'sometimes a fool speaks well'. However bad your barrister he may just have a good day.

Inter nos 'between us'. '*Inter nos* (between you and me), the judge evades tax'. Use of this expression does not make the assertion any the less potentially slanderous.

Inter pares 'among equals'. See *primus inter pares.*

Interregnum 'between reign'. An interval between reigns or between successive governments or régimes. A word used in the Church of England in respect of a vacant period between an incumbent rector or vicar.*

In terrorem 'to terrify: as a warning'. In times past convicted felons were hung, drawn and quartered *in terrorem*. See *Clodius Albinus.*

Inter vivos 'between living people'. Relates in law usually to a gift.

Intolerabilius nihil est quam femina dives 'nothing is more insufferable than a rich woman'. Juvenal 6.460. See *crescit amor nummi, donec eris, dummodo sit, esurientes implevit, felicitas multos* and *inopem me copia fecit.*

In toto 'completely, as a whole, exhaustively'.*

In vino veritas 'in wine the truth'. The drinking of wine impairs caution and inhibition so that the truth will out. See *bonum vinum, fecundi calices, nunc bibemus, nunc est bibendum, nunc scripsi totum,* and *nunc vino pellite curas.*

In vitro 'in glass'. Hence *in vitro* fertilisation: in a test-tube . . . a glass one.

Ipse dixit 'he himself said it'. A statement relying for truth upon the fact that it has been said: and which is not independently justified or corroborated. A dogmatic statement.

'For he himself hath said it, And its greatly to his credit. That he is an Englishman'. (in spite of all temptation to belong to another nation!)
W.S. Gilbert 1836-1911: from Gilbert and Sullivan's HMS Pinafore.

'Ipse dixit. 'Ipse' autem erat Pythagoras' 'he himself said it. He himself, however was Pythagoras'. Cicero. *De Natura Deorum*, 1.v.10.

Ipsissima verba 'the very or exact words'. The long term memory of the ageing can often quote poetry learned in youth, but usually there is some small error and the *ipsissima verba* are not reproduced.

Ipso facto 'by the fact itself'. By the very fact or act. He says some pretty stupid things, but is not *ipso facto* necessarily an idiot.*

Ira furor brevis est 'anger is a brief madness'. Horace Epistles 1. ii.62.

Irritabis crabrones 'you will stir up the hornets'. You will set the cat among the pigeons. See *oleum addere*.

Ite missa est 'go, the Mass is finished'. The last words in the Latin Roman Catholic Mass. See *dies irae*.

Item is, ex cuius coenaculo . . . . habitabat, dejectum effusumve aliquid est, ita ut alicui noceretur . . . . dupli quanti damnum datum sit, constituta est action 'So too, he who occupies an apartment from which anything has been thrown or poured down, which has done damage to another (is liable) and an action is given for double the damage done'. Justinian Institutes. Book iv, Title vi.

In the streets of Rome there was a problem with refuse and sewage etc., thrown or poured from windows onto passers by. As a deterrent the law provided a more than compensatory remedy, the proceeds of which went half to the State and half to the party bringing the action. See *Justinianus*.

J

There was no letter "J" in classical Latin literature, which convention-ally came to an end with Juvenal (c. AD 55-130). The letter J came to be used by Renaissance Italian Humanists to distinguish consonated from non-consonated forms of I. The expressions following are now commonly spelt with a "J" and for convenience are listed under this letter.

Jehova quam multi sunt hostes mei 'O Lord how numerous are my enemies'. Set to music by Henry Purcell this piece was performed as part of the Sir John Taverner 60th birthday Anthem Concert Series in the Temple Church on 13th May 2004. The liberal translation used was: 'Lord how are they increased that trouble me'.

Jesus Nazarenus Rex Judaeorum 'Jesus of Nazareth, King of the Jews'. The inscription placed at the head of the cross of Christ cruci-fied. Abbreviated to INRI in paintings depicting the crucifixion (there being no letter J in classical Latin). Saints Luke and John tell us that it was written also in Greek and Hebrew. Only St John (Ch xix. V. 19) records that it was Pontius Pilate, the Roman governor of Judaea, who wrote it. See *accepta aqua, ecce homo, quid est veritas* and *quod scripsi scripsi.*

Jubilate Deo 'rejoice in God or be joyful in The Lord'. Psalm 100: to be said or sung (alternative to *Benedictus* see above) after The Second Lesson at Morning Prayer in accordance with the Church of England Book of Common Prayer. 'O be joyful in the Lord, all ye lands: serve the Lord with Gladness and come before his presence with a song'. See too Psalm 66.

Julius necuam 'Julius worthless, good for nothing' (German 'Taugenichts'). Graffiti on a wall (of the casa delle nozze d'argento) at Pompeii. On the same wall is: '*Julius cinaedus*' 'Julius dancer' (homosex-ual). Poor Julius (if he be the same person).

Justinianus 'Justinian'.
Roman emperor of the later eastern empire who ruled from Constantinople AD 482-565. Christian, soldier, law giver he is probably

best remembered for his *corpus juris civilis* 'complete civil law' and for his Institutes (see *justitia est*) the introduction to which says all: *In nomine Domini nostri Jesu Christi. Imperator Caesar Flavius Justinianus Alamannicus Gothicus Francicus Germanicus Anticus Alanicus Vandalicus Africanus pius felix inclytus victor et triumphator semper Augustus cupidae legum juventuti* 'in the name of our Lord Jesus Christ, The emperor Caesar Flavius Justinian vanquisher of the Alamani, Goths, Francs, Germans, Antes, Alani, Vandals, Africans, dutiful, happy, glorious, triumphant conqueror, ever August, to the youth desirous of studying the law greeting'.

Tribonian masterminded production of his legal works while his remarkable military successes were due in large part to his great general Belisarius. See *Gaius* and *item is*.

Justitia est constans et perpetua voluntas jus suum cuique tribuens 'justice is the constant and perpetual wish to render every one his due'. The opening words of Book I title I, *de justitia et jure* 'about justice and law', of Justinian's Institutes. But what is a man's due?

The emperor Justinian (see *Justinianus*) 482–565 caused to be compiled the whole of the ancient Roman Law in fifty books called the Digests. From these were extracted four briefer volumes for practical use in learning the law, the Institutes. The emperor's personal commendation, given in 533, might bring a smile to the faces of modern law students. *Summa itaque ope et alacri studio has leges nostras accipite* 'Receive therefore with eagerness and study with cheerful diligence these our laws'. How many nowadays would even qualify to enter a competition for an emperor's prize for the most eager, cheerful and diligent student of the law? See *Gaius, redde cuique* and *reddite ergo*.

Justitia Thronam Firmat 'justice strengthens the throne'. Inscription on coinage of Charles I (on half-groats and pennies).

L

Laborare est orare 'to work is to pray'. The Benedictine monk's motto. Varied to '*Orando laborando*' 'by praying and working' it is the motto of Rugby School.

Labor omnia vincit 'work conquers all things'. Probably an abbreviation, with change of tense, of Virgil's statement in Georgics *labor omnia* *vicit improbus* 'ceaseless work overcame all'. An expression adopted by capitalists to exhort workers: productive of stress related illness.

> 'One of the symptoms of approaching nervous breakdown is the belief that one's work is terribly important, and that to take a holiday would bring all kinds of disaster'.
> Bertrand Russell 1872-1970. Conquest of Happiness 1930.

'Arbeit macht frei' 'work makes for liberty' was the terrible cynical message inscribed above the entrances to Auschwitz and other extermination camps created by the Nazis 1940-45. See *amor vincit omnia*.

Lacrima Christi 'a tear of Christ'. Expression used as the name for a sweet Italian wine. One might have hoped for something more exalted relating to these words.

Lactrodectus mactans Latin classificatory name for the deadly poisonous black widow spider. In UK, during November of 2002, three such spiders were found amongst grapes in separate purchases from supermarkets. Nobody was bitten.

Lacuna 'gap; void, pit, hole, chasm or defect'. A word of many meanings with a common thread. Used particularly by lawyers where there are frequently to be found *lacunae* (plural) in the law or in legislation. See eg., R v Duggan Times 7th October 2002.*

Lapsus linguae 'a slip of the tongue'.

Latet anguis in herba 'a snake lies hidden in the grass'. Virgil Ecl. III. 93. Virgil writes of a herdsman telling children, who are gathering flowers, to beware of a hidden danger.

In English the expression 'snake in the grass' may refer to a person who is treacherous and not to be trusted or to a lurking danger.

> 'It is the bright day that brings forth the adder;
> And that craves wary walking'.
> William Shakespeare. Julius Caesar II.I.14.

See *fide sed cui* and *vipera berus*.

Latine dictum 'spoken in Latin'. See *Anglice, Gallice* and *Latine scriptum*.

Latium. Name of a district in central Italy lying near the sea on the left bank of the river Tiber, which included ancient Rome. The language of this district was Latin. *Latius* means belonging to *Latium*. Latin is an engaging language and a model of brevity but nobody should pretend that it is easy.

'The Romans would never have found time to conquer the world if they had been obliged first to learn Latin'.
Heinrich Heine.

Latium was reputed to produce good wines and Horace tells us that it was the done thing to produce it on one's own estate. Epistles ii.2.160. Horace also relates:

Graecia capta ferum victorem cepit et artes
Intulit agresti Latio.
'Once overcome, Greece overcame her wild conqueror and brought the arts (culture) to rustic Latium'. Epistles ii.I.156.

See *oratio obliqua* and *vivat lingua Latina*.

Laudate Dominum 'praise the Lord'. Set to music by W. A. Mozart. *Vesperae solennes de Dominica* K321. First words of Psalm 150. 'Praise God in his holiness: praise him in the firmament of his power'. See too Psalms 117,147 and 148.

Laudator temporis acti 'a praiser of times acted out', of times past. Horace. Ars Poetica 173. The familiar observation of those who begin to grow old: 'things aren't what they used to be'. Probably they never were: this is nothing new. We think now of *homo antiqua virtute et fide* 'an old fashioned man of probity and loyalty'. Terence Adelphi III.iii.88. Terence died c. 159 BC? See *probitas laudatur, o tempora* and *quae fuerant vitia mores sunt.*

Laus est facere quod decet, non quod licet 'it is laudable to do what you ought to do, and not just what the law permits'. Observation of Cardinal Wolsey (recorded by his gentleman usher, George Cavendish in his 'Life and Death of Cardinal Wolsey') in the course of a conversation with one Master Shelley, who had brought the King's (Henry VIII's) commission demanding that Wolsey's House at Westminster, York Place, be made over to the King, since it was required as a Royal Palace. Wolsey, who was Lord Chancellor at the time, told Shelley in effect that the request was lawful, since the King was the King, but explained that the property belonged to the Bishopric of York and really ought to be paid for. Shelley replied that the King *could* pay twofold. The gist of Wolsey's response was that whatever he could do, there seemed to be no indication that he intended any payment at all.

Wolsey was quoting Seneca: *id facere laus est quod decet, non quod licet* 'it is praiseworthy to do what one ought to do not (only) what one is permitted to do:' ie., one should do the decent thing, not just what one can get away with.

Cicero was of much the same view: *Est aliquid quod non oportet, etiamsi licet* 'there is something which is not fitting, even if lawful'. Some things just won't do!

Legatus a latere 'legate (sent) from the side (of the Pope)'. Name given to a Papal office once held by Cardinal Wolsey. When Thomas Wolsey was Archbishop of York, he could not head the Church in England while Archbishop Warham of Canterbury lived. But he could supersede Canterbury by becoming *legatus a latere*. First he had to become a Cardinal. To this, at the request of King Henry VIII, the Pope agreed. Three years later, in 1518, he further reluctantly agreed to make Wolsey *legatus a latere* and, in 1524, made this a lifelong appointment. Wolsey headed the church in England, *primus inter pares* (see below) with the Archbishop of Canterbury.

Ultimately this was to be Wolsey's undoing. In 1529, after his failure to secure annulment of the King's marriage, he was indicted in the King's Bench. By publishing his papal bulls of appointment as *legatus a latere* within the realm of England he had offended against the Statute of *Praemunire* (which *inter alia* made it an offence to assert the supremacy of the Pope over the Crown of England). See *ego et rex meus* and *plus quam valor*.

Lege feliciter 'read happily'. Bede.

Legem brevem esse oportet 'a law should be brief'. Cicero. The long and convoluted Civil Jurisdiction and Judgements Act 1982 (at the time the most important chapter of community law since the European Communities Act of 1972) made clear why; and on its passage through the legislature drew the following comments:

'I rather think that it should be accompanied by a Government Health warning. There is nothing whatever I can do to make my speech short, and those who expect to find it of throbbing human interest will, I fear, be wholly disappointed. The road lies uphill all the way'.

Lord Hailsham. Lord Chancellor. HL, December 3, 1981, Vol. 425 Col, 1126.

'This mind-boggling myriad of legal complexity'.

Mr. Barry Porter. HC, March 24 1982, Vol. 20, col. 1126.

' . . . this is on any showing a Bill of enormous complication. I would go further and say that the measure gives to the word complexity a new dimension'.

Lord Foot HL, December 3 1981, Vol 425, col 1141.

Lege refertus 'stuffed with law', Motto on the Coat of Arms of Sir Christopher Staughton (*quondam* Lord Justice). Chosen by him as a pun on his name, it was received by The College of Arms with acclaim, since such a pun is in the finest heraldic tradition. Esoteric and Delphic it might have been baffling to many: 'by the law filled up, made rich, browned off'?

Legum idcirco servi sumus ut liberi esse possimus 'we are the bondsmen of the law so that we may be free'. Cicero.

Levavi oculos 'I will lift up mine eyes' (to the hills from whence cometh my help). Opening words of Psalm 121.

Lex talionis 'the law of retaliation'. A norm by which one does not turn the other cheek: one replies in kind on the principle 'an eye for an eye and a tooth for a tooth'. See Exodus: 21 'And if a man cause a blemish in his neighbour; as he hath done so shall it be done to him. And if any mischief follow, then thou shalt give life for life, eye for eye, tooth for tooth, hand for hand, foot for foot'. This directive is exemplified in full measure by the murderous tit for tat retaliative measures seen in Northern Ireland and more recently in the Israeli/Palestinian conflict: particularly in 2002-4. Cf., Leviticus 24:20 and Deuteronomy 19:21. See and note *nemo me impune*, *non revertar* and *qui mihi*.

Libenter enim sufferes insipientes cum sitis ipsi sapientes 'for ye suffer fools gladly seeing you yourselves are wise'. Vulgate. St. Paul epistle to the Corinthians II.ii.19. Source of the expression 'not to suffer fools gladly'. Note that those who are wise do suffer gladly their less gifted brethren to whom destiny has not been so kind: not to do so is unworthy and not to be applauded.

Remember: 'Be not wise in your own conceits'. Romans 12:16 and: 'The fool doth think he is wise, but the wise man knows himself to be a fool'. William Shakespeare As You Like It. Act V Sc.1. l.34. See *sapere aude*

Libinossima 'the most lusty (sexy) woman'. How many women would like to be so described?

Libra 'scales or balance'. The sign of the zodiac for those born between 22nd September and 22nd October inclusive.

It is nothing new for us to read our horoscope, now usually in the newspaper. The emperor Vespasian, 69-79 had supreme confidence in these predictions. Suetonius (23) tells us that this emperor was reputed to have dreamed of a pair of scales hanging in the palace: Claudius and his adopted son Nero were at one end and exactly balanced against himself, Titus and Domitian at the other. In the event this proved right, since the families ruled for equal periods of time. The emperor Augustus (27 BC-AD14) also laid store by his birth sign, capricorn and the historian Cassius Dio tells us that the emperor Septimius Severus (180-92) was a great believer in his horoscope. *Libra* was also the Roman pound weight. See *augur, aureus, bonis avibus* and *sagittarius*. For further detail see appendix 3.

Licet 'it is permitted'. A formal mode of granting permission. *Non licet:* it is not allowed.

Lictor. An officer attending a consul or other Roman magistrate. See *fasces.**

Lignum vitae 'wood of life'. The second hardest wood in the world (after snakewood). So called because, powdered, it was once thought to have medicinal properties. Resin in the wood can act as a lubricant and made it suitable for use by John Harrison in making moving parts, which would not corrode, for some of the timekeepers he produced between 1730 and 1760 in his (ultimately successful) pursuit of the Longitude Prize: for a full account read 'Longitude' by Dava Sobel 1995. This wood grows in the West Indian islands, Colombia, Venezuela and Central America.

Lingua Franca 'Frankish language'. *Lingua* is the Latin for a tongue or language. Franca is Italian. In the middle ages the Arabs called all Europeans Franks. The Frankish language evolved as a trading language, a mixture of Italian, French, Greek and Spanish. The expression *lingua franca* has come to be used as jargon, meaning the language used by two speakers of different tongues who communicate by a third language.

Lingua Latina occasionibus omnibus 'Latin for all occasions'. Title of a book of Latin light entertainment written by Henry Beard and published by Harper Collins in 1993.

Liquam(en) antipol(itanem) exc(ellens) L(uci) Tett(i)i Africani. Afri(cani) 'Lucius Tettius Africanus's finest fish sauce from Antibes; (product) of Africanus'. Abbreviated information (that in brackets is amplificatory gloss) painted in black on the neck of a first/second century *amphora* (clay vessel or jar usually with handles) found in London and exhibited in the Museum of London. See *condimentum*.

Literae humaniores 'the more humane writings or literature'. The humanities; secular as opposed to sacred learning. The University of Oxford Examination Statutes (to the end of Trinity 1958) provide: 'The examination in the honour school of *Literae Humaniores* shall always include as stated subjects: (1) The Greek and Latin languages. (2) The histories of Ancient Greece and Rome, to be studied as far as possible in the original authors. (3) Logic, and the outlines of moral and Political Philosophy. . .' This was referred to as 'reading greats' or 'reading classics'.

Litus arare 'to plough the sea shore . . . sand'. To labour fruitlessly or to no purpose.

Loco citato 'in the place cited'. Abbreviated to: *loc, cit.* e.g., in a foot-note it refers to a passage previously cited.

Locum tenens 'holding the place'. Used to refer to one who stands in for a cleric or, more commonly, a doctor '*locum*'. A substitute. Yet the word vicar is derived from *vicarius* meaning one who acts as a substitute or deputy.*

Locus 'a place'. A position or point. *Locus in quo* 'place in which': an expression used regularly in the past by lawyers when referring to the scene of an accident or crime or other matter under consideration.*

Locus classicus 'the classic place or source'. A reference to the most authoritative or most commonly cited passage or authority used to explain or illustrate some matter. The '*locus classicus*' of Latin Grammar was (and perhaps still is) Kennedy's Revised Latin Primer, published by Longman. See *fabulae faciles*.

Longissime a sapientia fors diffidet, Sed multa perficiet tamen simillima. Words of Sir Walter Raleigh in his great work 'The History of the World' (at section 15 in chapter one of the first part) and elegantly translated by him thus:

'From wisdom fortune differs far,
And yet in works most like they are'.

Written during his imprisonment between 1605-1616 this work was published in 1614. It achieved great popularity and by the 1640s was the most popular book in the library of the poet Henry Oxinden at Elham, near Canterbury in Kent. It deals with Egyptian, Greek and Biblical history from the creation to 168 BC. Oliver Cromwell rated it second only to the Bible. See *soles occidere*.

Lucilla ex corpore lucra faciebat 'Lucilla has been making money from her body'. Graffiti on the Basilica at Pompeii. See *sum tua*.

Lucri bonus est odor ex re qualibet 'the smell of money is good wherever it comes from'. Juvenal 14. 204-5. 'Money is like muck, not good unless it be spread'. Francis Bacon 1561-1626. Of Seditions and Troubles. 'Where there's muck there's brass' is the modern Yorkshire adage. See *ab honesto virum, dona clandestina, nec prece, nolite thesaurisare, omnia Romae, oportet ergo, pecunia non olet, radix malorum* and *si possis recte*.

Lupus in fabula 'the wolf in the story'. Terence, Adel. 1.21. Used of one who appears when spoken of. Speak of the devil. Not a Roman Little Red Riding Hood equivalent.

Lux et veritas 'light and truth'. Motto of Yale University. One up on Harvard, which has in its motto truth but not light. See *veritas* below. See also *ego sum, fortis est, magna est, quid est* and *veritas*.

Lux gentium lex 'light of the nations (of the peoples of the world), law'. The motto incorporated in the trade logo of Sweet and Maxwell Ltd, publishers of law books and periodicals.

Lux mundi 'the light of the world'. Vulgate. St. John. Viii.12. Jesus said: 'I am the light of the world: he that followeth me shall not walk in darkness, but shall have the light of life'.

'*Lux mundi*' is the title to Holman Hunt's famous painting of Christ standing by a door and holding a lamp which John Ruskin described as one of the noblest works of sacred art ever produced in this or any other age. Completed in 1854 it entered a private collection before being presented to Keble College, Oxford where it still hangs. Mr. Holman Hunt was unhappy with the way the College kept his painting and painted the subject matter again, much larger. This was first displayed in 1904 and was then exhibited around the world before ending up in St. Paul's Cathedral where it can be seen still hanging on the south side of the nave.

The painting (of Christ standing with a lamp and knocking at a door) is based upon the Book of Revelations Ch 3 v. 2. 'Behold, I stand at the door, and knock: if any man hear my voice, and open the door, I will come in to him, and will sup with him, and he with me'. In the picture there is no handle on the door. It is for whoever is inside to open it, trusting in The Light of the World. See *Dominus illuminatio mea.*

M

Macte nova virtute, puer, sic itur ad astra 'blessings on your young courage, boy: thus you go to the stars'. Virgil.
Compare: *audaces fortuna iuvat, audentis fortuna favet, fortuna favet fortibus* and *per ardua ad astra.*

Magister artium 'master of arts'. Abbreviated to MA.

Magister juris 'master of law'. Abbreviated to M. Jur. Post graduate law degree of Oxford University introduced in the academic year 1992-1993. Like the older BCL, (Bachelor of Civil Law) it is a Master's degree. The M. Jur. is a one year taught degree for students from a non-common law background while the BCL caters for students from a common law background. From the year 2001-2002 the M. Jur. syllabus has included business taxation law.

Magna Carta 'the great charter'. A charter of liberty and political rights forced from King John in June 1215 on the small island of Runnymede in the river Thames near Windsor. It outlined the Royal powers and rights of barons and freemen.
    A child once wrote in his scripture lesson: 'when Mary heard that she was to be the mother of Jesus, she sang the *Magna Carta*'.
See *Magnificat.*

Magna cum laude 'with great or high praise'. See *summa cum laude.*

Magna (est) veritas et praevalebit 'great is truth and it shall prevail'. From 1 Esdras 4.41. The books of Esdra form part of the Apocrypha (a Greek word meaning 'hidden things') which is a collection of Jewish writings of about 300 BC-AD 100. The Council of Trent (1548) of the Roman Catholic Church accepted that some of its content should be treated as part of the scriptures. The thirty nine articles of the Anglican Church lay down that the Apocrypha may be read 'for the example of life and the instruction of manners but may not be used to establish doctrine'. 'Someone says it's a lie. Well I am reminded by that of the remark of the witty Irishman who said: "there is a terrible lot of lies about the world, and the worst of it is that the half of them are true"'. Winston S. Churchill. See *ego sum via, fortis est, lux et, quid est, utilius* and *veritas*.

Magnificat 'it magnifies'. The Virgin Mary's reaction to the Annunciation. Gospel of St. Luke i. 46-55. The song of the Blessed Virgin Mary to be said or sung in English at Evening Prayer after a lesson from the Old Testament in accordance with the Church of England Book of Common Prayer: 'My soul doth magnify the Lord: and my spirit hath rejoiced in God my saviour' *Magnificat anima mea Dominum: Et exsultavit spiritus meus in Deo saluteri mea.* Vulgate. Set to music *inter alios* by J.S.Bach. See *esurientes implevit bonis* and *Magna Carta*.

Magnum opus 'a great work'. A writer's or artist's best work. A great work of art or literature. See *ave Maria* and *opus magnum*.

Major e longinquo reverentia 'respect is greater from a distance'. Familiarity breeds contempt. Cf., St. Matthew Ch 13 v 57. *Jesus autem dixit eis. Non est propheta sine honore nisi in patria sua et in domo sua.* (Vulgate) 'But Jesus said unto them, a prophet is not without honour, save in his own country and in his own house'. Said after Jesus had been rejected by his own town of Nazareth.

Most parents, whose children ignore their wisdom, will understand this. Yet older parents will be aware of the converse: 'Dad/Mum you must become more computer literate'. Cf., *omne ignotum* and see *credite posteri* and *est adulescentis majores*.

Majusculae 'capital letters'. Twenty two of the twenty six letters in our alphabet come from the Roman alphabet. There was no W or Y in the Roman alphabet and J was written as I. U and V were both written as V. See *Trajan* and *minusculae*.

Malum in se 'bad in itself'. Intrinsically bad.

Mappa mundi 'map of the world'. Perhaps the most famous of maps known by this Latin expression is that in Hereford Cathedral. A late 13th century wall map, it has survived in its entirety. The world is drawn on vellum as a circle with Jerusalem at its centre. How it came to Hereford is unknown: the first reference to it being 1682. Little sketches (of buildings, animals, monsters, devils etc) and cartoons cover it: related commentary and information is in Latin.

It is headed by Christ seated at the day of judgement. To his right an angel with a trumpet summons the blessed to joy. To his left another promises doom to the lost.

This '*mappa*' is still in Hereford Cathedral thanks to Sir Paul Getty's generous three million pound gift in the early 1990's.

Margarita 'a pearl'.

Masada. An ancient mountain fortress near the dead sea made famous by the great siege AD 66-74. Zealots of the Jewish revolt against Roman rule held out astonishingly against besieging legions initially under Vespasian (who became emperor during this time). The resolute Romans built and manned an encircling wall with regular attached forts but succeded finally through the construction by Flavius Silva of a huge siege ramp: a wondrous feat of engineering. With defeat staring them at last in the face the defenders all committed suicide.

In AD 71, well in advance of the fall of Masada, the Romans issued coinage of Vespasian with the legend *Judaea Captiva* 'Judaea captive' showing a Jewish woman guarded apparently by a soldier.

See *ecce agnus Dei*, *plus quam valor* and *una salus*.

M. Casellium Marcellum, aedile bonum, et numerarium magnum 'Marcus Casellius Marcellus a generous *aedile* (see *cursus honorum*) and generous sponsor' (of gladiatorial contests).

Graffiti in the Via Augustus on the wall of a house where probably the *aedile* lived in Pompeii.

Mea culpa 'by my blame or fault'. Mine is the blame . . . I am to blame. *Mea maxima culpa* 'mine is the greatest blame/fault'. I am extremely sorry. An apology.

Me consule 'in my time as Consul'. During my stewardship or term of office. See *consule Planco*.

Medici, causa morbi inventa, curationem inventam putant 'when doctors have found the cause of a disease, they think they have found the cure'. Cicero. *Tusculanae Disputationes 3.23.*

For medical men, diagnosis is the exciting, professional and intellectual challenge. Not infrequently thereafter it seems that whether there is anything curative to be done, is of lesser interest. See *graviore quaedam*.

Medicinae Doctor 'doctor of medicine'. An advanced medical degree from universities abbreviated to MD.

Medio tutissimus ibis 'the middle way is the safest for you to take'. Ovid. Metamorphoses ii. 137.

Me judice 'in my opinion or judgement'.

Meliores priores 'the better first'. Motto.

Melita 'honeyed'. Roman name for Malta from which the island's present name is derived. The island was very fertile at the time of its Roman occupation.

Memento mori 'remember that you are to die'. Expression used of anything that reminds of death's inevitability. One's last will and testament is a *memento mori* (if one has made one: if not, one really must, otherwise much money may be wasted on lawyers and more than necessary may go to the state). So too is the skull-and crossbones, the 'Jolly Roger' of pirate history. This emblem of death warned of what would follow resistance (and often in any event). Sometimes the pirate symbol took the form of a skull and cross swords.

Memorabilia 'things to be remembered'. Also objects by which things, people or events are to be remembered.

Mens sana in corpore sano 'a sound mind in a sound body'. Juvenal. X. 356. Something to be prayed for *orandum est ut sit mens sana in corpore sano*. But for some there may be something more to be desired. E.M. Forster wrote:

> 'They (public schoolboys) go forth into a world . . . of whose richness and sublety they have no conception. They go forth into it with well developed bodies, fairly developed minds and underdeveloped hearts'.
>
> Abinger Harvest 1936. 'Notes on English Character.'

See *compos mentis* and *Vegetus*.

Mens sibi conscia recti 'a mind conscious of its own righteousness'. Virgil. Aeneid. I. 601. Aeneas is talking about himself. See and Cf., *conscia mens recti*.

Meo periculo 'at my risk'.

Mero motu 'by or on one's own initiative'.

Merobibus. A word descriptive of the drinking of wine without water. As a young military officer the emperor Tiberius was seen as a hard drinker. His full name was Tiberius Claudius Nero. He was nicknamed 'Biberius Caldius Mero' 'drinker of wine unmixed with water'. Suetonius. Tiberius 42. For a sympathetic depiction of this unpopular (misunderstood?) emperor see Allan Massie's immensely readable historical novels 'Augustus' and 'Tiberius' published by Sceptre. See *aqua vitae damnatio memoriae, rescripsit boni* and *verbosa et grandis*.

**Meum est propositum
In taberna mori,
Ut sit vinum propius
Morientis ori.
Tunc cantabunt laetius
Angelorum chori:
Sit Deus propitius
Huic potatori**

'my intent is to die in a pub so that the wine shall be closer to my dying mouth. Then shall the choirs of angels sing more happily may God be more merciful to this imbiber'. Medieval doggerel Latin verse.

Militat omnis amans 'everyone in love is at war'. Ovid. Amores. I.ix.i. The poet compared lovers with soldiers: he also wrote *militiae species amor est* 'love is a kind of war'.

What do others think?

'And love's the noblest frailty of the mind'.
The Italian Emperor. John Dryden 1631–1700.
'La coeur a ses raisons que la raison ne connait point'.
Pensées. Blaise Pascal.
'The magic of first love is our ignorance that it can ever end'.
Henrietta Temple. Benjamin Disraeli. See *felix heu*.
'Oh, 'tis love, 'tis love that makes the world go round'.
Lewis Carroll (Charles Dodgson) Alice's Adventures in Wonderland.
'It lies not in one's soul to love or hate,
For will in us is overrul'd by fate . . . .
Where both deliberate, the love is slight;
Who ever loved that loved not at first sight'.
Christopher Marlowe 1564 – 93. Hero and Leander.

The last line appears in Shakespeare's As You Like It.

'Experience teaches us that to love is not to gaze at one another but to gaze together in the same direction'.

Antoine de Saint-Exupéry.

See *amor vincit, amare et sapere* and *Cestilia*.

Millenium 'a thousand years,' or the anniversary thereof. M in Roman numerals. MM is 2000. See appendix two.

Minimus 'smallest'. Some will remember single sex schools where boys were called by their surname only. If there were Smith brothers, the eldest would be "Smith" and his younger brother would be Smith *minor* (smaller Smith). If there was yet another brother, younger than both, he would be Smith *minimus* (Smith the "littlest").

"Minimus: Starting Out in Latin*"* is also the title of a Latin teaching course for children aged 7 to 10. Written by Barbara Bell, it was published in September 1999 by the Cambridge University Press. Following positive press coverage, it has met with great success in reviving enthusiasm for Latin: and has inspired grandparents in large numbers (well in excess of 1,000) to volunteer as teachers of the language in breaks and after school.

Minutiae 'small things', small matters or trifles. To fuss over the *minutiae* is to waste time with unnecessary detail. Cf., in the law *de minimis non curat lex* 'the law does not concern itself with the smallest things', trifles. Francis Bacon letter 282.

Minusculae. Small Roman cursive script (as opposed to *majusculae* above). See *Brittunculi* and *Trajan*.

Mirabile dictu 'miraculous to say'. Wonderful or amazing to relate. Virgil Georgics ii.30. An expression often used (in the Latin) with irony in relation to information or a story which is either inherently unlikely or utterly predictable.

A portrait in London's National Gallery, thought to be of St. Ivo (patron saint of lawyers) from the workshop of Rogier van der Weyden (*circa* 1450) bore the inscription *Sanctus Ivo erat Brito. Advocatus sed non latro. Res populo miranda* 'St. Ivo was a Breton. A lawyer but not a robber. Something miraculous to the people'. Instead of the last three words of the Latin there might just as well have been *mirabile dictu*.

M. Mirenius Julius bucinator cohortis vii vigilum 'Marcus Mirenius Julius trumpeter of the seventh watch cohort'. Graffiti at Pompeii.

Misce stultitiam consiliis brevem: Dulce est desipere in loco
'mix a little stupidity with wisdom: it's such fun to let one's hair down on occasion'. Horace. Iv. xii. 27.

'Every man has his follies . . . and often they are the best things he has'. Josh Billings 1818-1885. Cf., La Rochefoucauld's (1613 – 80) view:

Qui vit sans folie n'est pas si sage qu'il croit 'whoever lives his life without some stupidity is not as wise (clever) as he thinks'.

See *muscae morientes*.

Miserere 'have mercy'. Psalm 51 (50 in the Vulgate) is referred to as 'The Miserere' and commences: 'Have mercy upon me, O God' . . . *Miserere mei, Deus*. A Psalm of David and one of penitence. Verse 3: 'For I acknowledge my transgressions: and my sin is ever before me'.

Misericordia 'pity, mercy'. Misericord is the name given to a type of seat found in the choir stalls of some cathedrals, monasteries and old churches. The "main" seat tips up on hinges to allow more standing room and reveals affixed to the underneath and towards the front a narrow wooden ledge seat. Often exquisitely decorated with ancillary carved images, this (alternative higher seat) allows the occupant, now standing, to adopt a sitting/standing position taking weight off his feet. In times past these accommodated arthritic and infirm ageing monks called upon to stand and sing Gregorian Chants for long periods: installed out of pity for their plight; to relieve their misery.

Monks are not alone in a calling which requires them to stand for long periods. There is a case for installion of such alternative seating arrangements to accommodate advocates in law courts.

Some of the earliest misericords, dating from 13th century, are in Bristol, Chester, Winchester, Lincoln, Gloucester and Carlisle Cathedrals and Maidstone All Saints Church. The fascinating, often mysterious, wood carvings associated with misericords depict everything from the bawdy, the superstitious, the legendary and the biblical to the Coat of Arms of the patron funding their installation eg., Archbishop Courtney (1381-97) at Maidstone. In Lincoln Cathedral is an exquisitely carved knight fallen with his horse as he is felled by the bolt from a cross-bow. For more see "A Little book of Misericords" by Mike Harding. Aurum Press Ltd. See *Missa in Dominica Resurrectionis*.

Missa. The ecclesiastical Latin term for the Roman Catholic Mass: set to music in B minor by Johann Sebastian Bach 1685-1750. The Missal, in the Roman Catholic Church, is a book containing the texts in the service of the Mass throughout the church year.

Missa in Dominica Resurrectionis 'Mass for the Lord's Resurrection' . . . for Easter Sunday (*Solemnitas Solemnitatum* . . . the Feast of Feasts . . . The Roman Catholic Latin name for Easter Sunday). A Gregorian chant (the name given to plainsong music sung by monks and introduced by Pope Gregory 1st [AD 590-604] who made a number of changes to the liturgy and concerned himself with liturgical music). Other notable Gregorian chants are:

Prima Missa in Commemoratione Omnium Fidelium; 'first mass in memory of all the faithful dead' and *Prima Missa in Navitate Domini Nostri Jesu Christi:* 'first Mass for the birth of Jesus Christ Our Lord' (first Christmas Mass).

In the year AD 529 the Emperor Justinian declared the feast of the Lord's birth a public holiday. See *Justinianus*. See *misericordia*.

Missa in tempore belli 'Mass in time of war'. Haydn's Mass No. 9 in C (1796) otherwise known as the 'Pankenmesse'.

Missa solemnis 'solemn Mass', High Mass, especially in the Roman Catholic Church. So called because the concluding part of the Latin liturgy is: *ite*, . . . *missa est* 'go . . . it is the dismissal' . . . the Mass is finished. Also the name by which Beethoven's Mass in D, op. 123 (1823) is known.

Mobile vulgus 'the fickle crowd or mob'. Statius. Silvae II.ii.123. The easily moved or duped general public. The English word 'mob' is derived from this but has a different shade of meaning with connotations of disorderly or unruly behaviour. Cf., *miserabile vulgus* . . . 'the wretched mob'. See *belua multorum*, *ad captandum vulgus*, *faex populi*, *plebs* and *profanum vulgus*.

Modus operandi 'way of operating'. The particular way in which an individual goes about a specific task. Readily understood in domestic terms. When cooking there are those whose *modus operandi* is to clear up as they go along and there are those whose it is not. The behaviour of those whose it is not is calculated to cause depression, even psychiatric illness, in those whose it is.

Modus vivendi 'way of living'. Lifestyle. When my wife was away he suggested that I was out on the razzle every night. I wondered if the observation reflected his own *modus vivendi* or wishful thinking.

Mortui non mordent 'dead men don't bite'. Erasmus Adages iii. vi. Nothing is to be feared from dead men. Dead men tell no tales. View perhaps of the Tudor Kings and Queens from 1509 onwards and of Oliver Cromwell. But not necessarily true if by putting a man to death you make him a martyr. 'Death solves all problems – No man – no problem'. J. V. Stalin

Multis timere debet quem multi timent
'he whom many fear should be afraid of many'.
'A man who is feared by many has cause to fear many'.
  Francis Bacon.

'Uneasy lies the head that wears a crown'.
  William Shakespeare. Henry IV Part ii Act iii scene I line 31.

See *oderint dum metuant*.

Multum in parvo 'much in little'. A tabloid newspaper with all essential information concisely presented is one of which it ought to be appropriate to say: *multum in parvo*.

Munera nunc edunt et, verso pollice vulgus cum jubet, occidunt populariter 'today they hold shows by slaying with the turn of a thumb whomsoever the mob bids them kill'. Juvenal 3. 36 f. Famous despairing comment on the times (c.AD 100) and the gladiatorial contests. Things never were what they used to be. Note *ave Caesar* above. See *Colosseum, editor, retiarius, secutor* and *silentium*.

Muscae morientes perdunt suavitatem unguenti pretiosior est sapientia et gloria parva ad tempus stultitia 'dead flies destroy the sweetness of an ointment: so doth a little folly in him that is in reputation for wisdom and honour'. Vulgate *Liber Ecclesiastes 10:1*. Source of the expression 'fly in the ointment'. See *cave quid* and *misce stultitiam*.

Muscosi fontes et somno mollior herba 'The mossy fountains and the green retreats!' Virgil, Eclogue 7 lines 45-46. Translated by Alexander Pope 1688-1744 and inspiration for what followed:

'Where-e'r you walk, cool gales shall fan the glade.
Trees, where you sit, shall crowd into a shade,
Where-e'r you tread, the blushing flowers shall rise,
And all things flourish where you turn your eyes'.

Set to music by George Frederick Handel in Semele and very popular in the 1930's as sung by John McCormack: pop music of the times. Attributed to Handel and comparably romantic is:

'Did you not hear my lady come down to the garden singing
Silencing all the songbirds and setting the alleys ringing'.

See *et vera incessu.*

Mutatis mutandis 'things having been changed which needed to be changed'. Making the necessary alterations.*

N

Nam et ipsa scientia potestas est 'for knowledge itself is power'. Francis Bacon 1561-1621. Religious Meditations. Of Heresies. But remember that a pessimist is too often a well-informed optimist. Francis Bacon was the first Queen's Counsel. Lawyers' appointment to this rank developed into the secret and too often apparently arbitrary system administered until June of 2003 by a Department of State which allocated Royal Patronage on behalf of the Crown. 'Patronage the companion of power' is the old adage.

Nam in omni adversitate fortunae infelicissimum genus est infortunii, fuisse felicem 'For in every turn of adverse fortune, the most unhappy kind of misfortune is to have been happy.' Boethius *De Consolatione Philosophiae* 'Consolation of Philosophy', Book ii, prose 4. Blissful happiness is rare and lesser happiness makes only sporadic appearance and seldom lasts. But does Boethius not say that once it is known, the later acute awareness of its absence makes it a misfortune? This was written during imprisonment. Severinus Boethius (c.AD 480 – 524) was a patrician Roman. Consul in 523 he was accused of treason and imprisoned (when the above work was written) before execution in 524. In the thousand years following his death this work was possibly the most widely read book after the Bible. He has been described as the last of the Roman Philosophers and the first of the scholastic theologians.

Nam risu inepto res ineptior nulla est 'there is no more foolish thing than a silly laugh'. Catullus 87-54 BC xxxiv. Cf.,

'And the loud laugh that spoke the vacant mind'.
  'The Deserted Village'. Oliver Goldsmith 1728-1774.

See *nullum quod tetigit.*

Nam tua res agitur, paries cum proximus ardet 'for it is your concern when your neighbour's wall goes on fire'. Horace Epistles 1.i.84.

If the house of a Roman went on fire when he was away on holiday and his neighbour extinguished the fire and then secured the roof, the neighbour could, by *negotiorum gestio*, recover the reasonable cost of his voluntary unauthorised good deed. English law is not so benevolent. You expend money to assist your neighbour at your financial peril.

Narcissus obvallaris. Botanist's Latin classificatory name for daffodil.

> 'Daffodils
> That come before the swallow dares and take
> The winds of March with beauty'.
> William Shakespeare. Winter's Tale. Act IV Sc 4 ll 118-120.

Global warming has daffodils flowering in February; no longer in April. So much the more poignant therefore are words of Robert Herrick 1591- 1674, 'To Daffodils':

> 'Fair daffodils, we weep to see
> You haste away so soon; . .'

And William Wordsworth 1770 –1850

> 'I wandered lonely as a cloud':
> . . . when all at once I saw a crowd,
> A host of golden daffodils;
> Beside the lake beneath the trees,
> Fluttering and dancing in the breeze.
> . . . . . . For oft when on my couch I lie
> In vacant or in pensive mood,
> They flash upon that inward eye
> Which is the bliss of solitude;
> And then my heart with pleasure fills
> And dances with the daffodils'.

See *beatus* and *nunquam minus.*

Natura abhorret a vacuo 'nature abhors a vacuum'.

Natura nihil agit frustra 'nature does nothing in vain'.

Natus 'born'. Sometimes on gravestones with date of birth and of death to show life-span. See *hic jacet, hic sepultus, tempus tacendi* and *obit.*

Naufragia 'shipwrecks, accidents, crashes'. Word used for the pile ups which occurred when chariots collided in the immensely popular Roman chariot races. See *circus* and *tabula ex.*

Ne cede malis 'do not yield to misfortune'. Virgil Aen., VI. 95. See *nil desperandum* and *tu ne cede*.

Nec prece nec pretio 'by neither prayer (entreaty) nor price (bribe)'. Not for love or money. Motto. See *ab honesto virum bonum, omnia Romae, si possis recte* and *probitas laudatur*.

Nemine contradicente (abbreviated to *nem con*) 'nobody speaking against'. Nobody dissenting or all agreed. See *ad idem, constat* and *una voce*.

Nem con. See *nemine contradicente*.

Nemo aspicit, quin ingemescat 'no one looks at you without groaning'. Cicero *In Vatinium*. For most of us there is someone who has this effect; evidently it is nothing new. See *Cicero*.

Nemo me impune lacessit 'no one attacks me with impunity'. Motto of Scotland and of the Order of The Thistle. Inset in the milling around those one pound coins which bear the Scottish insignias on their reverse.

A boy saw a little wild rose growing. 'War so jung und morgenschön' it was so young and beautiful as the morning that he ran quickly to see it close up:

'Knabe sprach: Ich brech dich
Röslein auf der Heiden!
Röslein sprach: Ich steche dich,
Dass du ewig denkst an mich'.

'The boy said: "I'll pick you little wild rose on the moor". The little rose said: "I'll prick you, that you should for ever think of me"'.

A delightfully gentle example of *nemo me impune lacessit* extracted from J.W.Goethe's lyric 'Heidenröslein'. Set to folk music with its refrain of:

'Röslein, Röslein, Röslein rot
Röslein auf der Heiden'

it is prominent in German culture. Rot means red. See *fidem qui, decus et tutamen, lex talionis, non revertar inultus* and *qui mihi*.

Ne quid nimis 'let there be nothing in excess'. Terence Andria 61. Inscribed on the temple of the God Apollo at Delphi in Greece. Should be inscribed all over the City of London as a *caveat* midst a damaging culture of heavy drinking. Note *auditque vocatus Apollo*. And Apollo hears when called upon. Virgil Georgics iv. 7. See *est modus in rebus* and *nosce te*.

Nescis mi fili, quantilla prudentia mundus regatur 'you do not know my son with what a small stock of wisdom the world is governed'. Attributed to Oxenstierna (Swedish statesman 1583-1654) and others. (Entry courtesy of Chambers 20th Century Dictionary). Look at the current world leaders and think on this.

Nescit vox missa reverti. See *et semel emissum*.

Ne sutor ultra crepidam 'let the cobbler not venture beyond his sandal (last)'. Erasmus. Adages 1.vi.16. Keep to what you know about.

Niger 'black'.

Nihil ad rem 'nothing to the thing (point)'. Nothing to the matter (in hand); irrelevant.

Nihil est ab omni parte beatum 'nothing is a blessing unmixed'. Horace Odes xvi. 27. Counterpart: it is an ill wind that blows nobody good.

Nihil illegitimis carborundum est. Non-existent ostensibly Latin phrase incorporating only *some* authentic Latin words (*carborundum* being a modern trade name for sharpening stones, grinding discs and abrasive compounds). A delightful expression with a deceptive and subtle look of Latin authenticity; understood to mean: 'Don't let the bastards grind you down'. An uplifting slogan for those who feel that they are being unfairly or improperly treated. See *hodie mihi*.

Nihil obstat 'nothing stands in the way'. The way is clear: we can go ahead.

Nihil sine Deo 'without God there is nothing'. Motto. Sometimes *sine Deo nihil*. In the coat of arms of Charles Dawes High Sheriff of Kent for 2002.

Nihil sub solum nec valet quis quam dicere ecce hoc recens est 'there is nothing new under the sun which can properly be said to be recent'. Vulgate *Liber Ecclesiastes* 1:10. Biblical source of the expression: 'there is nothing new under the sun'.

Nil 'nothing'.*

Nil desperandum 'nothing is to be despaired of', never give up. From

Horace's Odes 1.vii.27. *Teucro duce et auspice Teucro* 'led by Teucer and watched over by Teucer' are the lesser known words following. How much more inspiring than the English translation. The gist of Sir Winston Churchill's exhortations in 1940. Useful slogan for the rugby scrum when you are twenty points to five down with five minutes to go. Obviously the gritty resolve of both crews in the epic boat race of 2003 when Cambridge fought to overhaul a slender Oxford lead but the latter held grimly on to win by a foot (how fitting that this was not expressed in metric terms!). See *at spes non fracta, carpe diem, tu ne cede malis* and *dum spiro spero*.

Nil obstat tibi dum ne sit te ditior alter 'nothing is a hindrance to you provided your neighbour is not richer than you'. Horace.

The problems of keeping up with the Jones?' 'Wealth: any income that is at least one hundred dollars more a year than one's wife's sister's husband'. H.L. Mencken 1880-1956. An increased comparable figure today will be arrived at by application of an appropriate inflation factor.

Nimbus 'a rain-cloud'. The word is used by aviators and meteorologists, frequently in conjunction with other Latin words, to describe cloud formation and potential. *Stratus*: a wide extended sheet of low cloud and *cumulus*, a heap. So various kinds of cloud may be called *cumulo-nimbus, nimbo-stratus, strato-cumulus*.

Note: a word to be learnt by any child (or person of any age with no prior knowledge of Latin) who is about to read J.K. Rowling's Harry Potter and the Philosopher's Stone (the English or the Latin version).

Nimiast miseria nimus pulchrum esse hominem 'what a great misfortune it is for a man to be too lovely'. Plautus. Miles Gloriosus. He was so madly handsome he could hardly breathe.

Nisi 'unless'.

Nisi Dominus frustra 'unless the Lord (build the house) it (the project) is in vain'. Edinburgh's motto from Psalm 127.1. Abbreviated from the Vulgate:

> *Nisi Dominus aedificaverit Domum, in vanum laboraverunt qui aedificant eam. Nisi Dominus custodierit civitatem, frustra vigilat qui custodit eam* 'unless the Lord build the house, its builders have laboured in vain. Unless the Lord guard the city, the guard stays uselessly awake'.

See *nihil sine Deo*.

Nocte 'by night', at night. Lawyers doing personal injury or professional negligence work will read doctor's and sometimes nurse's reports and notes where the word *nocte* is often found, denoting things done or drugs given or to be given in the night.

Nolens volens 'unwillingly, willingly'. Willy-nilly. *Nolens volens* that child will do as he is told.

Noli me tangere 'do not touch me'. From St. John's Gospel Ch 20 V 17. When the risen Christ was approached by Mary Magdalene, these are words he spoke. The subject of many paintings.

Nolite thesaurisare vobis thesauros in terra ubi erugo et tinea demolitur ubi fures effodiunt et furantur. Thesaurisate autem thesauros in caelo . . . . ubi enim est thesaurus tuus ubi est cor tuum 'lay not up for yourselves treasures upon earth where moth and rust doth corrupt and thieves break through and steal. But lay up for yourselves treasures in heaven . . . For where your treasure is there will your heart be also'. Vulgate. St. Matthew Ch.6. v.19-20.
Insufficiently heeded advice in our modern acquisition culture. Stop chasing growth stocks!
See *amor nummi, crescit amor nummi, esurientes, inopem, intolerabilius, lucri bonus, oportet ergo, pecunia non olet, radix malorum* and *si possis recte*.

Non Angli sed angeli 'not Angles but angels'. Observation attributed to Pope Gregory 1ˢᵗ (before he was Pope) when he saw fair haired Saxon youths for sale as slaves in Rome. See *Missa in Dominica Resurrectionis* and *Vegetus*.

Non bene pro toto aureo venditur libertas 'it is not a good thing for liberty to be sold (even) for all the gold (in the world)'. Motto of Dubrovnik (Roman *Ragusa*). Cf., *fidem qui perdit*. See *beneficium accipere*.

Non compos mentis 'not (having) control of mind. Of unsound mind. Not in one's right mind'. Opposite of *compos mentis*.

Non constat. See *constat*.

Nones. In the Roman calendar the ninth day before the *ides*. See *ides*.*

Non est pax dixit Deus meus impiis 'there is no peace to the wicked saith my God'. Vulgate Liber Isaie 57.21. Biblical source of the expression: there is no peace for the wicked.

Nonis Februariis (Vettia accepit) a Faustilla (denarios) xv: usura asses viii 'on the ninth February (Vettia has received) from Faustilla xv *(denarii)* with eight asses as interest (on the loan)'. Graffitti on a tavern at Pompeii. See *denarius* and *salve lucrum*.

Non ipsa pericula tangunt. See *Ditior in toto non . . .*

Non olet see *pecunia non olet*.

Non omnia possumus omnes 'all men are not able to do all things'. We can't all do everything. Virgil. Eclogues viii. 63. Too true. Those who try must not become neurotic and downhearted when they fail. After all 'Our business in this world is not to succeed, but to continue to fail in good spirits.' Robert Louis Stevenson: and 'Nothing matters very much and very few things matter at all'. Arthur Balfour 1848-1930 (a bit strong for schoolmasters or parents vis-à-vis the young but *sub specie aeternitatis* perhaps: see below). See *dimidium facti, possumus quia, Principia Mathematica* and *pons asinorum*. But remember:

> 'Our doubts are traitors,
> And make us lose the good we oft might win
> By fearing to attempt'.
>   Willliam Shakespeare. Measure for Measure Act 1 Sc.4 ll 77-79.

Non omnis moriar 'I shall not wholly die'. Horace Odes III. xxx.6. The writer's poetry, a part of him, would live on. Horace was acutely aware of his own mortality. See *aere perennius, domus et placens* and *qui fugiebat*.

Non placet 'it does not please'.
Used in the past in court and ecclesiastical circles to denote refusal. More usual nowadays is: 'Dad, I'm afraid I've bumped your car'. Usually an understatement. Dad's reaction: '*non placet*'.
See *persona non grata* and *placet*.

Non revertar inultus 'I shall not return unavenged'. Motto. Revenge is sweet but note *inhumanum verbum est ultio* 'revenge is an inhuman word'. Seneca Dialogi IV.xxxii.1.Cf., *lex talionis* above and note Christ's view at St. Matthew 5:38 – 39.

> 'Ye have heard that it hath been said, an eye for an eye and a tooth for a tooth: But I say unto you, that ye resist not evil: but whosoever shall smite thee on thy right cheek, turn to him the other also'. And St. Paul: 'Vengeance is mine; I will repay, saith the Lord'. Romans 12:19.

See *fidem qui perdit, nemo me impune, potius mori* and *sit sine*.

Non semper erit aestas 'it will not always be summer' (from Hesiod. c. 700 BC. One of the earliest known Greek poets).

We should all try to make some provision for the rainy day even if we are likely to find it plundered by fiscal measures to provide too often for the feckless who could but don't.

'Rough winds do shake the darling buds of May,
And summer's lease hath all too short a date'.
William Shakespeare. Sonnet xviii.

And yet:

'If winter comes can spring be far behind?'
Ode to the West Wind. Percy Bysshe Shelley.

This eternal optimism gives way to the real joy of "Spring is coming" from Handel's Otho sung if possible by Kathleen Ferrier.

Non sequitur 'it does not follow'. Used in English as a noun to describe something which does not follow logically from what went before. 'Because he has a degree he is intelligent' is a *non sequitur*.*

Non sum qualis eram 'I am not what I used to be'. Horace Odes iv. i. 3-4. Thought which comes, sooner or later, to all of us for so many reasons. The words following are: '*bonae sub regno Cinarae*' 'when I was under good Cinara's rule'. In Horace's poem the poet presses the goddess of love to tempt him no more. He does not have his old strength. See *corpora lente, senex* and *volo non valeo*.

Norma 'a rule, measure or carpenter's square'. Norm. Pomposity is the norm for lawyers. Infantile behaviour in Parliament is now the norm for too many of its members.

Nosce te ipsum 'know yourself'. Inscription on the temple of Apollo at Delphi where was to be found the famous oracle. This is the Latin version of the Greek and an expression used by Cicero. See *ne quid nimis* and *tecum habita*.

Nota bene 'note well'. Abbreviated to NB. Observe what follows with care.*

Notabilia 'notable things'.

Novi 'new persons'. Word used to describe new boys (virtually right-less underlings) at a number of English public schools. Falling into desuetude.

Novissima hora est 'the final hour is here'. The approach of death. Voice of Gerontius from the dream of Gerontius by (Cardinal) John Henry Newman. See *apologia pro vita sua, o lente* and *profiscere anima Christiana.*

Novissima verba 'newest or most recent words' last words.

Novum opus facere me cogis ex veteri 'out of something old you have compelled me to make something new'. Opening words of St. Jerome's letter to Pope Damasus I after the latter had commissioned him to translate the Bible into Latin. These words are reproduced at the beginning of the Lindisfarne Gospels, which were written and illuminated on vellum for God and St. Cuthbert (jointly!) at the end of the seventh century by Bishop Eadfrith at the Lindisfarne Monastry on Holy Island (off the coast of Northumberland). These constitute one of the world's greatest masterpieces of manuscript painting and are now housed in the British Library. For an original and beautifully produced study read 'Embracing Change – Spirituality and the Lindisfarne Gospels' by Ewan Clayton and Robert Cooper. Ewan Clayton 2003. 15, Sillwood Rd., Brighton, BN1 2LF. See *Vulgate.*

Novus homo 'a new man'. Self-made man, upstart, parvenu. One who reached high office in Rome, and who was without one of consular rank in the male line of his ancestry, was a *novus homo.* The expression was one of disdain and contemptuous mockery. Cicero was a *novus homo* as was Augustus, despite being the son of Caesar's sister Julia's daughter, Atia, and having been adopted as Julius Caesar's son. See *Augustus* and *Caesaris.*

Nulli malum pro malo reddentes 'recompense (render) to no man evil for evil'. Vulgate. Romans 12:17. Integral part of that multi-sourced composite prayer read often in schools at the end of term when there is an exodus.

    'Go forth into the world in peace.
    Be of good courage,
    Hold fast to that which is good;
    Render unto no man evil for evil;
    Support the weak;
    Help the afflicted;
    Honour all men . .'

What better code of living for humans whatever their religious denomination. See *quaecumque sunt.*

Nulli secundus 'second to none'.

Nullum quod tetigit non ornavit 'he touched nothing which he did not adorn'.

Dr. Johnson's epitaph on Oliver Goldsmith c.1728-1774. The full inscription was: *Olivarii Goldsmith, Poetae, Physici, Historici, qui nullum fere scribendi genus non tetigit, nullum quod tetigit non ornavit* 'of Oliver Goldsmith, a poet, philosopher and historian who left no form of writing untouched (by his pen) and touched none that he did not adorn'. On the 1776 monument in Westminster Abbey, Poet's corner.

Some of Goldsmith's friends were not happy with this epitaph. James Boswell records in his Life of Johnson (16th May 1776) that other eulogies, not in Latin, were proposed and taken to Johnson by Sir Joshua Reynolds in the form of a Round Robin (a petition with signatures in a circle which conceals the order of writing). Johnson received them with good humour but declared stoutly that nothing would induce him to disgrace the walls of Westminster Abbey with an inscription in English. The inscription remained in Latin.

See *dum spiro spero* and *nam risu inepto*.

Nullus amor populis nec foedera sunto . . . .
   Litora litoribus contraria, fluctibus undas . . .
   Imprecor, arma: pugnent ipsique nepotesque.
   'There shall be neither love nor pact between the peoples. Let your shores oppose their shores, your waves their waves, their arms your arms. My prayer is that their sons and their son's sons should fight eternally'.

Declaration of Dido Queen and foundress of Carthage in Virgil's Aeneid iv, 62ff. Vehement prophecy of the mutual hate to develop between Rome and Carthage during the Punic wars BC 265-242, 218-201 and 149-146 when Carthage was finally destroyed by Scipio Africanus.

A silver coin (a tetradrachm) struck by the Carthaginians in Sicily (4th Century BC) depicts a female head possibly that of Dido but more probably that of a female deity: there is one in the British Museum. See *bellum maxime, cunctator, delenda est Carthago, fides Punica, Hannibal ante portas*, and *summa sedes*.

Numerus 'a number'.
Note that as a matter of form the Roman number V (5) is in fact half of the character or symbol X (ten) . . . the top half. Roman numerals are

frequently seen on buildings and epitaphs. From fifty and above they are seldom remembered and so are set out in appendix 2. See *apostrophus*.

Nunc bibamus 'now let us drink'. See *ergo bibamus, fecundi calices, in vino veritas, merobibus, nunc est bibendum, nunc scripsi totum* and *nunc vino pellite curas*. The wealth of drink related expressions must say something for the average Roman.

Nunc demum redit animus 'now at last our spirit returns'.
Usually the case, sooner or later, however big the set back. See *dum spiro spero*.

Nunc Dimittis 'now you dismiss'. The full text is from St. Luke's gospel Ch 2. v. 29: *nunc dimittis servum tuum, Domine*. Literally 'now you dismiss your servant Oh Lord' but usually rendered as: 'Lord now lettest thou thy servant depart in peace according to thy word'. To be said or sung in English at Evening Prayer after a lesson from the New Testament in accordance with the Church of England Book of Common Prayer. The *Nunc Dimittis* is also known as 'The song of Simeon'.

Nunc est bibendum 'now is the time to drink'. Horace Odes Ixxxvii I. The words are etched on decorative drinking glasses sold at the Bodleian Library shop in Oxford. Horace's famous ode celebrates the downfall of Cleopatra. In further celebration Octavian struck coins with the inscription *Aegypto capta* (Egypt captive). When Octavian (by then Augustus) was later honoured by having the name of the month Sextilis changed to August (see *anno Domini*), one reason for this was that in that month he had brought Egypt into the Roman empire.
See *bonum vinum cor, ergo bibamus, fecundi calices, in vino veritas* and *nunc bibamus, nunc scripsi totum . . .* and *nunc vino pellite curas*.

Nunc scripsi totum pro Christo da mihi potum 'now that I have written so much for Christ, give me a drink'.
An inscription sometimes used by scribe monks and found at the foot of their manuscript works. This might also be translated as: 'Now I've written the lot, for Christ's sake give me a drink': the expression has a Delphic quality to be expressed in the translation according as to where breath is drawn or a comma inserted. See *bonum vinum, in vino veritas, nunc bibamus, nunc est bibendum* and *nunc vino pellite curas*.

Nunc vino pellite curas 'now drive off your cares with wine'. Horace Odes 1.vii.31. The benefits of drinking wine are well documented in the classical writings. Now we learn that regular modest intake of red wine benefits the cardio-vascular system. Keep on pouring it down! See *bonum vinum, ergo bibamus, fecundi calices, nunc bibamus, nunc est bibendum* and *nunc scripsi totum pro*.

Nunquam minus solus quam cum solus 'never less alone than when alone'. Based on Cicero *De Republica* i.27. Usually the case for one who is usually alone in a crowd; a loner. See *narcissus obvalaris* and *solus*.

Nunquam non paratus 'never not ready'. Motto of the clan Johnston. *Semper paratus* 'always ready'. *In omnia paratus* 'ready for all things'. *Nunquam paratus* 'never ready'. *Ad utrumque paratus* 'ready for either case or event'. Latin mottos cater for most states of readiness.

O

Obit 'he died'. Often on gravestones, usually followed by the date. See *hic jacet, hic sepultus* and *natus*.

Occasionem cognosce 'recognise opportunity'. Cf., *carpe diem*. Note Shakespeare's Julius Caesar Act iv. Scene iii. Marcus Brutus to Cassius:

> 'Our legions are brim full, our cause is ripe:
> The enemy increaseth every day;
> We, at the height are ready to decline.
> There is a tide in the affairs of man,
> Which, taken at the flood, leads on to fortune;
> Omitted all the voyage of their life
> Is bound in shallows and in miseries.
> On such a sea are we now afloat;
> And we must take the current when it serves,
> Or lose our ventures'.

But Brutus was wrong. At the battle of Philippi in 42 BC ventures were lost in defeat by the forces of Octavian Caesar (later the emperor Augustus) and Mark Anthony. Amongst the soldiers in Brutus's defeated army was a young poet called Horace who, *Deo gratias*, destiny spared (see *qui fugiebat*).

The expression should perhaps be coupled with *carpe diem . . . occasionem cognosce et carpe diem*. See *Augustus, Caesar, carpe diem, et tu Brute, omnem crede, Planco consule*, and *triumviri*.

Oculi omnium spectant in Te, Deus! Tu das illis escas tempore opportuno. Aperis manum Tuam et imples omne animal Tua benedictione. Mensae caelestis nos participes facias, Deus, Rex aeternae gloriae. Amen 'The eyes of all look to Thee O God! Thou givest them food in due season. Thou openest Thy hand and fillest every living thing with Thy blessing. Make us participants at the heavenly banquet, O God, King of eternal glory. Amen'.

A random example of an Oxford College grace medieval in origin.

Though in the days of 'Jock's stewardship' (*Jocko consule?*) at the unidentified College the dinners were always very good, there were those who thought that just occasionally they could not properly stand with, or be properly described by, the words: *mensae caelestis nos participes facias* 'make us participants at the heavenly banquet'.

The colleges each have their own Latin grace. See *Benedictus benedicat* and *Quicquid appositum*.

Oderint dum metuant 'let them hate so long as they fear'. I don't mind if they hate me so long as they are afraid of me. Accius *Atreus* fragment 4. Quotation often repeated by the Emperor Caligula. Suetonius. Caligula 30.1.

Note Latin's word economy. Cf., *multis timere debet, quem multi timent* 'he who many fear ought to fear many'. Francis Bacon. Note too: *regnare non vult, esse qui invisus timet* 'he who fears to be hated does not wish to rule'. Seneca.

The excesses of the Emperor Caligula's gratuitous cruelties are notorious. Suetonius, describing one of that Emperor's preferred methods of execution, records a familiar official order: *ita fere ut se more sententiat* 'make it so that he can feel that he dies', gives us an understanding of why this Emperor regularly quoted Attius' words. The emperor Tiberius used an adaptation. 'Let them hate me so long as they respect me'. Suetonius. Tiberius lix.2.

In February 2003, during the build up to war in Iraq, J.B. Kiesling (an American career diplomat) wrote in his letter of resignation from the US State Department that US foreign policy seemed to be seriously insensitive to the feelings of other nations and was one of *oderint dum metuant*. See *multis timere debet*.

Odium 'hate'. General or widespread dislike. *Veritas odium parit* 'truth begets hatred'. Terence Andria 1:1:68. See *veritas*.*

Odora canum vis 'the sharp scent of the hounds'. Virgil.

O fortunati nimium, bona si sua norint 'Oh too fortunate, if only you had known how lucky you were'. Edward Hyde Earl of Clarendon 1609-1674. The famous English statesman and historian, who lived through the horrors of civil war, was speaking of his time at Oxford.

O fortunatos nimium, sua si bona norint agricolas 'Oh happy farmers, if only they knew their good fortune'. Virgil. Georgics ii.458.

How many farmers in how many EC countries believe this now? See *Beatus ille*

O lente, lente currite noctis equi 'oh horses of the night run slowly, slowly'. Dr. Faustus. Christopher Marlowe 1564-1593.

With 'one bare hour to live' before he must fulfil his pact with the devil and be damned eternally, Dr. Faustus wills time to pass slowly while he ponders what might just permit salvation. See *novissima hora* and *quid enim.*

Oleum addere camino 'to add oil to the furnace'. To make things worse or stir things up. See *irritabis crabrones.*

Omne ignotum pro magnifico 'all things unknown are thought to be magnificent'. Tacitus Agricola 30. A Caledonian, chieftain (*Calgacus,* before the Romans' famous encounter with the highlanders at *Mons Graupius)* attempts explanation as to why the Romans should wish to subjugate Scotland. See *agricola* and *ubi solitudinem.*

The real thing which follows a pipe dream is too often disappointing. Cf., *maior e longinquo.*

Omnem crede diem tibi diluxisse supremum 'believe each day to have dawned as your last'. Horace, epist., I. IV.13. The old adage is: 'live each day as though it were your last: one day you will be right'.

'Look thy last on all things lovely
Every hour ——— let no night
Seal thy sense in deathly slumber . . .'
   'Fare Well'.
      Walter De La Mare

See *age dum, carpe diem, eheu fugaces, ille potens, in extremis, quid sit futurum* and *ut saepe summa.*

Omnem movere lapidem 'to move every stone'. To leave no stone unturned.

Omne trinum est perfectum 'all in threes is perfect'. Ménage a trois?

Troilism? Is the gooseberry always welcome? And the chaperon? . . if such an entity exists in 2004.

Omnia mors aequat 'death levels all things'. Charles de Gaulle had a much loved handicapped daughter, Anne. She was born in 1928 and died young in 1948. At her graveside he found solace in saying 'now she is like the others'.

Omnia mutantur. See *tempora mutantur.*

Omnia Romae cum pretio 'everything in Rome comes at a price'. Juvenal iii. 183. Is modern London (and other world capitals) any different? See *lucri bonus, nec prece, salve lucrum* and *si possis recte.*

Omnia tuta timens 'fearing all things even those which are safe'. Not much in life is safe. In the financial turmoil of 2003 pension funds made the point. Tsar Nicholas, the last Tsar of Russia, suffered seriously from depression and was not infrequently heard to observe: 'no sooner do I think upon a disaster than it befalls me'. See *quid sit futurum.*

Op. cit. See *opere citato* 'in the work (already) cited'.*

Ope et consilio 'by aid and counsel'. Aid and abet.

Opere citato 'in the work (already) cited'. Abbreviated to *op. cit.;* and used as reference to a work previously cited.*

Opinio juris sive necessitatis 'whether the opinion of the law is compulsory'. An expression of public international law which too many students encounter and then waste too much time seeking explanation. Custom as a source of international law involves the repetition or recurrence of acts. Recurrance of usage leads to an expectation that in similar future situations the same conduct will be repeated. When this expectation evolves into custom and then to a general acceptance by States that the conduct is a matter of legal right and obligation, then the transition through usage and custom to law is complete. This is termed the *opinio juris*: the concept of a fictitious juristic determination that usage, practice and custom have evolved to the point of becoming law.

Oportet ergo episcopum . . . . non violentium non percussorem, sed modestum, non litigosum, non cupidum 'a Bishop then must be . . . not given to wine, no striker, not greedy of filthy lucre; but patient, not a brawler, not covetous'. Vulgate. Timothy 3 1-3.

This is authorised King James' Bible translation, some eighty per cent of which was taken from William Tyndale's translation. 'Filthy lucre' is from Tyndale who is the apparent source of that expression, which appears to show inventive genius. Maybe he took it from the Greek or Hebrew. See *amor nummi, crescit amor nummi, esurientes, inopia me copia, intolerabilius, lucri bonus, nolite thesaurisare, pecunia non olet, radix malorum, si possis recte* and *Vulgate*

Opus artificem probat 'the work proves the workman'. A man's works speak as to his skill. In almost all fields one must look to a man's actual work in order to judge him. The well qualified may be incompetents, hopeless when it comes to the practicalities of a job.

Opus Dei 'work of God'. Opus Dei is the name given to a Roman Catholic lay religious order founded in Spain in 1928 by a Spanish cleric, Jose Maria Escriva de Balaguer, to maintain Christian ideals by the example of its members. A controversial, semi-secret ultra conservative society, it gained very considerable power and influence in the late 1960's Spain of General Franco and after through its membership in governmental and professional circles. Balaguer died in 1975. In February of 2002 the Vatican announced that he would be canonised and this was duly effected on 6th October 2002 at St. Peter's Square in Rome. The miracle approved as one pre-condition of canonisation was the medically inexplicable cure of a Spanish surgeon in 1992 after he had prayed to Escriva for intercession. See *advocatus diaboli.*

Opus magnum (usually *magnum opus*) 'great work'. Any writer's or artist's masterpiece. See *magnum opus.*

Orandum est ut sit mens sana in corpore sano. See *mens sana in corpore sano.*

Oratio congratulatoria 'a congratulatory speech'. Often laden with sycophantic humbug this type of speech tends to mark a meeting between heads of state. True or false, sincere or otherwise each spouts as much as possible of what the other wants to hear. All politicians should familiarise themselves with Plutarch's *quomodo adulator ab amico internoscitur* below. See *fere libenter.*

Oratio obliqua 'indirect speech'. Expression descriptive of areas of grammar and syntax in the Latin language. For explanation and examples see Kennedy's Revised Latin Primer 16th edition 1987 at section 458 *et seq.* inclusive. An expression too often dreaded (in the days when the learning of Latin was for nearly all compulsory) by those who adjusted ill to the subject. See *Fabulae Faciles, Latium* and *vivat lingua Latina*.

Ovem lupo committere 'to entrust the sheep to the wolf'.

O tempora! O mores 'what times, what customs (behaviour)'. Cicero. In Catalinam I.2. Words with which Cicero opened his attack on Catiline accusing him of conspiracy to organise revolution.

Another lament that things are not what they used to be. See *laudator temporis, munera nunc, panem et circenses, quae fuerant, rem tene* and *tempora mutantur*.

Oxoniensis 'of Oxford'. An Oxonian is one who is or has been at Oxford University. Oxonian means of or relating to Oxford or Oxford university. See *Cantabridgiensis*.

P

Pallida mors pulsat pede pauperum tabernas regumque turres 'pale death's foot kicks impartially the mean abodes of the poor and the towers of kings'. Horace Odes 1.iv.13-14.

'All human things are subject to decay,
And when fate summons, Monarchs must obey'.
    Mac Flecknoe. John Dryden 1631-1700.
See *quid sit*.

Panem et circenses. See *circus*.

Panis angelicus 'bread of heaven'. Title of music by César Franck (1822-1890). 'Bread of Heaven, Feed me till I want no more:' from a 16th century Welsh hymn (hymn number 397 in the English Hymnal. 'Guide me o thou great Redeemer, Pilgrim through this barren land'. [Argtwydd arwain trwy'r antlwch]). Rousingly tuneful, the refrain is often sung by the Welsh crowd at rugby internationals.

'And Jesus said unto them, I am the bread of life: he that cometh to me shall never hunger: and he that believeth in me shall never thirst.' St. John Ch. 6 v 35. *Panem nostrum quotidianum da nobis hodie* 'Give us this day our daily bread'. The Lord's prayer. St.Matthew Ch 6 v 11.

Pares cum paribus ut est in reteri proverbio facillimi congreguntur 'like with like, as in the old proverb, most easily gather together'. Latin version of 'birds of a feather flock together'. Cicero *de Senectute* iii. This expression seems to be of great antiquity.

Pari passu 'at an equal step' or equal double pace. At the same speed. Someone who works on two projects and divides his attention between them equally, works on them *pari passu*. *a, side by side,*

Pari ratione 'by equal reason', parity of reasoning.

Parva domus magna quies 'small house; great peace'. Inscription on a very old farmhouse in the Calf of Man (a small island off the southern tip of the Isle of Man).

Parva leves capiunt animos 'frivolities take over light minds'. Ovid Ars Amatoria i.159. Little things please little minds.

Passim 'everywhere'. In various places. The word is used in text and reference books to indicate that a topic is considered here and there in the work. All over the place, throughout. *Sic passim* 'so throughout'. See *sic.**

Paterfamilias 'patriarch or head of the family'. There is no English equivalent of the relationship between the Roman father (*paterfamilias*) and his son(s). The Roman *paterfamilias* had power *vitae necisque* (of life and death) over his son, who (if he survived) in turn was liable to inherit his father's debts (a *damnosa hereditas*, an injurious inheritance. Institutes of Gaius, ii,163). The *paterfamilias* could also sell his son with varying legal consequences according to circumstance; these included his becoming a slave.

At the time of the Catiline conspiracy (63 – 62 BC) Fulvius, the son of a senator, had joined the conspirators. His father had him pursued, brought back to Rome and put to death. (Sallust. Catiline, cap.39.5). See *Gaius, patria potestas* and *sui juris*.

Pater Noster 'Our father', (which art in heaven). Opening words of the Lord's Prayer (St. Mathew Ch 6 v 9-13) called the Paternoster. The Paternoster is also the name given to a large bead in a rosary at which, in the course of telling, the Lord's Prayer is repeated. The word may describe the rosary itself and has come to be used to mean anything strung like a rosary: in particular that part of a coarse fishing angler's line to which is attached hooks and weights at intervals.

'St. Agnes' Eve . . . Ah, bitter chill it was!
The owl, for all his feathers was a—cold;

The hare limped trembling through the frozen grass,
And silent was the flock in wooly fold:
Numb were the beadsman's fingers, while he told
His rosary . . .'
>   The Eve of St. Agnes. John Keats.

Paternoster Row and Paternoster Square lie just north of St. Paul's Cathedral in London EC4. See *Ave Maria*.*

Patria potestas 'a father's power'. The Roman father had extensive powers over his family. For some see *paterfamilias*.

Patris est filius 'he is his father's son'.

Paucis verbis 'with few words'. See *cave quid*.

Pax 'peace'. So in the days when the Roman Empire maintained a known world stability, there was the *Pax Romana*. More recently, in the heyday of the British Empire, there was the *Pax Britannica*. Now, perhaps, there is the *Pax Americana*. *Sed quaere* in 2002-4, in relation to Iraq. In English the word *pax* denotes a call for peace or a truce. See *pax quaeritur bello*, *si vis pacem*, *tu regere* and *ubi solitudinem*.*

Pax possessori 'peace to (the/my) owner'. Inscription appearing on a partly gilded Saxon pocket sundial found in 1938 during excavations of the cloisters girth at Canterbury Cathedral. The maker made clear that he reserved a little something to himself with the additional words *salus factori*, salvation to (the/my) maker: tempting *addenda* for all craftsmen. See *ad unguem*, *fecit* and *pinxit*.

Pax quaeritur bello 'peace is sought by war'. Together with *si vis pacem, para bellum* a useful expression for President George W. Bush in his autumn 2002 call for war against Iraq and Saddam Hussein. *Sed quaere.*

>   'Now the world has to learn all over again that weakness in the face of a tyrant's threat is the surest way not to peace but to war'.
>   Tony Blair on the 18ᵗʰ March 2003 when seeking a House of Commons mandate for UK to join America in imminent war against Iraq.

See *pax*.

Legend inscribed on the reverse of a broad, a coin of the Commonwealth bearing the head of Oliver Cromwell circa 1656 (a twenty shilling gold piece with milled edge). See, *decus et tutamen*, *has nisi periturus* and *si vis pacem*.

Pax vobis(cum) 'peace be with you'. *Pax Domini sit semper vobiscum . . .* the peace of the Lord be always with you.

Pecunia in arboribus alienorum crescit 'money grows on other people's trees'. Wishful self justificatory thinking of those who are takers, have fists which are tight or who experience difficulty with putting their hands in their own pockets. Note the comment of Philip Green in June 04 after some investors had dismissed as derisory his initial (ultimately withdrawn) bid to take over Marks and Spencer: "People flippantly dismiss £8 billion or £9 billion as though I found it on a tree on the way to the office but no one has ever raised £9 billion before in Europe". See *aliam excute.*

Pecunia non olet 'money does not smell'. Observation attributed to the Emperor Vespasian in answer to resistance by his son Titus to the former's taxation of urinals. See *lucri bonus* above and Suetonius. *De vita Caesarum*. Vespasian 8. 23, 2. The words were quoted on 19th February 2002 by Mr. Justice Jacob in the High Court in London when ruling that Value Added Tax (VAT) was payable on vice transactions (in principle; the practical mechanics of actual tax collection apart). Why should illegal transactions escape taxation when legal business must pay? His Lordship concluded: 'In this case, as the Latin poet said *"pecunia non olet"*. I allow the appeal'. With use of Latin deplored at the time by the law, the aside was politically incorrect (and none the worse for that) but the emperor Vespasian was no poet. He was an accomplished soldier and commanded the second legion 'Augusta' during the conquest of Britain in AD 43-47. See *veni vidi vici*; see also *Masada*.

The rudimentary, 'leave little of what was going on to the imagination' urinals in the Paris of the 1950s, called pissoirs, were known to an erudite élite as 'vespasians'.

A gold aureus of Vespasian was found near a Roman villa excavated near Finstock in Oxfordshire during the 19th century. It had been minted in Judaea! On the reverse is a standing figure of *justitia*. It is on view in the Ashmolean Museum, Oxford. See *Apollinaris medici, crescit amor, lucri bonus est, omnia Romae, oportet ergo, rescripsit boni* and *si possis recte.*

Pelli meae consumptis carnibus adhesit os meum et derelicta sunt tantummodo labia circa dentes meos 'my bone cleaveth to my flesh, and I am escaped with the skin of my teeth'. Vulgate Book of Job Ch. 19 v. 20. Source of the expression 'by the skin of my teeth'.

Pelliparii 'preparers of furs'. Name originally given to the guild of the furriers when Edward III granted their charter in 1327. The medieval guild governed the use, production and sale of furs when they were used for trimming the garments of the wealthy and controlled the conditions of apprenticeship in the craft. The Skinner's Company, as the guild or livery company is now called, no longer controls the craft but administers its property and assets which are used in large part for charitable purposes in particular education of the young: in Kent at Tonbridge School founded in 1553 by Sir Andrew Judde and at later foundations, the Judde School and the Skinner's School (1888 and 1886 respectively). The Skinner's Hall, built after the great fire of 1666, is at 8, Dowgate Hill, beside Cannon Street Station in the City of London.

Per 'through,' usually, but it is a word of many meanings. Can mean during, according to, out of etc.*

Per ardua ad astra 'through difficulties to the stars'. Motto of the Royal Flying Corps approved by King George V in 1913 and still in use by the Royal Air Force. We succeed by enduring hardship . . through determination and struggle . . . with a stiff upper lip! There are other phrases along the same lines: *per aspera ad astra* through adversities to the stars and per *angusta ad augusta* through difficulties to honours. See *macte nova* and *pervenire ad*.

Per capita 'by heads'. For each person. Individually. The rations will be shared equally *per capita*.*

Per centum 'by the hundred' per cent, in every hundred. Percentage: rate or proportion per cent.

Per diem 'by day,' daily, for each day.*

Pereunt et imputantur 'our days pass away and are scored to our account'. Martial. Epigrammata 5:20:13. Inscription above entrance to the Codrington Library in Oxford. Translation courtesy of Reginald Adams. Latin in Oxford. Perpetua Press 1994.

Perfecto in spiritu 'perfect in spirit'. Tatoo of David Beckham. See *habendum* and *ut amem*.

Per Jovem 'by Jupiter'. English by jove. Jupiter was the pre-eminent Roman god (originally the Greek god Zeus). God of the sky, thunder and lightning.

Per omnia saecula saeculorum 'through all the centuries of centuries'. World without end. See *in aeternum* and *in perpetuum*.

Per se 'through or in himself or itself'. Intrinsically. Intellect is not *per se* enough for the job: there must also be common sense.*

Persona grata 'acceptable person'. Used originally in relation to a diplomatic representative acceptable to the régime to which he was sent.

Persona non grata 'unacceptable person or one who has incurred disfavour'. Opposite of *persona grata*. The libertine who had cuckolded a husband. The teenage child who has bumped father's car (see *non placet*) or one whose dog has lifted his leg in another's house.

Pervenire ad summam sine industria non potest 'one cannot reach the top without industry'. Quintilian. However great a man's talent, aptitude and intellect, if he is to reach the top, there is no substitute for industry. See *per ardua ad astra*.

Pinxit 'he painted'. Frequently beside the name of the artist on paintings. See *fecit*.

Piscator-non-solum-piscatur. Motto of the Flyfisher's Club, the official translation of which is 'it is not all of fishing to fish' though the words are more usually rendered as: 'there is more to fishing than catching fish'. Founded in 1884 for gentlemen interested in fly-fishing the club provides an esoteric bonhomie for a dedicated and genteel body with premises situate in Brook Street, London, UK.

Placebo 'I will please'. *Placebo Domino* 'I will please the Lord'. First words of the first antiphon (i.e., a hymn or religious chant sung by two parties or groups alternately, the one responding to the other) of vespers for the dead in the Roman Catholic Church.

Also the name given to a medicine, which (unknown to the patient) will have no physiological effect but may do good for psychological reasons, the patient feeling an unwarranted confidence in some beneficial effect. White pills made from chalk are an example and used to be prescribed with suitable *gravitas* (see above) as *tab cretae* 'chalk tablets'.

Placebos are also used for testing drugs: they are interspersed with the experimental drugs and given to the human guinea pigs so that none knows whether or not he has been given the real thing. The resulting effects reported are thereby less likely to reflect subjective thought producing psychological symptoms and should therefore be more reliable. See *pruritis ani.*

Placet 'it pleases'. *Non placet* 'it does not please'. Used in the past in ecclesiastical and court circles to denote agreement or disagreement in the sense of permission, assent or the opposite.

In the conclusion to Dorothy L. Sayers' 'Gaudy Nights' (1935) Lord Peter Wimsey proposes marriage in New College Lane (Oxford) with the words *placetne magistra* ('does the lady whose prerogative it is agree?'). *'Placet'* is her reply. See *non placet.*

Platanus hybrida. Classificatory name for the London plane type of tree found in London; e.g., in the Temple and along the Embankment. The Plane Tree has a distinctive bark and the wood a unique fine speckled grain. It is frequently to be seen lining the old Route Nationale roads in France and typifies the beauty of travel in that country. Indifferent to pollution, it thrives in towns

Plebs 'the common people, lower classes'. See *belua multorum, faex populi, mobile vulgus, profanum vulgus* and *veto.*

Plenus et optabilis coitus 'full sex and desirable,' (as much as you want?). Fond memory (and perhaps continuing wish and ambition) of the poet Lord Byron 1788–1824 (abbreviated to: *plen* and *optabil. Coit.*): written in a letter of 22nd June 1809 to C.S. Matthews. See *et vera incessu.*

Plus quam valor valet Valette 'Valette is worth more than valour (courage)'. Inscription upon a sword and dagger (poniard) given by King Philip II of Spain to Jean Parisot de la Valette, Grand Master of the Order of the Knights of St. John of Jerusalem after the great siege of 1565, when the latter had led the lengthy, heroic and successful resistance to a massive Turkish invasion ordered by the Sultan Suleiman the Magnificent to wrest the island of Malta from the Knights.

The hilt of the sword and poniard are of enamelled gold set with diamonds and pearls and are in the Bibliotheque Nationale, Paris being one of the treasures looted by the French during the Napoleonic occupation of Malta from 1798.

Only one English Knight participated in this epic struggle. Sir Oliver Starkey had escaped from England, where the reformation meant that this catholic order could no longer survive. A number of Knights who remained in England were executed under the provisions of the Statute of Praemunire, which made it a capital offence to assert the supremacy of the Pope over the crown of England. See *legatus a latere*.

A pun seems to have been intended by this inscription. See *ecce agnus Dei, virtutis fortuna* and *vivat Hispania*.

Pons asinorum 'the bridge of asses'. The fifth proposition in the first book of Euclid. The bridge which must be crossed by those who are obtuse before they will understand. See *non omnia possumus omnes* and *Principia Mathematica*.

Pontifex maximus 'chief priest'. In Rome the chief of a college of priests who had conduct and control over religious matters. Julius Caesar was elected Pontifex Maximus in 63 BC.

Portant armas ad naves et hic trahunt carrum cum vino et armis 'they are carrying weapons to the ship: and here they are pulling a cart with wine and arms'. Extract from the Latin narrative to the pictorial Bayeux tapestries in which preparation for Duke William of Normandy's 1066 invasion of England is portrayed. The barrel of wine on the cart is noticeably large: plainly an indispensable accoutrement of war for a Frenchman. See *bonum vinum, Harold Rex* and *in vino veritas*.

Positura. Name given to a mark or symbol (like the number 7) used by medieval scribes to indicate the end of a piece. Punctuation as it is now understood did not come in until the rise of printing in the 14th and 15th centuries. See *scriptio continua*.

Possunt quia posse videntur 'they are able because they (are seen to be able) think they can'. Virgil. Aeneid v. 231. Self belief and confidence are formidable assets for anybody in any field, particularly for advocates. Note *non omnia possumus* above (especially the Shakespearian quote).

Post cibum 'after food'. Words to be found (often abbreviated to PC) in medical notes or on prescriptions, directing that something is to be taken or administered after food. See *ante cibum, bis die* and *nocte*.

Post hoc ergo propter hoc 'after this therefore on account of this'. Application of the expression is often responsible for first blush conclusions which turn out to be erroneous. Because one thing follows another, the later is not necessarily caused by the earlier. The reasoning is fallacious; the expression is a *non sequitur*.

Post mortem 'after death'. Words used in English (hyphenated: post-mortem) as the name for the examination of a body (usually by a pathologist) with a view to determining the cause of death: synonymous with autopsy.*

Post mortem patris pro filio 'for the son after the death of the father'. Inscription struck on coinage at Pontefract in 1648 after King Charles I had been executed on the orders of the regicides. See *dum spiro spero*.

Post scriptum 'written after'. Postscript. Abbreviated to PS. Additional material added, often at the end of a letter. Frequently used as a noun. 'I didn't read the PS in his letter'.*

Potius mori quam foedari 'rather die than be dishonoured'. With the progressive decay of honesty and honour fewer and fewer are moved by shame. See *fidem qui perdit, nemo me, non revertar* and *sit sine*.

Potius sero quam nunquam 'better late than never'. Livy iv.2.

Praemonitus, praemunitus 'forewarned is forearmed'. Motto. In war soldiers must be alerted to the propensities of their allies. In the course of the US/British conflict in Iraq during 2003, a US jet injured a British soldier, lance corporeal Stephen Gerrard. He observed: 'I'm trained for combat. What I've not been trained to do is to look over my shoulder to see if an American is shooting at me'. See *emeritus*.

Praetor. Generalised name for one who held executive state authority in Rome (*imperium*). The *praetor urbanus* administered justice as between Roman citizens and the *praetor peregrinus* as between those who were not (who were peregrines).

The Praetorian Guard (the Praetorians) comprised the household troops of the emperors and was formed by Augustus in 27 BC. An elite and powerful body it brought the emperor Claudius to power in AD 41, murdered the emperor Elagabalus in AD 222 (appalled by his obscenities and excesses). Yet it had stood more than acquiescently by while Roman soldiers murdered the worthy emperor Pertinax in AD 193 and had abandoned Nero to his fate in AD 68. See *Clodius Albinus, qualis artifax* and *verbosa et grandis*.

Prescriptio. A published list of outlawed Roman citizens whose property was to be confiscated by the state and who soldiers were licensed to kill on sight. Rewards and punishments were used to encourage informers. First used by the dictator Sulla in 82–81 BC this measure was invoked by the second triumvirate and Cicero was one of its victims. See *Cicero* and *triumviri*.

Prima facie 'at first sight or on first impression': on the face of it. A *prima facie* case is one which, subject to further scrutiny and to as yet unforeseen circumstances, seems good. Likewise with *prima facie* evidence.*

Prima luce 'at first light or at dawn'. To hear the birds dawn chorus is one of the uplifting joys of life. Can it really be for them such bliss to greet another day? See *arcus (pluvius)*.

Prima officina Londinii 'first workshop of London'. Name of the London Mint set up c. AD 303 – 310 as part of the Roman imperial system of mints in Europe. See *Carausius*.

Primo 'in the first place', first.

Primum non nocere 'first do no harm'. Expression used by Dr. Richard Nicholson (editor of the Bulletin of Medical Ethics, writing in The Times for 9:7:03 during the debate which followed the death of the Iranian Siamese twins, Ladan and Laleh Bijani, after surgery in the Raffles hospital, Singapore, to separate them) to describe a doctor's primary duty. When is a doctor entitled to undertake treatment for which a patient asks (pleads) when the risk inherent in that treatment is very great?

Primus inter pares 'first among equals'. There is always one who is top dog even among ostensible equals. Probably best known is George Orwell's 'All animals are equal but some are more equal than others'. Animal Farm 1945. Fifteen (plus: there were substitutes) magnificent men won the rugby union world cup (the Webb Ellis Trophy) for England in 2003 by defeating Australia in the final in Australia, but was Jonny Wilkinson not perhaps *primus inter pares*? See *utinam noster*.

Principia Mathematica 'principles of mathematics'. Title of Sir Isaac Newton's work, written in Latin and published in 1687: a work in a subject which for so many may prompt acute awareness of the *pons asinorum* (see above).

Sir Isaac (1642-1727) was the first to perceive and state the laws of gravity and light and to make a reflective telescope. Alexander Pope wrote an epitaph intended for Sir Isaac in Westminster Abbey:

'Nature and Nature's Laws lay hid in night.
God said, let Newton be! And all was light'.

See too *non omnia possumus omnes*.

Pro 'for'. To be *pro* means to be well disposed to. To be *pro* in an argument means to be supportive of one or other side. See *pro bono publico* below.*

Probitas laudatur, et alget 'integrity is praised and feels the cold'. Juvenal i. 74. Crime too often pays. Whilst lip service is paid to the praise of honour, integrity and honesty, in a cynical real world these qualities are frequently seen as naïvety, which advances one little and too often achieves nothing.

Charles III of western France 898-929 (never emperor) was derided as 'Charles the Simple'. He was not so much confused as straightforward and honest: qualities which do not befit men to rule.

Of Austen Chamberlain it was said: 'He always played the game . . . and he always lost'.

Yet Lloyd George said of Bonar Law that he was 'honest to the verge of simplicity'. After the tricky spin of Lloyd George that was just what the country wanted in the Britain of 1922 and he became Prime Minister. See *ab honesto virum, laudator temporis, nec prece* and *quae fuerant*.

Pro bono 'for good' (literally: not in the sense of 'for ever'). Abbreviation of *pro bono publico* for the public good. The expression *pro bono* has however come to mean much the same as *gratis* (for favour, without payment or obligation: *gratis* is *de facto* English). The provision of free legal services is known as *pro bono*. From 1997 onwards the Lord Chief Justice of England, Lord Woolf, campaigned to eliminate the use of Latin in the courts and, so far as possible, in English law generally. At a presidential luncheon of Ilex (the Institute of Legal Executives) in June of 2002 he said:

> 'I think one reason why *pro bono* is not playing its part in the provision of legal services as it should do is because of the very words *pro bono*. I would like someone to provide me with a plain-English substitute'.

ILEX organised a competition to find it. The winning entry was 'law for free'. Plain if ugly English and awful grammar. Fortunately *pro bono* is not to be abandoned. Known world wide it is to be alternative. A lawyer can work *pro bono* but he cannot work 'law for free'. As a successor this cannot be a universal substitute.

On the second of December 2003 in the Court of Appeal Criminal Division sitting in the Royal Courts of Justice, London the exchange following took place: senior Lord Justice to the applicant's counsel:

'Do we understand correctly that you appear *pro bono*'?
'My Lord, yes'.
'We would like to thank you and are sorry that we cannot do more'.

The old Latin terminology seems to be holding its own. See *gratis* and *progressus per*.

Pro bono publico 'for the public good'. See *pro bono*.

Profanum vulgus 'the vulgar herd or mob'. The fuller text (from Horace Odes iii.i.1) is: *odi profanum vulgus et arce* 'I hate the vulgar mob and steer clear of it'. This was not an unattractive class driven observation. The word *vulgus* might be translated as uninitiated or even philistine. The intended meaning was that the poet did not wish to mix with those who did not appreciate poetry and literary talent. See *ad captum vulgus, belua multorum capita, faex populi* and *plebs*.

Profiscere, anima Christiana, de hoc mundo 'go forth upon thy journey Christian soul. Go from this world'. Voice of the priest in John Henry Newman's 'The Dream of Gerontius'.

John Henry Newman 1801-1890 was made a cardinal in 1879. The Dream of Gerontius was set to music as an oratorio by Sir Edward Elgar. See *Apologia pro vita sua* and *novissima hora est*.

Pro forma 'for form', as or being a matter of form. A pro-forma invoice is sent in advance of goods supplied.*

Progressus per peritiam 'progress through skill (practical knowledge)'. Motto of the Institute of Legal Executives (ILEX) until November 2002 when it was replaced by English: 'Progress through knowledge'. Have they abandoned skill? See *pro bono*.

Pro hac vice 'for this turn' (on this occasion only).

Pro mundi beneficio 'for the benefit of the world'.
Motto of Panama and reference to its canal.

Pro patria 'for one's native country'. *Pro patria et rege* 'for king and country' (reversed). A rousing acclamation of patriotism. See *dulce et decorum est*.

Pro rata 'according to the rate'. Proportional or in proportion.*

Pro Rege, Lege, Grege 'for the King, the law and the flock (the people)'. Motto on the standard of Captain Withers in the Civil War

1641-1646. Standards and banners of the civil war are exhibited in the British Museum. See *exurgat Deus* and *ut Rex noster*.

Pro tanto 'by so much', to that extent, as far as it goes.

Pro tempore 'for the time being'. Abbreviated to *pro tem.**

Proximo 'next', in the next. Abbreviation of *proximo mense* 'in the next month'. Used in commerce. See *ultimo* below.*

Prunella modularis. Classificatory Latin name for the hedge sparrow or dunnock.

Pruritis ani 'itching of the backside'.
Classificatory medical name for a common affliction, particularly in men; frequently when under stress. Often psychological it may sometimes be cured by placebo medical advice to scratch the back of the head. See *placebo*.

Ps. See *post scriptum* above.

Puella Carthaginis ridebat
Quam tigris in tergo vehebat.
Externa profecta
Interna revecta
Sed risus in tigre manebat.
> There was a young lady of Carthage
> Who rode with a smile on a tiger.
> They returned from the ride
> With the lady inside
> And the smile on the face of the tiger.

A well known English limerick slightly varied and translated delightfully into Latin. Used by Silenus, Hannibal's tutor, to assist in teaching him Latin (in Ross Leckie's 'Hannibal'. Abacus 1986).

Subtle differences in pronunciation of the French language may be highlighted for appeal to English students by vaguely comparable doggerel, viz:
> '*Le bon-bon fondit dans les dents du bon bandit*' 'the sweet melts in the teeth of the good bandit'. *Une multitude de Turcs, musclés et turbulents* 'a crowd of muscular and rowdy Turks'.
> Source Mr. Logie Bruce-Lockhart *circa* 1954.

See *bellum maxime omne, cunctator, delenda est Carthago, fides Punica, nullus amor populis* and *summa sedes*.

Pulvis et umbra sumus 'we are dust and shadow'. Horace Odes IV. vii. 16. Cf., '. . . earth to earth, dust to dust, ashes to ashes . .' part of the Order for the Burial of the Dead in the Church of England Book of Common Prayer. 'We brought nothing into this world and it is certain we can carry nothing out'. Note too Genesis 3:19 *terra es et terra ibis* 'for dust thou art and to dust thou shalt return'. We really musn't get above ourselves! See *inopem me copia fecit* and *nolite thesaurisare vobis*.

Puto deus fio 'I think that I am becoming a god'. Suetonius. Vespasian xxiii. By the time of the emperor Vespasian (emperor 69–79) the emperors Augustus and Claudius had been deified. This was Vespasian's way of saying 'I think that I am dying'. He was suffering from a fever which he had not taken sufficiently seriously and, not long after, stricken by a violent spasm he struggled to his feet saying 'an emperor should die standing': and so indeed he did. Suetonius xxiv. More recently a greatly respected elder statesman, stricken by sudden infirmity, was attended by a very young doctor. 'Who are you?' inquired the patient. 'I'm a doctor' came the reply.' 'Ah, do not distress yourself young man. The main thing is that we should die with our boots on.' But he didn't: he lived on and vigorously.

The quotation is now sometimes used by way of erudite and esoteric exaggeration as when the dire symptoms of mega hangover hit their peak.

Q

QED. See *quod erat demonstrandum*.

Qua 'in the capacity of; in so far as'. He cheats at golf then sends people to prison *qua* judge! She was unattractive in many ways, but not *qua* woman.*

Quadragesima. First Sunday in Lent. From *quadragesimus*, forty. Lent has forty days. Hymn number 73 English Hymnal, a Lent hymn:

> *'Forty days and forty nights*
> *Thou wast fasting in the wild;*
> *Forty days and forty nights*
> *Tempted and yet undefiled.'*

See *retro me satana* below.

Quaecumque sunt vera, quaecumque sunt pudica, quaecumque sunt justa, quaecumque sunt sancta, quaecumque sunt amabilia, quaecumque sunt bonae famae si quis virtus, si qua laus, haec cogitate 'whatsoever things are true, whatsoever things are honest, whatsoever things are just, whatsoever things are pure, whatsoever things are lovely, whatsoever things are of good report; if there be any virtue and if there be any praise, think on these things'. Philippians Ch.4 v. 8. (From the Vulgate: *In epistulis Pauli Apostoli ad Philippenses*). In a world, threatened since the events of 11ᵗʰ September 2001 with a new dark age of the Antichrist, things to ponder in any language. See *nulli malum*.

Quae Deus conjunxit nemo separet 'what God has joined together, let no man put asunder'. From St. Matthew Ch.19, 6. Incorporated into the form for solemnisation of matrimony in the Church of England Book of Common Prayer. King James I however invoked the expression for another purpose. After union of the Crowns of England and Scotland in 1603, he had it inscribed on the larger silver English and Scottish coins.

First steps towards separation came nearly four hundred years later with the setting up of the Scottish Parliament by the Blair government. On many English, Scottish and Irish coins of James I are the inscriptions *tueatur unita Deus* 'may God guard these united (kingdoms)' and *faciam eos in gentium unam* 'I will make them one nation' Ezek 37.22. See *exurgat Deus et dissipentur*.

Quae fuerant vitia mores sunt 'what were vices are (now) the fashion'. Seneca. The prostate used to be a taboo topic verboten in conversation. Now, alert to the diminishing efficiency (or surgically restored state) of their plumbing, men over a certain age seem to talk of little else.

Barristers 'corporate' entertaining and touting for work: something unthinkable, unprofessional and disciplinable not so long ago. When some barristers urged that they should be permitted use of business cards, praying in aid that these were used by accountants and solicitors, their supplications were declined; 'they are businessmen, we are gentlemen'.

It is hard to know where 'corporate' entertainment ends and bribery begins. He who greases his way travels easily. In such pursuit the noses of some are said to become brown.

In business the word 'bribe' has fallen into desuetude, being replaced by the more palatable 'facilitating payment'; something increasingly necessary for survival in international commerce.

Modesty used to be a virtue and any *disposition* to the vulgar commercial was unacceptable. One does not survive in the rat-race turmoil of 2004 unless one has ample breath with which to blow one's own trumpet; and the sound offends few. But remember *laus propria sordet* 'self praise is to be despised' and beware *malus pudor* 'false modesty'.

'The past is a foreign country: they do things differently there'.
L.P.Hartley 1895- 1972. The Go–Between 1953..

See *adolescentem verecundum*, *beneficium accipere*, *honores mutant*, *munera nunc*, *o tempora*, *potius mori* and *tempora mutantur*.

Quae fuit durum pati, meminisse dulce est 'what is hard to suffer is sweet to remember'. Seneca. Early schooldays at the English Public Schools of the 1950's and before: sweet to remember? A lifelong low grade negative happiness ought to ensue, since very little in life thereafter should be worse. Likewise with the nightmare memories of barrister's first court appearances. The greatest horrors relate to the throng and bustle of the companys court in London's Royal Courts of Justice as it was on Monday mornings; when orders for the winding up of companies were made, usually after incantation of a formula and request for 'the usual compulsory order'. Two episodes involving once very young barristers (each instructed at the eleventh hour) illustrate. After recital of the formula one asked for the 'usual compulsory order'. 'And what exactly is that order?' inquired the judge. Excruciating silence preceded mortifying admission: 'My Lord, I don't know'. Another was briefed to resist the 'usual order'. 'Does nobody oppose?' said the judge to the seething masses below. 'I do . . my Lord' said a faint voice from beneath the whitest wig. 'Yes, on what grounds?' An ugly panic pause: 'The usual grounds'. See *forsan et haec*.

Quae nocent docent 'what hurts teaches'. We learn from bitter experience. But: 'We learn from experience that men never learn anything from experience'. George Bernard Shaw.

Quaere 'question'. An imperative. See *sed quaere* below.

Quare fremuerunt gentes? 'Why do the people so furiously rage together?' Psalm 2 v.1. Set to music to be sung in English by a bass voice in Handel's Messiah.

Quaesivit sibi Dominus virum juxta cor suum 'the Lord hath sought him, a man after his own heart'. Vulgate *Primus liber Samuhelis* (first book of Samuel) Ch.13: 14. Source of the expression 'a man after my own heart'.

Quaestor. A Roman magistrate.

Qualis artifex pereo 'what an artist I die'. Suetonius Nero xlix. I. One of the last things said by the emperor Nero before his suicide in AD 68 after the Praetorian Guard had abandoned him. Nero had been devoted to the arts, particularly music. See *praetor*.

Qualis rex, talis grex 'as the king is, so are the people (flock)'. It is all a question of following example. The lead comes from the top. 'Like father like son'. Based on Petronius Satyricon lviii. 4: 'as the master, so too the slave'. See *arbiter elegantiae*.

Quam plurimi 'as many as possible'.

Quam pulchra es 'how beautiful you are'. Name given to a three part motet written by King Henry VIII 1491-1547 (one of his thirty four surviving compositions). Henry was taught music from an early age and it featured prominently at his court. See *et vera incessu*.

Quasi 'as if'. A useful word permitting a wide degree of approximation in relation to things which have a nexus but do not fit comfortably into a given category or classification. *Quasi* may also mean: sort of, almost, nearly. It is a word much used by lawyers who cannot find the verbal exactitude they seek eternally. So, quasi-contract, quasi-judicial etc.

One who was inordinately fond of his dog once boasted to a friend of its obedience, except when it picked up an irresistible scent. 'Don't equate him with humans' said the friend 'he's really just a wild animal'. He told this to his handsome, athletic, intelligent, mannerly paragon of a dog who was indignant but prepared to agree that he was *quasi-*human. See *homini fidelissimi*

Quem di diligunt adolescens moritur 'he whom the gods love dies young'. Plautus. Bacchides 1.817.

Quercus. Basic classificatory Latin name for the many species of oak. *Quercus robur* is the common oak.

Quicquid agas, prudenter agas, et respice finem 'whatever you do, do it cautiously and keep the end result in view'.
Thomas à Kempis c.1380 – 1471.

Quicquid appositum est, aut apponetur, Christus Benedicere dignetur, in Nomine Patris, et Filii, et Spiritus Sancti 'may Christ think it right to bless whatever has been or will be set before (us). In the name of the Father and of the Son and of the Holy Ghost'. 'Amen' is said by way of response.

A random example of a Cambridge College pre-meal grace. All the Colleges have their own. See *Benedictus benedicat* and *oculi omnium spectant in Te Deus*.

Quicunque vult servari 'whosoever will be saved'. Opening words of the Athanasian Creed (ie., that based on the teaching of St. Athanasius c.296 – 373) known as the '*quicunque vult*'. There are three Creeds [summary articles of religious belief] which, by article viii of the Anglican Articles of Religion 'ought thoroughly to be received and believed: for they may be proved by most certain warranty of holy scripture': namely: The Apostle's Creed (the oldest form of Creed attributed to the Apostles) that named after St. Athanasius and the Nicene Creed (based on the decisions of of an ecumenical council at Nicaea in 325.

Quid ais 'what do you say?' A judge might say to one counsel, after hearing the other, '*quid ais?*'. If he were to receive a most unintelligent answer, he might go on: '*ain vere?*' (abbreviation of *aisne vere* 'do you really mean it?'). Two very useful shorthand expressions which ought surely to be in judicial use?

Quid enim proderit homini, si lucretur mundum totum, et detrimentum anima suae faciat? 'For what shall it profit a man, if he gain the whole world and lose his own soul?' Vulgate. St. Mark Ch 8 v 36 (compare St. Matthew Ch.11 v 26).

E.M. Forster asked (Howard's End Ch. 15) 'what shall it profit a man, if he gain his soul and lose the whole world?'

Verse 37 goes on: *Aut quid debet homo commutationis pro anima sua?* . . . 'or what shall a man give in exchange for his soul?' Does every man have his price? Marlowe's Dr. Faustus sold his soul to the devil in return for twenty four years of life in which he should have whatever he asked. See *ab honesto virum, o lente* and *non bene*.

Quid est veritas? 'What is truth?'

'Pilate therefore said unto him, Art thou a King then? Jesus answered Thou sayest that I am a King. To this end was I born, and for this cause came I into the world, that I should bear witness unto truth. Everyone that is of the truth heareth my voice. Pilate said unto him, what is truth?'
St. John 18:38.

Christ's answer, if any, is not recorded. Unfortunately, apart from his involvement in the events leading to and immediately after Christ's crucifixion as recorded in the gospels, little that is reliable is known of Pontius Pilate the then Roman governor of Judaea.

English and Irish coins of Mary Tudor bore the inscription: *veritas tempora filia* 'Truth the daughter of Time'.

There are plenty of unanswerables. What is time? . . . not how do you measure it? and does the universe end? . . . if so what lies outside it?

See *accepta aqua, ecce homo, ego sum, fortis est, Jesus Nazarenus, lux et, magna est, quod scripsi* and *veritas.*

Quid faciam? Invenias argentum 'what am I to do? You are to find the money'. Terence. Phormio 539. Often the best legal advice. To attempt delay of the inevitable is to waste money on lawyers. See *felix qui nihil.*

Quid faciant leges, ubi sola pecunia regnat 'what may laws do where only money reigns?' What power has the law where only money speaks? Petronius. Satyrica 14. Money too buys the best lawyers: 'Justice in England is open to all, like the Ritz Hotel'. Lord Justice Sir James Mathew 1830 – 1908. See *inter arma silent leges* and *quid leges.*

Quid faciendum 'what's to be done?' Goes well with *nil desperandum* see above. *Nil desperandum. Quid faciendum?* Or *vice versa.*

Quid leges sine moribus vanae proficiunt 'without morals what can futile laws do?' Horace. Carmina 3.24.35. An increasingly relevant observation as dishonesty and corruption at the highest levels of corporate and accounting business come more and more to light. See *fama clamosa* and *quid faciant leges.*

Quid pro quo 'something for something'. Return made for a gift or favour. Thing given by way of compensation. If a large political donation is made, the *quid pro quo* may be a knighthood or even a peerage. Fundamental (termed 'consideration') to the validity of a simple contract in English law.*

Quid sit futurum cras, fuge quaerere et Quem fors dierum cumque dabit lucro Appone 'refrain from asking what will be tomorrow and count as profit (a bonus) the time that destiny gives you'. Horace Odes 1 ix. 13.

'And God shall make thy soul a glass where eighteen thousand Aeons pass

And thou shalt see the gleaming worlds as men see dew upon the grass'.

   'The Gates of Damascus' James Elroy Flecker 1884 – 1915.

'But in this world nothing can be said to be certain except death and taxes'.

   Benjamin Franklin 1706 – 1790.

See *age dum, carpe diem, ille potens, omnem crede, omnia tuta, pallida mors, rapiamus amici* and *sub specie aeternitatis.*

Quieta non movere 'not to move things which are quiescent'. Let sleeping dogs lie. Leave well alone. When the expression is actually applied to dogs, it relates as much to gorgeous puppies (who, when awake, rampage and trash everything with ferocious energy) as to fierce, hostile big dogs. See *draco dormiens nunquam titillandus.*

Qui fugiebat rursus proeliabitur 'he who has fled will fight again'.

   'For he who fights and runs away
   May live to fight another day;
   But he who is in battle slain
   Can never rise and fight again."

   Oliver Goldsmith. Art of Poetry on a New Plan Ch. XIX.

The poet Horace (Quintus Horatius Flaccus 65-8 BC)' as a young man, fought on the losing side at Philippi. He fled the field and survived to write some of the world's most famous poetry, *aere perennius;* and to observe *non omnis moriar* (see above).

   But, for the Roman soldier's ordinary prospects, see *decimare.* Note *tempori cedere* and see *immortalia ne, occasionem cognosce* and *triumviri.*

Qui maxime clamat ei ultimo ministrabitur 'who shouts loudest shall be served last'. During the writing of this book the author's wife deserted him for several months whilst on a horse she made the pilgrimage from Canterbury to Santiago de Compostela in Spain. She left a number of animals to be looked after including a very aged half Siamese cat called 'Winnie', whose endlessly demanding deep throat gravel voice was often answered with these words: but she wasn't!

Qui me tangit vocem meam audit 'whosoever touches (strikes) me hears my voice'. Inscription (in moulded grooving) on an old brass bell to be found outside the back door of a 17th century house at Bonnington, Nr.Ashford in Kent.

Qui mihi VILBIAM involavit sic liquat comodo aqua . . . qui eam involavit Velvinna, Exsupereus, Verianus, Severinus 'may he who has stolen *Vilbia* from me become as liquid as water . . who has stolen it (or her) *Velvinna, Exsuperius, Verianus, Severinus*' etc.

Restored text of the original 'Bath Curse' (*defixio*, curse or spell) found in 1880 as later were others amongst items recovered from the sacred spring at the Temple of Sulis Minerva at Bath (UK). The text is 'restored' ie., deciphered by scholars, with gloss where letters are missing or illegible or where deficient literacy in the scribe is suspected and because curses were usually written on lead sheet, often with words jumbled or the letters of the words reversed or also jumbled and the lead rolled up, inferentially so that only the gods would understand what was asked. *Vilbiam* is probably a reference to a slave girl. *Velvinna* is the first of an apparent short-list of ten named suspects with Roman and Celtic names. A number of curses were found in the vicinity suggesting regular theft of clothing and effects from those taking the sacred waters.

Directing curses appears to have been resorted to as a means of getting even or achieving a rough justice by appeal to the gods. Curses were however invoked for other purposes. See *Circus*. There is some not very strong evidence that there were those in business who, for a fee, would undertake all scribing and other necessary procedural steps to direct a curse.

Some curses were straight-forward as one ('The London Curse' London Museum) found in London's Prince's Street:

> *Titus Egnatius Tyranus est et Publius Cicereius Felix defictus est*
> 'Titus . . . . is hereby cursed, likewise Publius . . .'

Others were much more specific and much nastier. In Britain these were usually prompted by theft incorporating notions of justice in that they were to operate only while and if the item stolen was not returned: like one found on lead sheet at the Temple of Mercury at Uley in Gloucestershire, the restored text of which reads: *Biccus dat Mercurio quidquid perdidit si vir si mascel ne meiat ne cacet ne loquatur ne dormiat ne ne vigilet nec salutem nec salutatem nessi in templo Mercurii pertulerit ne conscientiam de perferat nessi me intercedente* 'Biccus gives Mercury whatever he has lost (that the thief) whether man or male (sic. Female was probably intended) may not urinate nor defecate nor speak nor sleep nor stay awake nor (have) well being or health, unless he bring it into The Temple of Mercury'. See *Aquae Sulis, Circus, lex talionis, nemo me* and *non revertar inultus*.

Quinque viae 'the five ways'. The five arguments put forward by St. Thomas Aquinas (1225-1274) in his great work *Summa Theologica* as proving, by *a posteriori* (see above) reasoning, the existence of God. Si Dieu n'éxistait pas, il faudrait l'inventer . . . 'if God did not exist, it would be necessary to invent him'. Voltaire. See *via*.

Quis custodiet ipsos custodes? 'Who is to guard the guardians themselves?' Juvenal vi 347-8. To the point if police corruption is in question. Juvenal's concern however was with the reliability of guards placed upon a wife to thwart a lover. Knowledge of the fuller context of this famous piece may be salutary.

"Pone seram, cohibe. Sed quis custodiet custodies? Cauta est ab illis incipit uxor." Bolt her in keep her in. But who is to guard the guards themselves? Your wife is careful and begins with them. See *casta est quam*.

Quis famulus amantior domini quam canis? 'what servant loves his master more than does his dog?' Columella. 1st century AD. Hailing from Spain he wrote *'De Re Rustica'* 'on farming'.

Ulysses' return to his old and faithful dog is touchingly portrayed in English verse by Alexander Pope's 'Argus' (the name of Ulysses'/Odysseus' dog in Homer's Odyssey):

'When wise Ulysses, from his native coast
Arriv'd at last, poor old disguis'd alone.
Long kept by wars, and long by tempest tost,
To all his friends and ev'n his Queen unknown;
Chang'd as he was, with age and toils and cares,
Furrow'd his rev'rend face, and white his hairs,
Scorn'd by those slaves his former bounty fed,
Forgot of all his own domestic crew;
The faithful dog alone his rightful master knew!
. . . . . .
Him when he saw – he rose, and crawl'd to meet,
('Twas all he cou'd) and fawn'd and licked his feet,
Seiz'd with dumb joy – then falling by his side,
Own'd his returning Lord, look'd up and dy'd!'

But the converse is true. 'One of the saddest things in life is the animals we outlive'. Brian Johnston. English commentator (particularly cricket) and broadcaster 1912-1994). See *canes timidi, canis ingens, cave canem, fide, homini fidelissime* (in particular), *quasi, semper fidelis* and *tene me ne*.

Quisque me cenam vocavit valeat 'whoever has asked me to a meal,

153

greeting'. Graffiti on the basilica at Pompeii. The grammar is wanting: *quisque* should be *quisquis* and *vocavit* should *be vocaverit*.

Quis umquam adparitor tam humilis, tam abjectis? 'what syco-phant was ever so servile and cringing?' Cicero. Philippicae II. See *Cicero* and *Quomodo Adulator*.

Qui timide rogat, docet negare 'he who asks timidly courts denial'. Seneca. To be noted in all walks of life and in particular by advocates.

Quoad hanc 'in regard to or vis-à-vis this (a particular) female person'. An expression used in the past by the law in relation to nullity of marriage on the grounds of non-consummation; where a man was capa-ble of performing but not with his wife. It has been conjectured that this syndrome afflicted the emperor Augustus in relation to his intelligent, patrician and fearsome wife Livia. This gave her an ascendancy over him so that it has been said (by Robert Graves in 'I Claudius') that perhaps Augustus ruled the world but Livia ruled Augustus.

Note Horace Epode 12: *Inachiam ter nocte potes, mihi semper ad unum mollis opus* 'you can manage Inachia three times a night but for me you are never even once man enough for the job'.

'Heav'n has no rage, like love to hatred turn'd,
Nor Hell a fury, like a woman scorn'd'.
    William Congreve 1670-1729 'The Mourning Bride'.

Frequently misquoted as: 'Hell hath no fury like a woman scorned'.

Quo animo 'with what intention'.

Quod erat demonstrandum 'which was to be shown or demon-strated'. An expression used as an appendage to a mathematical (partic-ularly a geometrical) solution and meaning that the answer to the proposition to be proved is set out. Usually it is abbreviated to QED.
In early September 1995 several national newspapers carried news that use of Latin tags was to be abandoned in the Treasury because too many did not understand them. In France, Francis 1 abandoned Latin as the language of State as long ago as 1539. An unpopular civil service official jargon, *langage administratif*, grew up in its place.

From late September 1995 the Sunday Telegraph ran a very success-ful "learn Latin by Christmas" course. It was called "QED" and written by Peter Jones.*

Quod erat faciendum 'what was to be done'.

Quod scripsi scripsi 'what I have written I have written'. St. John xix.22 in the Vulgate. Pontius Pilate wrote and placed above Christ on the cross the inscription 'Jesus of Nazareth the King of the Jews'; written in Hebrew, Greek and Latin (*Latine scriptum*, see above, *Jesus Nazarenus, Rex Judaeorum.*"). Classical Latin did not have a "J" hence the abbreviation INRI often seen in paintings and on crucifixes, especially in Roman Catholic churches and cathedrals.

The chief priests of the Jews protested and demanded variation to state, not that he was King of the Jews, but rather that he had maintained that he was. Pilate answered with: '*quod scripsi scripsi*'. In the King James Bible this appears in English, not in Latin. The Latin version has however come into general usage denoting that a person will not compromise his integrity by a convenient change of mind, by persuasion from what is truth or is right or by alteration of something properly done. See *accepta aqua, ecce homo, Jesus Nazarenus* and *quid est veritas*.

Quod vide 'see which thing'. Abbreviated to q.v. A reference to somewhere else in a book.

Quo jure 'by what right or law?' A questioning of authority.

Quomodo 'how or in what way?'

Quomodo Adulator Ab Amico Internoscatur 'how a flatterer is to be distinguished from a friend'. Title to a treatise in Latin by the Greek biographer, historian and moral philosopher Plutarch (c. Ad 46 – c. 120). A useful work in any age, particularly for those in positions of power or authority. 'Let me have men about me who are not sycophants': after Shakespeare's Julius Caesar. See *fide sed cui* above. Motto: beware of men with brown noses. See *cucullus non facit, fronti nulla fides, quis umquam* and *timeo Danaos*.

Quomodo sedet sola civitas. In the epilogue to Evelyn Waugh's 'Brideshead Revisited' is the passage following: 'The builders did not know the uses to which their work would descend; they made a new house with the stones of the old castle; year by year the great harvest of timber in the park grew to ripeness; until, in sudden frost, came the age of Hooper; the place was desolate and the work all brought to nothing; *Quomodo sedet sola civitas.* Vanity of vanities, all is vanity' (see *Vanitas vanitatum* below). The words are from The Lamentations of Jeremiah (Ch.1 v.1 Vulgate) and are followed by the words *plena populos;* the whole translating as: (King James Bible translation) 'How does the city sit solitary and alone, that was full of people!'

Quomodo vales? 'How are you faring? How are you? Comment allez-vous? Wie geht's ihr?' Roman greeting.

Quondam 'sometime'. One who in his youth played rugby for England is a *quondam* rugby international.*

Quorum 'of whom, of which (persons)'. Used in English as a noun (a quorum . . of whom there should be two, three etc.) to specify the number of persons who must be present to validate the proceedings of an assembly or society. '*Quarum*' perhaps in the women's institute!'*

Quot homines tot sententiae: suo' quoique mos 'so many men so many opinions; each has his own right way'. Terence Phormio II. IV. 14. A reference to how hard it is to find consensus in 'a world composed of men who are as various as the sands of the sea'. E.M. Forster. Abinger Harvest 1936. Notes on the English character. Cf., *pectoribus mores tot sunt, quot in orbe figurae* 'there are as many characters in men as there are shapes in the world'. Ovid.

Quo vadis 'where do you go?' or 'Whither goest thou?' Outside Rome, on the *via Appia* (the Appian Way) is a small church (of St. Maria dell Piante, usually called *Domine quo vadis)* which commemorates the tradition (based on the apocryphal 'Acts of St. Peter') that St. Peter was running away from Rome, probably from Nero's persecution of the Christians, when, confronted by a vision of Christ, he asked: '*Domine quo vadis?*' ('whither goest thou Master?') and, on hearing the answer that Christ was going to Rome to be crucified again, St. Peter was ashamed and himself returned to Rome to be crucified, at his own request, head down, because he was not worthy of crucifixion in the same manner as Christ.

The expression appears also in the Gospel according to St. John Ch. 16 v 5.

'But now I go on my way to him that sent me: and none of you asketh me.Whither goest thou?'

Name given to a 1951 film starring (Sir) Peter Ustinov as the emperor Nero.

R

Radix malorum est cupiditas 'greed is at the root of all evils'. From the Vulgate. I Timothy 6:10. This expression heads the 'Pardoner's Prologue' (to the Pardoner's Tale in Geoffrey Chaucer's Canterbury Tales). Note that it is not money but the love of money, greed and avarice, which are at the root of evil. See *amor nummi, crescit amor, dummodo sit dives, esurientes, Lucilla ex corpore, inopem me copia, intolerabilius nihil, lucri bonus, nec prece, nolite thesaurisare, omnia Romae, pecunia non olet* and *si possis recte.*

Rapiamus amici occasionem de die 'friends let us snatch our opportunity from the passing day'. Horace. See *age dum, carpe diem, ille potens, occasionem cognosce, omnem crede* and *quid sit futurum.*

Rara avis 'a rare bird'. Juvenal, vi. 165. A person of exceptional virtue, talent etc., a paragon. *Rara avis in terris nigroque simillima cygno* 'a rare bird on the earth and very like a black swan'. See *augur* and *bonis avibus.*

Redde cuique quod suum est 'render to each that which is his own'. Inscription on Henry VIII groat (coin). See *reddite ergo* and *justitia est.*

Reddite ergo quae sunt Caesaris Caesari: et quae sunt Dei, Deo 'render therefore to Caesar the things which are Caesar's; and to God the things which are God's'. Vulgate. St. Matthew. Ch.22 v.21.

With a view to compromising Christ the Pharisees asked him whether he thought it lawful to pay tribute to Caesar. Did allegiance to God come before that to Caesar? Jesus invited them to show him a coin of the Empire. They tendered him a *denarius* (a silver coin showing the head of the Roman emperor). Jesus asked them whose was the head and inscription shown upon it. 'Caesar's' they replied in triumph before receiving the above reply by which they were disconcerted and went their way.

The coin is known as the 'tribute penny'. It is generally accepted that the head shown upon it would have been that of the Emperor Tiberius but *denarii* of Augustus, who died in AD14, could still have been in circulation at what is an uncertain date.

The passage is sometimes abbreviated to *Caesaris Caesari* 'Caesar's things to Caesar' and used to mean that rights or chattels should go to those entitled. See *Augustus, denarius, justitia* and *redde cuique.*

Reductio ad absurdum 'reduction to absurdity'. Expression used to describe how the logical consequences of propositions lead to nonsense.

Regina 'queen'.*

Regius 'royal or splendid'. A regius professor is one whose chair was founded by a king, usually Henry VIII. At Oxford there is a regius professorship of Ecclesiastical History and of Medicine. In April 2002 the Queen approved the appointment of John Bell, professor of clinical medicine and head of the department of clinical medicine, to the Regius Chair of Medicine.

Rem tene, verba sequentur 'stick to the point and the words will follow (come)'. Cato. Only fragments of the speeches of this great orator survive but he deserves for ever to be remembered for this piece of advice to us all.

Marcus Porcius Cato (234 – 149 BC) became Censor at the age of fifty. Seeing Romans degenerate in headlong pursuit of money, luxury and debauched living, he sought Canute-like to turn back the tide by urging the old values which had made Rome great; tilling the land, austerity and honour. Cf., Juvenal in *circus* above: see too *fidem qui perdit* and *munera nunc*. See *delenda est Carthago*.

Renuntium Coh VIIII Batavorum, omnes ad loca qui debunt et impedimenta. Remuntiarunt optiones et curatores. Detulit Arquittius, opto, crescentis 'report (date) ninth cohort of Batavians. All men and equipment present and correct. Certified by the deputy centurions and quartermasters. Arquittius, deputy centurion of Crescens, reports'.

Military routine efficiency. Content of a letter excavated at Vindolanda on Hadrian's Wall (see *Brittunculi*). Batavians seem to have been recruited into the Roman army from the Batavi, a tribe in the low countries; modern Holland. Taken from 'Roman Records from Vindolanda on Hadrian's Wall' with permission of the author, Robin Birley. See *C.L. Lepidina* and *Claudius Karus*.

Requiem aeternam dona eis, Domine et lux perpetua luceat eis 'give them eternal rest O Lord and may light perpetual shine upon them'. Opening words of the Roman Catholic Church's mass for the dead. The word 'requiem' (mass) takes its name from the first word of the introit. The mass has been set to music *inter alios* by Mozart 1791 (unfinished), Berlioz 1837, Verdi 1874 and by Dvorak. Benjamin

Britten's War Requiem of 1961 combines the Latin texts with the war poems of Wilfred Owen. See *dulce et decorum est*.

Requiescat in pace. See RIP and *requiem aeternam*.

Rescripsit boni pastoris esse tondere pecus, non deglubere 'he wrote in answer that the good shepherd shears his sheep, he does not skin (flay) them'. Governors in the provinces had recommended to the Emperor Tiberius burdensome taxes. This was the emperor's reply. Suetonius. Tiberius xxxii.

Latin for chancellors of the exchequer to note (despite a ban on use of Latin in the treasury since 1995 See *quod erat demonstrandum*). It is not recorded whether stealth taxes were those proposed.

In St. Luke's gospel 3.1 there is reference to various things which came about in the fifteenth year of the emperor Tiberius Caesar's reign when Pilate was governor of Judaea. See *damnatio memoriae*, *Merobibus*, *pecunia non olet*, *sicut pastor* and *verbosa et grandis*.

Res loquitur ipsa, quae semper valet plurimum 'the thing itself speaks and that is always of the utmost value'. Cicero Pro Milone 53. The variant expression *res ipsa loquitur* (the thing itself speaks) is a maxim of the law, where it has (had) a technical meaning relating to who must prove what in a negligence claim. The expression is one of the law's Latin maxims which is well known to many non-lawyers. However current efforts to exclude use of legal Latin may have made this no longer acceptable in the courts. See Fryer v Pearson The Times 4th April 2000 and Lawyers' Latin by John Gray. Robert Hale 2002.

Res perit domino 'the thing perishes to the owner'. At the owner's risk.

Respice finem 'look to the end'. See *quicquid agas*.

Retiarius 'gladiator with trident and net'. The name given to one of a number of categories of gladiator; they being named according to the nature of their opponent and the weaponry and protection permitted to each of them. The *retiarius* had his net, trident and a long dagger. He wore no helmet and had no armour except the *manica* and *galerus*, a leather or metal arm and shoulder guard respectively. He was pitted against the *secutor* who had a *manica* on his arm, a shield and a short sword. He had also a helmet, which was completely enclosed with only small eye holes to protect his face and eyes from the trident. Such a helmet may be seen in gallery 69 showcase 20 at the British Museum.

Another more ornate one (from the gladiatorial barracks at Pompeii) is displayed in the Museo Archaeologico Nazionali di Napoli (Naples). Both are bronze and first century AD. See *Ave Caesar, Colosseum, editor, munera nunc, secutor* and *silentium*.

Retro me, satana 'get thee behind me satan'. Stop trying to tempt me. Matt. XIV. 23. Mark VII. 33. Luke IV. 8. Jesus had sought to prepare his disciples by warning of terrible things he was destined to endure. Peter began to rebuke him and assert that this could not be. Christ replied with these words. In the Vulgate *vade retro me satana*. See *quadragesima*.

Ricinus communis. Latin classificatory name for the castor oil plant; a member of the pumpkin family from the seeds of which the lethal poison ricin is made. The poison is a favourite of dissident and extremist groups. Literature relating to its production was found in Kabul after the Taleban retreat from that city in the Afghan war of 2001, when British and American allies sought (unsuccessfully) to find and capture Osama Bin Laden who was thought to be responsible for the greatest ever terrorist outrage in New York on September 11th 2001.

This poison attracted much publicity in 1978 when used by Bulgarian secret agents to kill the dissident Georgi Markov in London. He was stabbed with an umbrella which had a ricin capsule fitted in a sharp tip.

Ridiculum acri fortius et melius magnas. Horace satires 1:10 lines 14-15.

'Jesting decides great things.
Stronglier, and better than earnest can'.
    Translation by John Milton 1608-1674.

RIP. Abbreviation of *requiescat in pace* 'may he rest in peace'. Taken generally in the English with the same letter commencing each word as simply: rest in peace . . . RIP. Seen on many gravestones. See *requiem aeternam dona eis.* *

Romani ite domum 'Romans go home'. On the plinth of an equestrian statue of the Roman emperor Nerva recently erected in Gloucester these words appeared in June of 2004. They were quickly removed by the council. Entry courtesy of letter from Geoffrey Johnston, Gloucester.

Roma semel quantum dat bis Menevia quantum 'to Rome gives twice as much as to Menevia'. Pilgrimages to sacred shrines were an important part of medieval life in Christendom. The ultimate was a pilgrimage to Jerusalem. Cheaper, safer and closer to home for most were those to the seven pilgrimage churches of Rome and to Santiago de Compostela, Galicia in north west Spain. In England there were pilgrimages from Winchester and London to the shrine of St. Thomas Becket in Canterbury (portrayed in Geoffrey Chaucer's Canterbury Tales). A number of Papal decrees declared the relative value to a pilgrim's soul of a journey to various shrines and holy places. The above Latin is from a Papal Bull of Calixtus II (1119-1124) stating that a pilgrimage to Rome was, in terms of accumulatable divine goodwill, worth twice as much as one to Minevia (the shrine of St. David on the Pembrokeshire coast in Wales). The concept may be understood in terms of 'brownie points' stored up in life to improve the prospect of ultimate salvation. See *capitulum hujus, Finis Terrae* and *salus factori*.

Romulus. Name of the traditional founder of Rome in 753 BC. Legend has it that in infancy, with his twin brother Remus, he was thrown into the river Tiber. For dynastic reasons the twins were to be disposed of. They were however washed ashore and suckled by a she-wolf before being taken in by a royal herdsman and reared. Romulus grew to manhood and founded Rome. See *ab urbe condita*.

Rostra. Name of the platform in Rome's forum from which speakers addressed the people. The word *rostrum* has come in English to mean any platform or pulpit for public speaking. See *Cicero*.*

Ruat caelum '(Though) heaven fall'. Words following *fiat justitia* . . . 'let justice be done though heaven fall'. That justice should be done is paramount.

Ruber 'Red'.

Rubicon. Name of a river which once marked the boundary between Italy and Cisalpine Gaul. In face of orders from the senate to disband his army, Julius Caesar crossed this river in 49 BC making civil war inevitable. According to Suetonius, after crossing, Caesar said *"iacta est alea"* 'the die is cast'. In common parlance 'to cross the Rubicon' has come to refer to an action from which there can be no going back. For more of this famous episode read Rubicon. Tom Holland. Little Brown 2003. See *Caesar*.

Rufus Callisuni salutem Epillico et omnibus contubernalibus certiores vos esse credo me recte valere si vos indicem [f]ecistis rogo mittite omnia diligenter cura agas ut illam puellam ad nummum redigas 'Rufus, son of Callisunus, greetings to Epillicus and all his fellows. I believe you know that I am very well. If you have made the list, please send it. See that you do everything carefully so as to reduce that girl to cash'.

Letter in Roman cursive script on a 'fir-wood' stilus tablet found c. 1927 near Walbrook at Lothbury. The address of the writer on the outside face is no more than *Londinio* (at London). One can only guess at why Rufus was so anxious that the sale of the (tiresome?) slave girl should realise as much as possible. Translation courtesy of The Roman Inscriptions of Britain R.G. Collingwood and R.P. Wright edited 1992 by S.S. Frere and Dr. R.S.O.Tomlin. See *Vegetus*.

Rus in urbe 'the country in the city'. Martial xii. Lvii. 21. London's great parks, Green Park, Hyde Park, Regent's Park and St. James' Park. Central Park in New York and the Capitol Gardens in Washington. The Retiro in Madrid and the Bois de Boulogne in Paris. The Botanical Gardens in Sydney.

Rutilans rosa sine spina 'a dazzling (reddening) rose without a thorn'. Inscription on small gold coins of Henry VIII. Of how many beautiful women can this truly be said? See *nemo me* (Röslein rot).

S

Sagittarius 'an archer'. From *sagitta* an arrow. A constellation (group of stars) in which can be discerned the figure of an archer. The ninth sign of the zodiac. One born when the sun is in this sign is a sagittarian. See *aureus, libra* and appendix 3.

Salus factori 'salvation to the maker'. Note *pax possessori* above and see *ad unguem, fecit* and *pinxit*.

Salus humani generis 'rescuer of the human race'. Amongst those who moved to act against Nero (whose appalling excesses, towards the end of his reign, had become intolerable) was one Gaius Julius Vindex who backed Galba and urged him to 'rescue the human race'. Galba became emperor and had *salus humani generis* inscribed on his coinage as well as *libertas restituta, Roma renascens* 'liberty restored, Rome being reborn'. Notwithstanding, too niggardly to pay the Praetorian Guard the price of their continuing support, he was brutally murdered a year later in 69 at the instance of his successor Otho. According to Plutarch his last words, spoken to his assassins were: 'do your work, if this is better for the Roman people'.

Salus Publica 'public well-being'. A legend on Roman coinage of the Emperor Hadrian, who was renowned for his interest in provincial affairs and the high moral quality of his administration. He visited Britain in AD 122 and his wall, or great sentry walk, spanning seventy miles across northern England, was completed in AD 133. It marked the northernmost frontier of the Roman Empire. See *Apud Lapidomurenses, Britannia, Brittunculi, Claudius Karus, CL Lepidina, renuntiam* and *veni, vidi, vici.*

Salve 'hail or hi–there'. Roman greeting.

Salve lucrum 'hail profit'. Words to be found all over Pompeii. The Romans were true capitalists. See *nonis Februariis, omnia Romae* and *sum tua.*

Sanctus 'holy'.

Sapere aude 'dare to be wise'. Horace Epist., I. II. 40. See *libenter enim.*

Sapientis est proprium nihil quod paenitere possit facere 'it is the characteristic of a wise man to do nothing of which he may repent'. Cicero. Analagous to the old adage: 'act in haste repent at leisure' See *ad poenitendum properat.*

Satis diu vel naturae vixi vel gloriae 'I have lived long enough for the demands of nature or fame'. Cicero. Pro Marcello. Famous sentence in Cicero's speech thanking Caesar for pardoning Marcellus when in 51 BC the latter, as consul, had launched an attack on Caesar which precipitated civil war. See Cicero.

Scilicet 'one is permitted to know', namely, that is to say. Abbreviated to sc. A word introductory to explanation.

Scintilla 'spark or smallest part of a thing'. 'There is not one *scintilla* of evidence to support . . . .' is (or used to be) a regular judicial expression. See *excelsior.*

Scio enim quod redemptor meus vivat et in novissimo de terra surrecturus sit 'I know that my redeemer liveth and that He shall walk at the latter day upon the earth'. Vulgate. Book of Job 19-25. Well known passage, the English being set to music for soprano voice in Handel's Messiah.

Scriptio continua 'uninterrupted things written'. Name used for the writings of early scribes who, when transcribing Latin, used no punctuation and initially left no gaps between the words. For more read 'Eats Shoots and Leaves' by Lynn Truss. Profile Books Ltd. 2003. See *consolamini* and *positura*.

Scrutamini scripturas 'search the scriptures'. St John 5: 39. 'Search the scriptures; for in them ye think ye have eternal life: and they are which testify of me'.

'These two words have undone the world'.
John Selden, 1584–1654.

Scutum fidei proteget eum (or **eam** as appropriate) 'the shield of faith protects him/her'. Words inscribed on much of the gold coinage of Edward VI and Elizabeth I.

Secutor 'pursuing gladiator'. Category of gladiator. Armed usually with a sword, helmet, shield *(scutum)* and *manica* (arm guard), he was pitted in the arena against a *retiarius* (with net and trident: see above). See *Ave Caesar, Colosseum, editor, munera nunc, secutor* and *silentium*.

Sed et benignitas et misericordia subsequetur me omnibus diebus vitae meae 'surely goodness and mercy shall follow me all the days of my life'. Vulgate Psalm 23 v.6. Seen to by a guardian angel? A comforting thought but hard to believe in a world of never ending violence and destruction. But see *una salus*.

Sede vacante 'the seat or benefice being vacant'.

Sed quaere 'but question'. Used to pose a query following statement of a proposition. It is not necessarily fatal for one person to drink a litre bottle of scotch in five minutes; *sed quaere*. Entry in a lonely hearts column might read: '. . . aged sixty five. Have teeth and hair, *sed quaere* marbles'.

Semen 'seed', or anything planted.

Semper eadem 'always the same'.

Motto of Queen Elizabeth I in her coat of arms. She was well versed in the Latin language and proud of her grammar. See *ditior in toto*.

Semper fidelis 'always faithful'. Motto. Dogs have more or less a monopoly of this expression. See *canis ingens, fide sed cui, homini fidelissime, quasi, quis famulus* and *tene me*.

Semper paratus 'always ready'. Motto. *Nunquam paratus* 'never ready'. See *nunquam non paratus*

Senatus 'senate'. The legislative council of Rome. See SPQR.

Senex 'an old man'. Word from which 'senile' is derived. If we live long enough the chances are that in greater or lesser degree we will become senile. We cannot draw upon the experience of old age because we have not been there before.

'Old age is the most unexpected of things that can happen to a man'.
Leon Trotsky 1879-1940. diary 8th May 1935.

See *non sum qualis* and *volo non valeo*.

Sepultus 'buried'. Seen on gravestones. See *hic jacet, hic sepultus, natus* and *obit*.

Seq. 'following'. Short for *sequens . . . sequentia . . .* singular and plural respectively. For example: *et seq.*, 'and the following'.

Sic 'thus'. Used following a word, which has the first sight appearance of being a misprint, a mis-spelling or otherwise in error, to indicate that what appears is what was intended by the writer or is what was written without qualification by an original author, who is quoted. Confirming that what is written is indeed correct or is as intended.

The word is used in particular by editors when quotation is involved so as to make plain that an apparent error has not gone unnoticed and is reproduced in its original form. See *passim*.

Sic semper tyrannis 'thus ever to tyrants'. Shouted by John Wilkes Booth in 1865 after he had shot and killed Abraham Lincoln.

'The Lord prefers common-looking people. That is why he makes so many of them'.
Abraham Lincoln. Attributed.

See *iniqua nunquam*.

Sic transit gloria mundi 'thus passes the glory of the world'.

Words spoken at the investiture of a new Pope. White flux is burned signifying the transient nature of worldly glory.

Sicut erat in principio, et nunc et semper 'as it was in the beginning is now and always (ever shall be)'. See *in principio*.

Sicut pastor gregem suum pascet 'He shall feed his flock like a shepherd'. Vulgate Isaiha 40:11. Set to music for Contralto voice in Handel's Messiah. See *rescripsit boni*.

Sic volo; sic jubeo, sit pro ratione voluntas 'I wish thus, I order thus: let my will be the reason'. Sometimes *hoc volo*. Juvenal vi.223.

What I wish and say goes. My wish is as good as a reason. You will do what you are told because I say so. The poet describes the awfulness of a dominant wife who demands that her husband crucify a slave who is without fault.

Signa inferre! Praege! Concursu! Ad gladios! Infestis pilis 'fetch the standards! Advance! At the run! Look to your swords! With weapons threatening!' Orders from a Roman commander to his legionaries about to engage Gauls in "Le Fils d'Asterix" (see *Asterix Gallus*). The splashed word "patchac" accompanies the pictured encounter and instant humiliating defeat of the Roman cohort. A French asterisked translation of the Latin goes: en avant! Marche! Pas de charge! Aux armes! En joue!

Silentium dormiant tauri 'silence let the bulls sleep'. A message depicted on a 3rd century AD Roman mosaic from Thysdrus (El Djem) in Tunis and now in the Bardo Museum, Tunis. Bulls were regular contestants with gladiators in the arenas (amphitheatres) of which there were many throughout the Roman Empire. The mosaic is reproduced on the cover of Colin Well's 'The Roman Empire' (second edition. Fontana Press 1992. An authoritative and immensely readable history) and shows the human contestants feasting before the games while the bulls are sleeping. See *ave Caesar, circus, Colosseum, editor, munera nunc, retiarius* and *secutor*.

Si monumentum requiris, circumspice 'if you seek a monument (to him), look around you'. Inscription on the tomb of Sir Christopher Wren in St. Paul's Cathedral, which he architected and built together with numerous other churches and buildings in London. See *exegi monumentum* and *digito monstrari*.

Simulatio maxima 'the greatest hypocrisy'. See *integer vitae*.

Sine amicitia, vitam esse nullam 'there is no life without friendship'. Cicero. See *nihil sine Deo*.

Sine dubio 'without doubt'.

Sine mora 'without delay'.

Sine qua non 'without which not'. See *causa sine qua non*. The ultimate fundamental. Combustion is a 'without which not' of smoke.

Sinistra manu 'with the left hand'.

Si possis recte, si non, quocumque modo rem 'if possible honestly, if not somehow, the thing (make money)'. Horace 65-8 BC. Epistles.
Alexander Pope 1688-1744 translates this as:

'Get wealth and place, if possible with grace,
If not by any means get wealth and place'.

'I'm opposed to millionaires, but it would be dangerous to offer me the position'.
Mark Twain.

The widespread decay of honesty and honour (see *laudator temporis acti*) and a culture of 'what's in it for me' marks the decline of any society. See *ab honesto virum, amor nummi, crescit amor, dona clandestina, esurientes, inopem, lucri bonus, nec prece, nolite thesaurisare, omnia Romae, oportet ergo, pecunia non olet* and *radix malorum*.

Sit sine labe decus 'let my honour be without stain'. High minded motto alas largely outmoded.

'What stronger breastplate than a heart unstained'.
William Shakespeare. Henry VI Part II. Act iii. sc. 2. l. 235.

See *fidem qui perdidit, nemo me, non revertar* and *potius mori*.

Si vis pacem, para bellum 'if you want peace, prepare for war'. Sometimes *qui desiderat pacem, praeparet bellum* 'who desires peace, let him prepare for war'. Vegetius 4th century AD; based on the prologue to his *Epitoma Rei Militaris* a four volume work on Roman military practice and the only work on the subject to survive intact. True of Britain in 1939 and relevant again since the Autumn of 2001 as the world pondered the threat from more terrorism and Saddam Hussein's alleged weapons of mass destruction in Iraq. See *pax*.

In 2001 a solicitor's instructions to counsel commenced: *Qui desiderat pacem, praeparet bellum.* The writer was not inhibited by the law's disapproval of Latin usage. The recipient was baffled. Advice as to preparation for impending trial was asked. Compromise negotiations had begun to avoid the daunting expense and uncertainty of a long trial. If tactical negotiating strength was to be maintained, a show of vigorous preparation was vital. Classic strategy is mutual bombardment with lorry loads of documents. This was followed until both crawled, broken and exhausted (their clients already impoverished) to the final settlement table. Conflict had been avoided by preparation for it. See *pax* and *pax quaeritur bello*.

Socius 'an ally or comrade'. A fellow, partner, associate.

Soles occidere et redire possunt. Nobis cum semel occidit brevis lux, Nox est perpetua una dormienda. Catullus. Poem 5. Translation by Sir Walter Raleigh 1554-1618:

'The sun may set and rise:
But we contrarywise
Sleep after our short light
One everlasting night'.

Sir Walter was a man of supreme diverse talent, intellect and ability: soldier, privateer, historian, scholar, poet, chemist and advocate (his defence of himself when facing death and prosecuted by as illustrious and formidable a lawyer as Sir Edward Coke was composed and masterly). He wrote verse in the death cell on the night before his execution and on the scaffold, when asked to face east, replied: 'what matter which way the head lie if the heart be right'. Worldly advice given to his son was: 'trust no man too much'.

His statue stood outside the Ministry of Defence for nearly forty years before being moved to the grounds of the Old Royal Naval College, Greenwich on the twentieth December 2001. *See longissime a sapientia.*

Solis terraeque vinum fructus 'wine is the fruit of the sun and the earth'. Inscription in glass relief on bottles of 2002 'La Chasse du Pape' (Côtes du Rhône). The wine is named after the chest which contained the reliquaries of the Popes residing in Avignon during the 14th century. See *bonum vinum.*

Solus 'alone'. To fly solo is to fly alone.

'Alone alone, all all alone, Alone on the wide wide sea.
And never a saint took pity on My soul in agony'.
    Samuel Taylor Coleridge 1772-1834. The Rime of the Ancient
Mariner.

'Nunquam se minus otiosum esse quam cum otiosus, nec minus solum quam cum solus esset' 'one is never less idle than when completely idle, nor less alone than when wholly alone'. Cicero. De Officiis III i I. See *nunquam minus*.

Spartacus. See *fasces*.

Spectatum veniunt, veniunt spectentur ut ipsae 'they come to see, they come to be seen themselves'. Ovid Ars Amatoria i.99. In Biarritz beautiful people come to the Royalty Bar in the Place Georges Clemenceau where, on balmy summer evenings, they sit outside and drink and see and are seen as the elegant world goes by. The poet however was writing of available women and Dryden translates these words and what follows thus: 'To see, and to be seen, in heaps they run: Some to undo, and some to be undone'.

Spero meliora 'I hope for better things'. Heartfelt lament of the commuter who has to use the 2002-2004 UK. railway network. See *at spes non, dum spiro spero* and *video meliora*.

Splendide mendax 'nobly untruthful'. Horace Odes iii.xi.35. Lying for commendable ends. Telling a white lie.

Sponte sua 'by his own choice,' of one's own accord. Usually rendered as *sua sponte*.

SPQR abbreviation of: *Senatus Populusque Romanus* 'the Roman Senate (government) and People'. The abbreviation was used on military standards at the head of Roman armies and is today on drain covers in Rome. See too *fasces* and *senatus populusque*.

Stabat Mater dolorosa, Juxta crucem lacrimosa Dum pendebat Filius 'with her Son suspended, there stood the sorrowing Mother, weeping beside the cross'. Hymn attributed to Pope Innocent III. Set to music by Rossini.

Stabit quocunque jeceris 'it will stand whichever way you throw it'. Legend on the Isle of Man coat of arms related to the island's three legged emblem which is an ancient sun symbol. Found on a stone cross (the Maughold Cross) and on the hilt of a sword of antiquity, it was adopted in the 12th century as the island's symbol. Both the emblem and the expression (*quocunque gesseris stabit*) appeared on copper coinage of the Island in 1709, when the Earls of Derby were Lords of Man. The legs are now usually shown clad in armour but this was not originally so. The same symbol has been found also on some early Norwegian shields.

Status quo 'the state in which. The existing state of affairs'. The *status quo ante* is the state of affairs existing before some event. If you kill a man the *status quo ante* cannot be restored: a point made so tellingly by Shakespeare as Othello steals with murderous intent into the bedchamber of the sleeping Desdemona, lit only by a candle's flame. (The Moor of Venice Act v. Scene II):

'Put out the light, and then put out the light:
If I quench thee, thou flaming minister,
I can again thy former light restore,
Should I repent me: — but once put out thy light,
Thou cunning'st pattern of excellent nature,
I know not where is that Promethian heat
That can thy light relume' –

In 1920 Sir Edward Marshall Hall KC used this passage to great dramatic effect when addressing the jury on behalf of a solicitor, Harold Greenwood, accused of murdering his wife. At that time a verdict of guilty meant the macabre donning of the judge's black cap and recital of that terrible prescribed form of words: 'The sentence of the court upon you is, that you be taken from this place to a lawful prison, and thence to a place of execution, and that there you suffer death by hanging; and that your body be afterwards buried within the precincts of the prison in which you shall have been confined before execution. And may the Lord have mercy upon your soul'.

Stet 'let it stand'. When a correction or alteration has been made in writing and cancellation of the correction or alteration is desired, so that what went before stands, this may be expressed or directed in useful shorthand by the Latin word (adopted by English) *stet*.*

Stilus 'a pen'. Not like those of today. A pointed instrument used usually to scratch into soft materials such as wax or clay. Used by the Romans and earlier. Made from anything from bronze to bone, they were usually shaped at the opposite end from the point so as to spread out, oar-like, to a flat end, which could be used to smooth the material being written upon eg., to permit correction of a mistake. The word stylus is now also used to describe the hard pointed item which follows the groove in a gramophone record for sound reproduction purposes.

Stipendium 'A Roman soldier's pay'. A clergyman's remuneration is now called a stipend.

Sua cuique voluptas 'to each his own pleasures' Statius. II ii 73. Silvae. Every man to his own taste. Chacun à son gout.

Suae quisque fortunae faber. See *faber est*.

Sua sponte. See *sponte sua*.

Suaviter in modo fortiter in re 'gentle in manner strong (resolute) in deed'. See *fortiter in re*.

Subfuscus 'brown, dusky, tawny (sometimes *suffuscus*)'. An abbreviation *subfusc* is used at Oxford University to describe the attire compulsory for the taking of examinations or attending graduation ceremonies: dark suit and shoes with mortar-board and white bow-tie.

Sub nomine 'under or by the name', abbreviated to *sub nom. (or s.n.)* Under a specified name (eg., 'Jones, see below *sub nom*. Smith').

Sub rosa 'under the rose'. The rose was a Roman symbol of secrecy. The expression is used to mean that something is secret or in confidence. Where a mole in the civil service leaks a Government document (officially or unofficially) to the media, the illicit transaction is *sub rosa*. Until the budget speech the Chancellor of the Exchequer's new measures are supposed to be kept *sub rosa*.

Sub specie aeternitatis 'under the view of eternity', ie., seen in the context of the eternal. See *quid sit futurum*.

Suggestio falsi 'suggestion of untrue things'. See too *suppressio veri* with which the expression is often combined.

Sui generis 'of his or its own kind'. Not belonging to, or fitting exactly into, a recognised class or category. Unique. This book is perhaps *sui generis*.

Sui juris 'in his own right'. Adult: recognised by the law as responsible for his actions: not a *minor*, (see above) infant or child. And not a 'patient' . . . i.e., not one of unsound mind. In Rome all persons were *sui* *juris* or *alieni juris* 'of independent status or in the power of another'. Those *alieni juris* were slaves and children of the *paterfamilias*. See *patria potestas* and *paterfamilias*.

Summa cum laude 'with the highest praise': greater than *magna cum laude* see above. In May 2001 the first nominated 'people's peers' were nominated. There was query as to whether the multi-honoured and talented professor of synaptic (relating to the joinder of nerve cells) pharmacology at Oxford university, Susan Greenfield, really qualified as 'one of the people'. Insofar as modest beginnings were a qualifying factor, it was suggested, she could claim membership *summa cum laude*. The expression is used in some American universities for grading degrees. The descent is from *summa cum laude*, through *magna cum laude* (with great praise) to *cum laude* (with praise).

Summarum summa est aeternum 'the sum of all sums is eternity'. Lucretius c. 99-55BC.

Summa sedes non capit duos 'the seat of supreme power cannot take two'. Supreme power cannot be shared. The thinking which prolonged the wars between Rome and Carthage. Something well understood by Al Capone as *seriatim* (one after the other) he 'rubbed out' challenging would-be godfathers amongst the mob of hoodlums in America's prohibition of the 1930s. See *bellum maxime omnium, cunctator, delenda est Carthago, fides Punica, Hannibal ante portas, Puella Carthaginis ridebat* and *nullus amor populis*.

Sum quod eris, fui quod es 'I am what you will be. I was what you are'. A wise old man to an impetuous youth?

Sum tua aeribus assibus II 'for two copper asses I am yours'. Graffiti on the wall of a Roman house at Pompeii in region xi. To evaluate this offer see *denarius*. There were twenty five organised brothels in Pompeii when mount Vesuvius erupted in AD 79. See *cave canem* and *salve lucrum*.

Sunt lacrimae rerum et mentem mortalia tangunt 'tears are at the root of things and matters mortal touch (affect) the mind'. Virgil Aeneid 1.462. Words famous as being Virgil's comment on the human condition. In context however the words seem to speak of no more than the capacity of man as a species to share and cry over the suffering of others.

Suo cuique judicio est utendum 'each must use his own judgment'. Cicero. However much advice we receive the final decision must always be our own. Admirable wisdom progressively eroded by the nanny state.

Suo gladio jugulatus 'throat cut with his own sword'. Hoist with his own petard.

Super flumina Babylonis ibi sedimus et flevimus cum recordaremur Sion 'by the rivers of Babylon, there we sat down, yea we wept when we remembered Zion'. Vulgate Psalm 136 vi.

To be captives in Babylon, despite the splendour of its hanging gardens (one of the Seven Wonders of the Ancient world, adjoining the palace of Nebuchadnezzar near Baghdad) was a terrible fate captured by G.K. Chesterton in his epic poem Lepanto (see *Vivat Hispania*):

'They are countless, voiceless, hopeless as those fallen or fleeing on. Before the High king's horses in the granite of Babylon'.

The rivers were the Tigris and the Euphrates in what is now Iraq.

These words (in English) were set to popular music in 1978 and, sung by Boney M, featured long and high in the charts of pop music. See *tanquam in speculo*.

Super montem excelsum ascende tu que evangelisas Sion. Vulgate. Isaiah 40:9. Rendered as: 'For thou that tellest glad tidings to Zion, get thee up into the high mountain': this is set to music in Handel's Messiah (sung by Kathleen Ferrier and recorded to near perfection circa 1951 with the London Philharmonic Orchestra conducted by Sir Adrian Boult).

Supra 'above'. Used in books to indicate prior mention or reference. See *Vide supra.**

Sursum corda 'lift up your hearts'.

Suus cuique erat locus attributus 'to each man his own place has been assigned'. Julius Caesar. The Church of England has left such thinking behind. No longer is what follows to be found in its hymn books:

'The rich man in his castle,
The poor man at his gate;
He made them high and lowly,
And ordered their estate'.

173

Symposium 'drinking party or banquet'. Latin adapted from Greek. Symposium in English is used to mean conference or meeting to discuss a project or subject. Lavish corporate entertaining no doubt retains something of the Latin meaning.*

T

Tabula ex (in) naufragio 'a plank in a shipwreck'. Means of survival. Rescue.

Tacet 'he is silent'. Word used in musical score to indicate that a performer is to keep silent. See *tempus tacendi*.
Talis qualis 'such like; such as'. Such as it is.

Tangere ulcus 'to touch a sore'. Open an old wound. Sometimes *ulcus tangere*.

Tanquam in speculo 'as in a mirror'.

'He sees as in a mirror on the monstrous twilight sea
The crescent of his cruel ships whose name is mystery;
They fling great shadows foe-wards, making Cross and Castle dark
They veil the plumèd lions on the galleys of St. Mark; . .'

It is the Pope who sees and the cruel ships are those of the Sultan Suleiman the Magnificent: in G.K. Chesterton's epic poem 'Lepanto'. *Alicia per Speculum Transitus* 'Alice through the Looking glass'. Lewis Carroll's (Charles Dodgson's) famous book has been translated into Latin and published in 1966 by MacMillan (as has Alice in Wonderland . . *Alicia in Terra Mirabile* . . likewise in 1994). See *Vivat Hispania*.

Tantum quantum 'just as much as'.

Tantum religio potuit suadere malorum 'only religion has had the ability to influence men to (so many) evils'. Lucretius *De rerum natura* 'on nature' i.107. One wonders what the poet/philosopher had in mind. He lived c.99 – c. 55 BC. Yet to come were Christ's crucifixion, Nero's vicious persecution of the Christians (making them scapegoats for the fire which consumed half of Rome in 64) and that of Diocletian begun in 303, King Richard's execution over three days during the third crusade of over three thousand Moslems after the siege of Acre in 1191 (the

Saladin was less brutal), the 13th century burning of Cathars in France and the 16th century burning of heretics in Spain by Torquemada (of the inquisition and Holy Office) and by Mary Tudor in England: to mention only some religion inspired evils. See *de Heretico Comburendo* and *te Deum*.

Tarde sed tute 'slow but sure'. Motto. 'Slow but sure combustion' was the inscription surrounding a delightful cast iron tortoise on the top of cylindrical 'tortoise' stoves which graced and warmed the huts on RAF and army units in 1940-5.

Tarpeian rock. Rock on the south west corner of the Capitoline hill in Rome from which convicted criminals were hurled to their death below. The name is legend based. When early Rome warred with the Sabine, Tarpeia, a Roman soldier's daughter, agreed to betray the citadel in exchange for the gold bracelets worn by the Sabines on their left arms. Far from rewarding her treachery, when the Sabines broke in, they crushed her with their shields carried also by their left arms. The Tarpeian rock symbolised the consequences of treachery and criminality.

Tecum habita 'live with yourself'. See *nosce te ipsum*.

Te Deum Laudamus 'we praise thee O God'. A hymn named in Latin (known as the *Te Deum*) but to be said or sung in English after the First Lesson from the Old Testament at Morning Prayer in accordance with the Church of England Book of Common Prayer. The opening words are: 'We praise thee O God: we acknowledge thee to be the Lord'. The concluding words are: 'O Lord in thee have I trusted, let me never be confounded'. *In te Domine, speravi: non confundur in aeternum* 'Lord I have based my hope in thee. I shall not for ever be destroyed'.

The hymn is set fittingly to powerful music by Charles Villiers Stanford 1852-1924, 'the Stanford Te Deum'. Other musical settings are by Handel, Sullivan, Parry and Walton. Charpentier's Prelude to Te Deum is inspired music.

On the accession of Mary Tudor to the throne of England in 1553 'there were bells, bonfires, banquets and *Te Deums*'. (Chronicle of Queen Jane and Queen Mary ed. Nicholls 9-11). The mood was to change when the burning of heretics began. Oxford acquired its martyrs and a pall of sinister black smoke hung over Smithfield in London. See *De Heretico Comburendo* and *tantum religio*.

Tempora mutantur et nos mutamur in illis 'times change and we change with them'. Harrison. Description of Britain 1577 III. iii 99.

In the early days of pocket calculators a judge of the High Court (Thompson J) said: 'We must check the mathematics in this case. I will operate by the old fashioned method. You may use those new-fangled machines'. He was also however heard to observe that he was pleased to note that expert's reports no longer told him that on motor cars the wheels went round. See *laudator temporis acti, munera nunc* and *quae fuerant vitia mores.*

Tempora si fuerint nubilia, solus eris 'if cloudy (hard/bad) times, come you will be alone'. Ovid 1. xi.5. A friend in need is a friend indeed. See *donec eris sospes.*

Tempori cedere habetur sapientis 'to yield to the occasion is considered (the characteristic) of a wise man'. Cicero.
'The better part of valour is discretion'. William Shakespeare. Henry iv Part 1. Act iv Sc.4 l.121. *Sed quaere.* Cf., *decimare* and *audentes fortuna.* See too *qui fugiebat, una salus* and *vae victis.*

Temporis ars medicina fere est 'of the healing arts that of time is to be rated highly'. Not just in recuperation from illness but from bereavement or the wounded and the broken hearts of youth. See *Cestilia.*

Tempus abire tibi 'it is time for you to go'. Horace. Something we think more often than we feel able to say.
   'Stand not upon the order of your going
   But go at once'.
      William Shakespeare. Macbeth Act iii Sc.4 ll, 119-120.
See *tempus tacendi.*

Tempus edax rerum 'time the devourer of things'. Ovid. Metamorphoses xv. 234. 'Time the subtle thief of youth'. John Milton 1608-1674.
   A child aged eight, fascinated by a flickover digital clock, once asked 'Dad. What is time. I don't mean how do you measure it: I mean what is it?' His father was without answer.

Tempus fugit 'time flies'. Cf., *sed fugit interea, fugit irreparibile tempus* 'but as it flies the while, time flies irretrievably'.Virgil.

Tempus tacendi et tempus loquendi 'a time to keep silent and a time to speak'. Vulgate Ecclesiastes ch. 3 v. 7. Verse 1 lets us know that

'To every thing there is a season, and a time to every purpose'. Verses 2-8 list some of the more important things for which there is a time. 'A time to be born and a time to die'. It is so important in so much of life to know when it is time to speak and when it is time to be silent. This passage is often read at funerals. See *paucis verbis, natus, nescit vox, tacet, tempus abire* and *vir sapit*.

Tenax propositi 'tenacious of purpose'. Steadfast. Motto.

Tene me ne fugia(m) et revoca me ad dom(i)num meu(m) Viventium in ara (area) Callisti 'hold me lest I run away and return me to my master Viventius on the estate of Callistus'. Direction on a Roman tag fitted to a dog's collar. The original is exhibited in the Greek and Roman Department of the British Museum (gallery 69 case number 7). Doubt lingers as to whether, disappointingly, this might be a slave's tag. See *canes timidi, canis ingens, cave canem, homini fidelissime, quasi, quis famulus, semper fidelis* and *vegetus*.

Tenere lupum auribus 'to hold the wolf by the ears'. Erroneously thought sometimes to be the Roman equivalent of 'to take the bull by the horns'. See *Immo id, quod*.

Terminus ad quem 'end point or boundary to which'. Finishing point.

Terminus a quo 'end point or boundary from which'. Starting point. *Terminus* means boundary.

Ter quaterque beatus 'thrice and fourfold blest'. Virgil.

Terrae filius 'son of the soil'. Person of humble birth. See *filius terrae*.

Terra firma 'firm land'. Dry land. Dream destination of those who are seasick. In childhood tales of adventure on the Spanish Main, sea-faring men were ever on the lookout for *terra firma*.

Terra marique 'by land and sea'.

Terra nullius 'nobody's land'. Land subject to nobody's ownership.

Thesaurus 'treasury, treasure, store or storehouse. That is exactly what that invaluable reference book in your bookshelves is.*

Thomas Edwardus Lawrence Arabiae jacentis vindex impavidus 'Thomas Edward Lawrence intrepid avenger of oppressed Arabia'. Part of the inscription on a bronze plaque above the porter's lodge of Jesus College Oxford. T.E.Lawrence, known as 'Lawrence of

Arabia', was an undergraduate there 1907-1910. After participating to great effect in the successful Arab revolt against the Turks, he was made a fellow of All Souls and wrote the Seven Pillars of Wisdom (published 1926) the name of which was taken from Proverbs 9.1.

'Wisdom has built her house, she has hewn her seven pillars'.

Timeo Danaos et dona ferentes 'I fear the Greeks even when they bring gifts'. Virgil Aeneid. ii.49. The wooden horse left by the Greeks was ostensibly a gift to the Trojans; but it was in fact filled with 'enemy commandos'. Take care with anyone who is inexplicably over generous, friendly or charming. He may be up to, or want, something.

Note the fuller context: *Equo ne credite, Teucri. Quidquid id est, timeo Danaos et dona ferentes* '. . . do not trust the horse, Trojans. Whatever it is I fear the Greeks even when they bring gifts'. See *fide sed cui, fronti nulla fides* and *quomodo adulator.*

Titus Andronicus. Name given to the leading Roman character in Shakespeare's play of that name. There is concern today for TV and screen violence. In this work however there is revenge, brutal murders, rape, cannibalism and a sentence of death by unusual means. The writer's sources are not known. There appears to be no such character in Roman history or literature. Entertainment? Not for the squeamish.

Totidem verbis 'in so many words'.

Toties quoties 'the one as often as the other'.

Trahit sua quemque voluptas 'each man's pleasure drags him on', everyone is lured by their own pleasure. Virgil Eclogues ii. 65. The smoker, the drinker, the gambler, the lothario and the nymphomaniac all spring to mind.

Trajan. Roman emperor AD 98 to 117. What is thought to be his statue stands at Tower Hill in London (go out of Tower Hill underground station exit, then turn right down stone steps and there he is, in bronze, on the left and at ground level).

Adopted son of Nerva and a Spaniard, he was the first emperor not born a Roman. His famous column, in Rome's Forum, records his victories over the Dacians and the Parthians. Lettering on the marble panel at the foot of this column is generally thought to be the finest example of formal monumental lettering in the best period of Roman inscription making. Nearly two thousand years later the classical Roman alphabet remains the criterion for evaluating lettering quality.

The capitals (*majusculae*) are accepted as ideal to use as a model alphabet because they are based on the simple geometrical forms of the square and circle, rectangle and triangle.

Based on Pliny's praise of this Emperor is the maxim: *bellum nec timendum nec provocandum* 'war must be neither feared nor provoked'. See *Classicianus* and *majusculae*.

Triumviri (triumvirs) 'three men'; joint commissioners or colleagues: members of a triumvirate (a ruling body comprised of three power sharing men). The historically famous triumvirates are, first, that of 60 BC. an informal arrangement between Julius Caesar, Pompey and Crassus. Pompey failed more than once to persuade the senators to provide for his veterans as he asked. This drove him into alliance with Caesar. Joined by Crassus, a banker of immense wealth, these two proven soldiers and statesmen quickly undermined the machinery of Republican Government and marked the beginning of a chain of events leading to civil war, Caesar's dictatorship and assassination.

In the confused power struggle, which followed Caesar's murder, the second triumvirate of 43 BC was formed. Caesar's great nephew, C. Octavius (then aged 19) entered the race for power, assumed the name of C. Julius Caesar Octavianus and, somewhat cynically, allied himself with Mark Anthony and Lepidus (a political lightweight) against Cicero and the forces of Republican Government. Cicero denounced Mark Anthony as an unscrupulous adventurer and was murdered (see *Cicero* and *prescriptio* above). The forces of republicanism under Brutus and Cassius were defeated at the battle of Philippi in October of 42 BC. heralding the era of Imperial Rome. See *Augustus, Caesar, et tu Brute, reddite ergo* and *Rubicon*.

Tu ne cede malis sed contra audentior ito 'do not yield to misfortunes but proceed the more boldly against them'. Virgil Aeneid vi. 95.

The Book of Job suggests that this may be very wearing advice. Virginia Woolf observed: 'I read the Book of Job last night. I don't think God comes well out of it'. (Letter to Lytton Strachey).

'Who do so beset him round,
With dismal stories,
Do but themselves confound–
His strength the more is . . .'
Hymn 402 in the English Hymnal. John Bunyan 1628-1688 (but not quite John Bunyan's original version).
See *nil desperandum*.

Tu regere imperio populos, Romane memento;
hae tibi erunt artes; pacisque imponere morem,
parcere subiectis, et debellare superbos.
'It is for you Roman to rule the nations: the objects of your talents shall
be these; to impose the habit of peace, to spare those who submit and to
crush the haughty'. Virgil 6 851-3.
Virgil's idea of early Rome's duty and destiny in the world. See *pax*.

U

Ubi caritas et amor. Ubi caritas Deus ibi est. 'Where there is reverence and love, God is present'. Title to hymn from the Taizé Community at 525 in Hymns Old and New. Anglican edition 1996. Latin is not completely abandoned by the churches.

Ubi lapsus? Quid feci? 'where did I fall down? What have I done?' A common, too often undeserved, reaction to distress, illness or misfortune. Why me? Why am I punished?

Ubi mel, ibi apes 'where there is honey there are bees'. The young men clustered round the pretty girl like bees around a honey pot'.

Ubique navigabimus 'we shall sail everywhere'. Inscription over the entrance doorway of Overseas House, centre of the Royal Overseas League, Park Place, St. James Street, london SW1 A 1LR.

Ubi saeva indignatio ulterius cor lacerare nequit (here lies the body of . . .) 'where savage indignation can tear his heart no more'. Part of the epitaph of Jonathan Swift, written by and for himself. To be seen in St. Patrick's Cathedral, Dublin. He died in 1745 the year of Bonnie Prince Charlie's (Charles Edward Stuart's) doomed Jacobite bid for the crown of England. See *ad infinitum* and *facit indignatio*.

Ubi solitudinem faciunt, pacem appellant 'where they create desolation they call it peace'. Famous words attributed by Tacitus (Agricola xxx) to the Caledonian highland leader Calgacus in AD 84 when he exhorted his troops before being defeated by Agricola at the battle of *Mons Graupius*. Equally astute is another of his observations (see above) made at the same time: *omne ignotum pro magnifico est* 'of what man is ignorant he sees as wonderful'. See *Agricola* and *pax*.

Ulmus procera. Latin classificatory name for the English Elm.

Ulterior 'more distant; further away'. Ulterior motive: one which is concealed, not obvious or not admitted.

Ultima ratio regum 'the last argument (resort) of kings'. Inscription on a cannon. In 2004 (substituting nations for kings) this could be inscribed on cruise and tomahawk missiles.

Ultimo. Abbreviation of *ultimo mense* . . . literally last month. Reference in a letter (especially in commerce) to 28th *ultimo* means the 28th of last month. See *proximo* above.

Una salus victis nullam sperare salutem 'the only safe course for the vanquished is to expect no mercy (have no hope of safety/salvation)' Virgil Aeneid ii 354. Conclusion to be heeded, especially when the enemy has announced that no prisoners will be taken. One reason why a defeated Roman fell on his sword. The above words are preceded by: *moriamur et in media arma ruamus* 'let us die as we rush into battle'. A notable exception was *Caractacus;* see above. Seneca wrote a three volume treatise (*de clementia* on clemency) on the need for clemency in a ruler, inspired perhaps by an exclamation of the emperor Nero (whose early reign was relatively mild) when unwillingly signing a death warrant: 'would that I had never learned to write'. See *Boudicca, Clodius Albinus, decimare, fasces, fidem qui perdit, homines enim, sed et benignitatis* and *vae victis.*

Una voce 'with one voice'. Unanimously. See *ad idem, constat.*

Uno animo 'with one mind or intent'. *Uno animo* the lemmings ran towards the sea. See *nemine contradicente.*

Uno flatu 'with one breath'. The child blew out the birthday candles *uno flatu.* The word *flatu* is from *flatus*, which may mean flatulence as well as breath. The expression *uno flatu* might, in appropriate circumstances (not in relation to candles on a birthday cake; *sed quaere* in the work of Émil Zola 1840-1902) accordingly admit of another translation.

Unus et idem 'one and the same'.

Ut amem et foveam 'that I should love and cherish'. Tatoo of David Beckham.To love and to cherish. See *habendum et tenendum* and *perfecto in spiritu.*

Utilius sensoria quam vera loqui. In November 2003 The Lord

Deedes of Aldington wrote in his (W.F.Deedes') Monday column of the Daily Telegraph: "Adrian Hodges, who altered history for the BBC series on the life of Charles II, declares it is 'more important to be convincing than authentic'. Translated into Latin what a fine motto that would be for spin doctors everywhere".

No reader responded with a translation. It is not easy with exactitude to capture in Latin the meaning of the English. Classical scholars (not the author!) have ventured (reproduced in order of receipt) the above, literally: 'things perceived through the senses (suppositions) are more useful (in the cynical sense of 'serve one's purpose') than speaking the truth' and: *fallere fictis utilius quam veritate suadere* literally: 'it is of more use (serves one's purpose better) to deceive by falsehoods than to persuade by truth': *vera dicere magnum; maius suadere* literally: 'it is a great thing to speak the truth: it is a greater thing to persuade': *vera loqui magnum; verbis convincere maius* literally: 'it is a great thing to speak the truth; to convince with words is something greater' (this happens to be a hexameter!): *persuasionem appetens quam veritatem* literally: 'seeking (desirous of) persuasion (rather) than truth': *praeferta vero speciosum* literally: 'the plausible preferred to the true' and *suave malet audire plebs quam scire vera* literally: 'people will prefer to hear what is agreeable (agreeably) than to know the truth (true things)'. One translator thought that there was a certain affinity with *magna est veritas et prevaelebit* (see above) and suggested *magna est simulatio et praevalebit* literally: 'great is pretence and it shall prevail'. Spin doctors have a wide choice. See *ego sum via, fortis est, lux et, quid est* and *veritas*.

Utinam noster esset 'would that he were ours'. Opponent's thought on David Beckham (football), Sir Don Bradman and Sir Leonard Hutton (cricket) and Jonny Wilkinson (rugby football). See *primus inter pares*.

Utopia. A *quasi-* (see above) Latin word used by Sir (St.) Thomas More as the title to his work 'Utopia' written in Latin and published in 1516. It depicted the perfect state with ideal customs and laws and a society without private property, where there was universal religious toleration and free education for men and women. Reason prevailed and there were no lawyers! The word 'Utopia' is constructed in Latin from the Greek meaning 'no place': no place of such idealistic perfection existed.

Ut Rex Noster sit Rex Noster 'that our King should be our King'. Inscription on the banner of Captain Gold in the civil war 1642-45.

Standards and banners of the civil war are exhibited in the British Museum. See *exurgat Deus*.

Ut saepe summa ingenia in occulto latent 'how often are men of the utmost ability lost in obscurity'. Plautus. See *carpe diem* and *occasionem cognosce*.

Ut sementem feceris, ita et metes 'as you sow so shall you reap'. Cicero. 'For whatsoever a man soweth, that shall he also reap'. Galatians 6:7. Yet: 'Behold the fowls of the air; for they sow not neither do they reap, nor gather into barns, yet your heavenly Father feedeth them'. St. Matthew 6:26.

Uxor 'wife'. One who is greatly and/or overtly fond of his wife is uxorious. See *domus et placens uxor*.

V

Vade in pace 'go in peace'.

Vade mecum 'go with me'. The expression (hyphenated) is used in English as a noun referring generally to a book containing information, to which there is or may be the inclination or need for regular reference, and which is small, light and manageable enough to be carried about in a bag or a pocket. A constant companion and/or manual.*

Vae victis! 'woe to the vanquished!' Livy V. xlviii. 9. Livy tells of an episode showing how, if the vanquished seek to extract conditions mitigating their plight, they are open to humiliation: unless luck intervenes. See *decimare, fasces* and *una salus*.

Vale 'goodbye'.

Vanitas vanitatum, omnis vanitas 'vanity of vanities all is vanity'. Ecclesiastes Vulgate I:2. As well as vanity however *vanitas* may mean emptiness, falsehood, uselessness etc. The expression seems therefore to be as much to do with all being in vain as with vanity as such. The fuller text from Ecclesiastes is: *Vanitas vanitatum, dixit Ecclesiastes; vanitas vanitatum, et omnia vanitas* 'vanity of vanities said the preacher; vanity of vanities and everything is vanity'. See *quomodo sedet sola civitas*.

Vare, redde legiones 'Varus, give me back my legions'. Suetonius. Augustus 23. In the year AD 9 the Romans were engaged in colonising parts of Germany. Their commander, Publius Quinctilius Varus, was not popular and was tricked by the chief of his German bodyguard, Arminius, so as to lead his army off the intended route and into impenetrable parts of the Teutoberg Forest where it was ambushed. Three legions, three cavalry regiments and six cohorts (the whole army) were annihilated and Varus committed suicide. It was a major disaster, towards the end of the Emperor Augustus's long reign (and while Christ lived on earth). So distressed was the ageing Emperor that he kept the anniversary as a day of deep mourning and would often beat his head against a door and cry out with these words.

His recurring anguish is well portrayed in "Augustus: a Novel" by Allan Massie: Sceptre edition 1987.

A legion was the principal formation of the Roman army and comprised 5,000 infantry with 120 cavalry and often auxiliaries attached. The magnitude of the disaster can be readily understood.

In the years AD 14-16 Germanicus avenged the slaughter of Varus' legions with victories over Arminius.

Varium et mutabile semper, femina 'woman is always fickle and changeable'. Virgil. Aeneid iv. 569. Cf., 'la donna è mobile' in Verdi's opera Rigoletto.

Vegetus Montani imperatoris Aug(usti) ser(vus) . . . emit (. . .) que accepit puellam Fortunatam . . . natione Diablintem de Albiciano (denariis) sescentis . . . ea(m)que puella(m)que sanam traditam esse erronem fugitivam non esse 'Vegetus, assistant slave of Montanus, the slave of the August emperor . . . has bought and received the girl Fortunata, by nationality a Diablintian, from Albicianus for six hundred *denarii*. The girl in question is transferred in good health and is warranted to be without known propensity to wander or run away'.

This is an extract from what is written on a wooden Roman writing tablet c.AD 80 – 120 unearthed in 1996 at Poultry in the City of London and on view in the Museum of London since early 2003 evidencing sale and purchase of a slave girl. Vegetus worked for the imperial procurator (the financial administrator for the province of Britannia). The legality of purchase of a slave by a slave is, from standard textbooks on Roman Law, unclear but plainly this happened in London. It was an expensive purchase. Six hundred *denarii* was a lot of money at the time (two years pay for a Roman soldier): and how one with the status of slave came by so much money is not obvious.

But what a lovely fragment from the lives of two people living long ago: enough to stir the fertile imagination of a romantic. The name 'Fortunata' means 'lucky'. As a Diablintian she came from the region around what is now Jublains, a small village in northwest France near Mayenne. One assumes her to have been young. Vegetus would have been an educated man. Did he see her in the slave market? Was she very beautiful? so that Virgil's '*et vera incessu patuit Dea*' (see above) sprang to his mind as he was overcome? Did he pay so much to wrest her from the clutches of some brute? Might the commercial acquisition of a human being have been in fact the very stuff of fairy tales, leading to lifelong companionship and happiness: 'Fortunata'? See *mens sana, non Angli, Rufus Callisuni* and *tene me ne*.

Vel capillus habet umbram suam 'even a hair has its own shadow'. Publilius Syrus. We are none of us wholly insignificant or ineffective?

Veni creator spiritus 'come holy ghost eternal God'. Great hymn sung in 1553 before her anointing at the coronation of Mary Tudor and heralding a precarious return to Roman Catholicism in England.

Veni, vidi, vici 'I came, I saw, I conquered'. Words attributed by Plutarch (in 'Parallel Lives') to Julius Caesar when reporting his final victory in 47 BC at Zela over Pharnaces, King of Pontus. However according to Suetonius, Lives of the Caesars, it was an inscription displayed in Caesar's Pontic Triumph. Suetonius. Caesar 37:2.

These words are often wrongly attributed to Caesar after his landings in Britain in 55 and 54 BC. These were however not very successful episodes. The effective conquest of Britain did not begin until the reign of Claudius when, in AD 43, Aulus Plautius invaded with four legions and with elephants as engines of war. The process was ongoing. The Emperor Hadrian visited Britain in 122 and the construction of his wall from Tyne to Solway was commenced in that year and completed in 133. See *Caesar, Caractacus, Cassivellaunus, Brittunculi* and *salus publica*.

Venite, exultemus Domino 'come, let us rejoice in the Lord'. Psalm 95. To be said or sung (except on certain days) during Morning Prayer in accordance with The Church of England Book of Common Prayer. 'O come let sing unto the Lord: let us heartily rejoice in the strength of our salvation'.

Verbatim 'word for word. In the same words exactly'. Presumably, despite the present onslaught against the use of Latin in the courts, continued use of this plainly now alternative English word may be permitted. Featuring as *de facto* English (see appendix four), it stands a better chance than *seriatim* (meaning in succession or one after the other and appearing in the main text of Chambers 20th Century Dictionary).*

Verbosa et grandis epistula 'long-winded and lengthy letter'. The poet Juvenal's famous description of the emperor Tiberius' letter denouncing Sejanus (then prefect of the Praetorian Guard) for plotting the emperor's overthrow.

The ageing emperor had retired to Capri and ruled through Sejanus in Rome. However he became ever more suspicious of the latter's ambitions. Sejanus was led to believe that the letter contained his tribunician power (as to which see *veto* below) and was surprised to find that it was his death warrant. See *damnatio memoriae, praetor* and *veto*.

Verbum non amplius addam 'I won't add a word more'. Horace, Satires I.I 121. Useful resolve for most wordy people in most circumstances.

Vercingetorix see *Caractacus.*

Veritas 'truth'. Motto of Harvard University. Note *quid est veritas* above: yet the Roman writers had quite a lot to say about truth. *Veritas nunquam perit* 'truth never dies'. Seneca Troades 614. *Veritas odium parit* 'truth begets hatred'. Terence Andria 1:I:68.

Truth featured prominently in the language of the notorious Lord Chief Justice Jeffreys at the bloody assizes of 1685, which followed the rout at Sedgemoor ending the protestant Duke of Monmouth's bid to oust the Catholic King James II. Fugitives from the battlefield were hunted down. At their trials this judge behaved with a cynical savagery probably without equal in the history of English justice. Some two hundred and fifty death sentences were handed down in addition to endless, floggings, deportations and other dire penalties. At the trials he was less than tolerant of any evidence which did not go to guilt. Witnesses and juries were alike bullied. Lady Alice Lisle was one of his victims. A frail widow of over seventy, she was said to have fed and watered two fleeing wretches (upon whom, it appears she may have taken pity). At her trial were the following truth related exchanges:

Judge to the witness Pope. 'I would not by any means in the world endeavour to frighten you with anything, or in any way tempt you to tell an untruth. I would however provoke you to tell the truth, and nothing but the truth. You have a precious immortal soul and there is nothing in the world equal to it in value'.

And when evidence did not point towards guilt, or worse, suggested innocence! he took fierce remedial action:

'Mr. Dunne, have a care, for it may be that more of this is known than you think'.

'My Lord I tell the truth'.

'Well I only bid you have a care. Truth never wants subterfuge, it always likes to appear naked, it needs no enamelling nor any covering. But lying and canting and snivelling always appear in masquerade . . .you are a prevaricating, lying, snivelling rascal'.

This judge after the most meteoric rise to Lord Chief Justice of the King's Bench was aged only thirty eight at this time. Lady Alice was convicted and sentenced to be burned alive, a sentence which was commuted by King James to beheading. Jeffreys was later made Lord Chancellor! See *ego sum, fortis est, lux et, magna est, odium, quid est* and *vincit veritas*.

Versus 'towards or against'. So, in cricket, England versus Australia.

Vesper in ambiguo est 'the evening is in twilight'. Inscription in a glass window on the upper floor of the Old Ashmolean Museum in Oxford. See *age dum*.

Veto 'I forbid, prevent, prohibit'. A word used in English to mean a right to reject or prohibit decisions or proposals of those in positions of authority. In Rome it appears early in relation to the Tribunate of the *plebs* (the common people) which was instituted in 494 BC to protect them from the arbitrary power of consuls. Its officials, the Tribunes, were immune from arrest and their power progressed until they were empowered to veto or annul acts of other magistrates and they acquired the right to sit in the Senate and initiate legislation. Such became their authority that Augustus and succeeding emperors caused themselves to be vested with tribunician powers.

Veto is used today to denote a power to reject or annul. So a permanent member of the UN Security Council has a power to veto and the same word, used as a noun, describes exercise of that power. Similarly for some purposes there are powers of veto vested in certain member states of the EU. See *plebs* and *verbosa et grandis*. *

Via 'by way, road, path or street'. Used in English as a preposition: by way of or through to indicate a route. One may travel on Eurostar to Paris from London, Waterloo to Gare du Nord (and back) *via* Ashford International in Kent. See *Ego sum via* and *Quinque viae* above.

Vice versa. Literally: 'things having been reversed'; but used to mean the position being reversed, conversely or the other way round.

Victor ludorum 'winner of the games'. In many schools a cup bearing this inscription used to be won by the pupil most successful in the athletics on sports day. The pupil's name and the date was usually then inscribed upon it.

Vide 'see, consult'. Used as an instruction in a reference to a passage in a book.

Videlicet 'it is permitted to see' Usually abbreviated to *viz.* Namely.

Video meliora, proboque. Deteriora sequor 'I see better things and approve them. I follow the worse'. Ovid Metamorphoses vii. 20-21. I know that to drink in moderation is good, but I can't resist the stuff! The old cliché, 'the road to hell is paved with good intentions' is well founded and *ad rem* for too many of us.

Vincit veritas 'truth wins (conquers)'.

Vipera berus. Classificatory Latin name for the common viper or adder. See *latet anguis.*

Viridis 'green'.

Vir sapit qui pauca loquitur 'he is a wise man who says little'. Note *paucis verbis* with few words. See *tempus tacendi.*

Virtutis fortuna comes 'fortune is the companion of valor'. Motto of the Duke of Wellington. Despite the language of his motto the Duke is said to have told new members of Parliament: 'Don't quote Latin; say what you have to say, and then sit down'. Not a new directive. Plautus (c.250-184 BC) in his play Miles gloriosus wrote; *quin tu istanc orationem hinc veterem atque antiquam amoves?* 'why do you not abandon that language of antiquity?' But he did not refer to Latin. See *commentarii* and *plus quam valor.*

Vitaque mancipio, nulli datur, omnibus usu 'and life freehold to nobody is given: it is for all leasehold'. Lucretius c. 99 – c.55 BC.

Vivat 'may he live'.

Vivat Hispania. Domino gloria 'may Spain live (long live Spain). To the Lord glory'. The words which follow are: 'Don John of Austria has set his people free'. From the ecstatic finale to the battle of Lepanto as immortalised in G.K.Chesterton's epic poem of that name.

Under Suleiman the Magnificent (1494-1566), Sultan of the Ottomans, Allah's deputy on Earth, the Ottoman Empire reached the peak of its glorious power and seriously threatened Christian Europe. In 1565 however, after a long and bitter siege marked by the astonishing tenacity and superhuman bravery of the defenders, he failed to wrest Malta from the sea faring Knights of St. John (for a gripping account read 'The Great Siege. Malta 1565' by Ernle Bradford, Hodder and Stoughton 1961), and, in 1571 Ottoman sea power in the Mediterranean was finally broken when a coalition fleet of Pope Pius V's Christian League (mainly Spanish and Italian) under the handsome and gifted Don John of Austria, half brother of Philip II, won a spectacular victory at Lepanto (the Greek Navpaktos).

Chesterton captures the suspense of titanic struggle in a stirring masterpiece of writing. His opening words set vividly the scene: 'White founts falling in the Courts of the sun'. The picture of awesome eastern magnificence is already complete. Uniquely brilliant alliteration sounds the tramp of armies on the march and the boom of cannonades. 'Don John pounding from the slaughter painted poop.' Nobody should depart this life without having read it . . . . more than once. See *ecce Agnus Dei, super flumina, plus quam valor* and *tanquam in speculo.*

Vivat Latina 'may Latin live or long live Latin'. See *vivat lingua Latina.*

Vivat lingua Latina 'may the Latin language live'. Abbreviated to *vivat Latina.* By analogy with vivat Regina (below) . . long live the Latin language. See *Fabulae Faciles, Latium* and *oratio obliqua.*

Vivat Regina 'may the Queen live'. Generally taken to mean 'long live the Queen'. The words appear in Sir Hubert Parry's anthem 'I was glad'; processional music written for the coronation of Edward VII and sung at all coronations since. If this music is performed, the words *Vivat Regina* (or *vivat rex* . . . may the King live or long live the king, as appropriate) should be included only if the performance is in Westminster Abbey and they are shouted by the scholars of Westminster School.

Viva voce 'by or with the living voice', orally. A *viva* is an abbreviation for a *viva voce* examination, i.e., one involving a live and spoken interview. Evidence from the witness box in court is given *viva voce*.

Vive hodie 'live for today'. *See age dum, carpe diem, dum vivimus, omnem crede* and *quid sit futurus.*

Viz. See *videlicet.*

Voce populi 'by the voice of the people'. These words appear inscribed around the head of King George III on crude copper token coinage minted in Ireland *(Hibernia)* in and about 1760 by one William Roche, a button manufacturer in Dublin. This was widely used in America by immigrants, there being no official US coinage until the 1790's. It is known as the *voce populi* coinage.

Volans 'flying'. The name, used now in English, of a flying fish found in southern waters.

Volo non valeo 'I am willing; I am not up to it'. Sprinting a hundred yards . . . ageing man's lament. (Currently ageing men in Britain still don't want to understand metres). But appreciating just when to call it a day is a problem beautifully portrayed in the taunting words of Gudurz (from Mattthew Arnold's tragic epic poem, 'Sohrab and Rustum') as he seeks to goad the mighty Rustum into assuming the role of Persian champion in single combat with Sohrab, the Tartar protagonist.

' . . . . Take heed lest men should say:
That like some old miser, Rustum hoards his fame,
And shuns to peril it with younger men'.
'O Gudurz, wherefore dost thou say such words?
Thou knowest better words than this to say'.
Matthew Arnold. 1822-88.

Mark Twain once observed: 'I'm pushing sixty and that's enough exercise for me'. See *corpora lente*, *non sum qualis eram* and *senex*.

Vox clamantis in deserto 'a voice crying in the wilderness'.Vulgate. St. Matthew Ch .3.3. John the Baptist *parate viam Domini rectas facite semitas eius* Prepare ye the way of the lord, make his paths straight.

Vox humana 'human voice'. Name given to organ stops intended to produce tones like those of the human voice.

Vox populi 'the voice of the people'. Public sentiment. In the temporarily hung US elections of 2000 President George W. Bush is reported as having announced: 'The American People have spoken but it's not yet clear what they've said'. The abbreviation '*vox pop*' is used by the media to refer to on street interviews.

Vulgate. Not Latin but often quoted in this text and appropriate here. The word is derived from the Latin *vulgare* (to make public) . . . . *Biblia sacra vulgata* Holy Bible (sacred books) made common or public. Vulgate is the name given to the ancient version of the biblical scriptures in common use in the western church since the seventh century. It was first compiled in Latin from sources in Aramaic, Hebrew, Old-Latin and Greek mainly by St. Jerome (commissioned by Pope Damasus I) in the 4th century: there is more of his work in it than of any other. The B*f*ook of Ecclesiasticus is pure Old-Latin untouched by Jerome.

Pope Sixtus V set up a commission to revise it, but, impatient with progress, took it upon himself to complete, and, on 2nd May 1590, published a version so full of blunders that, after his death, it had to be withdrawn. The Pope following him, Urban VII, was Pope for only twelve days, dying from malaria before his coronation. His successor, Pope Gregory XIV, arranged for revision but was Pope for less than a year and his successor (Pope Innocent IX), in turn, for less than three months; so it fell finally to Pope Clement VIII to publish a corrected version (the Clementine edition). This he did in 1592 and his version remained authoritative until the 20th century.

When in due course William Tyndale sought to make the Bible public by translating it into English and publishing in 1525, he ran into fierce opposition from powerful factions who thought that the Bible should be read only by clergy. Tyndale was driven from England and to ultimate execution. It was not until 1611 that the English version authorised by King James 1st was published. Winston S. Churchill's History of the English Speaking Peoples (Vol II at pages 123-4. Cassell and company 1956) sets out concisely how the latter came into being.

See *biblia sacra vulgata* and *novum opus*.

W

Winnie ille Pu. Winnie-the-Pooh. In 1958 Dr. Alexander Lenard translated into Latin and then printed for private distribution A.A. Milne's classic "Winnie-the-Pooh". This was published in 1960. See *Domus Anguli Puensis*.

APPENDIX ONE
The Hippocratic Oath

I swear by Apollo the physician. By Aesculapius, Hygela and Panacea*, and take to witness all the gods and goddesses, to keep according to my ability and judgment the following Oath: To reckon him who taught me this Art as dear to me as my parents, to share my substance with him and relieve his necessities if required; to look on his offspring as as my own brothers and to teach them this Art without fee or stipulation if they wish to learn it; that by precept, lecture and every other mode of instruction I will impart a knowledge of the Art to my own sons and sons of the master who taught me and to disciples bound by stipulation and oath according to the law of Medicine, but to none others.

I will follow that system of regimen which according to my ability and judgement I consider best for the benefit of my patients and abstain from whatever is deleterious and mischievous. I will give no deadly medicine to anyone if asked, nor will I suggest any such counsel. In like manner I will not give a woman a pessary to procure an abortion. Nor will I cut persons labouring under the Stone**, but will leave this to men who are practitioners of this work.

With purity and holiness will I pass my life and practice my Art. Into whatever houses I enter I will go into them for the benefit of the sick and will abstain from all intentional ill-doing and especially from the pleasure of love with those I come into contact with therein, whether they be women or men, free or slaves.

All that may come to my knowledge in the exercise of my profession or daily commerce with men which ought not to be spread abroad I will keep secret and never reveal.

While I continue to keep this Oath unviolated may it be granted to me to enjoy life and the practice of the Art, respected by all men and in all times, but should I trespass and violate this Oath may the reverse be my lot!

* Aesculapius was the mother of Hygela (Hygeia) the goddess of health. Panacea is a universal medicine or healing plant.
** Persons labouring under the stone were those with bladderstones. Their removal used to mean a hazardous operation and most died. Samuel Pepys survived such an operation.

APPENDIX TWO
Roman cardinal numerals

Roman	Arabic	
I	1	unus
II	2	duo
III	3	tres
IV	4	quattuor
V	5	quinque
VI	6	sex
VII	7	septem
VIII	8	octo
IX	9	novem
X	10	decem
XI	11	undecim
XII	12	duodecim
XIII	13	tredecim
XIV	14	quattuordecim
XV	15	quindecim
XVI	16	sedecim
XVII	17	septendecim
XVIII	18	duodeviginti
XIX	19	undeviginti
XX	20	viginti
XXX	30	triginta
XL	40	quadraginta
L	50	quinquaginta
LX	60	sexaginta
LXX	70	septuaginta
LXXX	80	octoginta
XC	90	nonaginta
C	100	centum
IƆ or D	500	quingenti
CIƆ or M	1,000	mille
MM	2,000	duo milia
IƆƆ	5,000	quinque milia
CCIƆƆ	10,000	decem milia
IƆƆƆ	50,000	quinquaginta milia

CCCIƆƆ	100,000	centum milia
IƆƆƆ	500,000	quingenta milia
CCCCIƆƆƆ	1,000,000	deciens centena milia

The reverse C (Ɔ) is called the *apostrophus*. The symbol IƆ is alternative to D for 500. If the *apostrophus* is used more than once it means 'multiplied by ten'. Thus IƆƆ equals 5,000 and IƆƆƆƆ equals 500,000.

Examples:

MCMLXXIX = 1,979.
MCMLXXX = 1,980.
MM = 2,000.

There were variations used in the Middle Ages and later. For detail see Chambers Twentieth Century Dictionary. For ordinals, distributives and numeral adverbs (ie., answering the questions which in order of number? how many each? and how many times? respectively, viz., *primus* first, *singuli* one each and *semel* once etc., see Kennedy's Revised Latin Primer published by Longman.

APPENDIX THREE
Signs of the Zodiac

The zodiac is a zone in the heavens through which the sun, the moon and principal planets travel. From earliest times astrologers divided this zone into twelve equal divisions each of which had in it a group of stars from which could be discerned a shape to which a name was given. These shapes are termed the signs of the zodiac. In some quarters it is thought that those born at a time of year when a certain sign is showing have common characteristics and even that a person's future can be forecast from stars showing at that time; their horoscope: this can be read in many newspapers and periodicals. The Roman emperors Augustus, Vespasian and Septimius Severus were all believers in their horoscopes. See in the main text: *Aureus* and *Libra*.

The signs of the zodiac all have Latin names. Only *sagittarius* and *libra* are noted in the main text. The full dozen with translation, symbol, date and when the sun enters each one are:

Aries	a ram	March 29th
Taurus	a bull	April 20th
Gemini	twins	May 21st
Cancer	a crab	June 21st
Leo	a lion	July 23rd
Virgo	a virgin	August 23rd
Libra	scales (balance)	September 23rd
Scorpio	a scorpion	October 23rd
Sagittarius	an archer	November 22nd
Capricorn	a goat*	December 22nd
Aquarius	drawer of water or Water bearer	January 21st
Pisces	fish (plural)	February 19th

* Literally a horned goat from *caper* a goat and *cornu* a horn.

APPENDIX FOUR

Some Latin, the majority of which is set out in the main text of the Oxford Modern English Dictionary 1992 edition, thereby adopted as de facto English.

Ad hoc Ad hominem Ad infinitum Ad lib Ad nauseam Aegrotat Affidavit Agenda Alias Alibi Aliquot Alma mater Alter ego Alumnus Animus Anno Domini Atrium Aqua vitae A posteriori A priori Augur

Bona fide Bona fides

Caveat Circa Circus Cognoscenti Coitus Compos mentis Concordat Consensus Consortium Contra Corrigendum Curriculum vitae

Data Delirium tremens Detritus Deus ex machina Dramatis personae

EG Eiusdem generis Emeritus E libris Ergo Erratum Et al Et cetera Et seq Ex cathedra Executor Exeunt Ex gratia Ex hypothesi Exit Ex officio Ex post facto Extant Ex tempore

Facsimile Factotum Fellatio Forum

Genus Gratis

Habeas corpus Homo Homo sapiens Honorarium

Ibid Ides Ignoramus Impedimenta Imperium Imprimatur Index Indices In extremis In flagrante delicto Infra In loco parentis In memoriam In situ Inter alia Interregnum Intra In toto In utero Ipso facto

Lacuna Libra Lictor Locus Locus classicus Locus tenens

Magnum opus MD Minor Modus operandi Minutiae Modus vivendi Mutatis mutandis

Nexus Nil Non compos mentis Nones Non sequitur Nota bene Nucleus.

Odium Op cit.

Passim Paternoster Pax Per Per annum Per capita Per diem Per pro Per se Persona Post mortem PP. Ps. Prima facie Pro Pro forma Pro rata Pro tempore Proximo

Qua Quantum Quasi Quid pro quo Quod erat demonstrandum Quod vide Quondam Quorum.

Re Regina RIP. Rostrum.

Scintilla Sic Sine die Sine qua non Status quo Stet Sub judice Subpoena. Sub rosa Sui generis Supra.

Thesaurus.

Ultimo

Vade mecum Verbatim Versus Veto Via Vide Viva voce.

Note that in the case of *consortium, corrigendum, referendum* and *ultimatum* the English plural is optional. An 'S' can be added (eg., consortiums) or the Latin 'a' thus: *consortia, corrigenda, referenda* and *ultimata*. In the case of *nucleus* the Latin plural *nuclei* is adopted and there is no English alternative.

Erratum and *index* adopt entirely the Latin plural and have no alternative English version, thus respectively: *errata* and *indices*.

The plural of *lacuna* and *thesaurus* is optional, *lacunae* or *lacunas* and *thesauri or* thesauruses. 'Stadium' however has only the one plural 'stadiums' (not *stadia*). It is derived not from Latin but from the Greek 'stadion'.

APPENDIX FIVE

List of the Roman Emperors

An asterisk denotes joint rule

27 BC – AD 14	Augustus.
AD 14 – 37	Tiberius.
37 – 41	Caligula (Gaius).
41 – 54	Claudius.
54 – 68	Nero.
68 – 69	Galba.
69	Otho and Vitellius.
69 – 79	Vespasian.
79 – 81	Titus.
81 – 96	Domitian.
96 – 99	Nerva.
98 – 117	Trajan.
117 – 138	Hadrian.
138 – 161	Antoninus Pius.
161 – 180	Marcus Aurelius.
161 – 169	Lucius Verus.*
180 – 192	Commodus.
193	Pertinax.
193	Didius Julianus.
193 – 194	Pescennius Niger.*
193 – 211	Septimius Severus.*
195 – 197	Clodius Albinus.*
211	Geta.*
211 – 217	Caracalla.*
217 – 218	Macrinus*
218 – 222	Elagabalus.*
222 – 235	Severus Alexander.
235 – 238	Maxinus I.
238	Gordian I.*
238	Gordian II.*
238	Balbinus.*
238	Pupienus.*
238 – 244	Gordian III
244 – 249	Philip the Arab.

249 – 251 Decius
251 – 253 Trebonianus Gallus.*
251 – 253 Volusian.*
253 – 260 Valerian.*

Between about 260 and 274 a breakaway empire consisting of Gaul, Britain and Spain (latterly only Gaul and Britain) became known as the 'Gallic Empire'. This was ruled by Postumus 260-269, Latinius and Marius in 269, Domitianus ? (see text) and by Tetricus until 274).

253 – 268 Gallienus.*
268 – 270 Claudius II
270 – 275 Aurelian.
275 – 276 Tacitus.
276 Florian.*
276 – 282 Probus.*
282 – 283 Carus.
283 – 284 Carinus.*
283 – 284 Numerian.*
284 – 286 Diocletian.

Western Empire	Eastern Empire
286 – 305 Maximian.	286 – 305 Diocletian.
305 – 306 Constantius I.	305 – 311 Galerius.*
306 – 307 Severus II.*	
306 – 312 Maxentius.*	309 – 312 Maximinus Daia.*
306 – 324 Constantine I.*	308 – 324 Licinius.*

324 – 337 Constantine I ruled East and West.

337 – 340 Constantine II.*
337 – 350 Constans.*
350 – 353 Magnentius.   337 – 353 Constantius II.

Between 353 and 364 the emperors following ruled both East and West:

353 – 361 Constantius II.*
360 – 363 Julian.*
363 – 364 Jovian.
364 Valentinian I.
364 – 375 Valentinian I.   364 – 378 Valens.
367 – 383 Gratian.*
375 – 392 Valentinian II.*
392–394 Eugenius.

                                    379 – 391 Theodosius I.
394 – 395 Theodosius I ruled East and West.

395 – 423 Honorius.

395 – 408 Arcadius.*

423 – 425 Johannes.

402 – 450 Theodosius II.*

425 – 455 Valentinian III.

450 – 457 Marcian.

455 – 456 Avitus. (Petronius Maximus for only weeks).

457 – 461 Majorian.

457 – 474 Leo I.*

461 – 465 Severus III.

465 – 467 (interregnum: no emperor).

467 – 472 Anthemius.*

473 – 474 Leo II.

472 Olybrius.*

474 – 475 Zeno.

473– 474 Glycerius.

475 – 476 Basiliscus.

474– 475 Julius Nepos.

476 – 491 Zeno.

475 – 476 Romulus Augustus.

491 – 518 Anastasius.
518 – 527 Justin.
527 – 565 Justinian.

For a full but succinct history of the emperors from Augustus to Romulus Augustus, the last western emperor in 476, read Chronicle of the Roman Emperors by Chris Scarre. Thames and Hudson 1995.

BIBLIOGRAPHY

Production of this kind of book involves reference to much varied literature drawn upon in greater or lesser degree. Information derived from that identified below has gone towards making the whole and it is invidious to differentiate in recording real thanks. I have however asterisked those works to which I am particularly indebted.

A Dictionary of Latin Tags and Phrases. Eugene Ehrlich. Robert Hale 1989.

A Dictionary of Latin Words and Phrases. James Morwood OUP 1998.*

A Garden of Latin Verse. Frances Lincoln Limited.

Agnes Bernauer. Friedrich Hebbel. Edited Mary Wiesener-Garland BA. George G. Harrap and Co. Ltd. 1953.

A.H.M. Jones article on The Origin and Early History of the Follis published 1959 by The Society for the Promotion of Roman Studies 31 – 34 Gordon Square, London W.C.1.

Alexander Pope. The Poetry of Allusion. Reuben Arthur Brower. Oxford at the Clarendon Press 1959.

Ancient Rome. Simon James. In association with the British Museum. Dorling Kindersley.

An Introduction to Roman Law. Barry Nicholas. Oxford. Clarendon Press 1961.

Asterix Gallus. Dargaud. Paris. 1974.

Augustus. Allan Massie. Sceptre 1988.

Biographical Dictionary. Chambers-Harrap Publishers LTD. 2002. Edited by Una McGovern.

Brideshead Revisited. Evelyn Waugh. Penguin books 1981.

Britain in the Roman Empire. Joan Liversedge. Reader's Union Routledge and Kegan Paul. London 1969.

Caesar. A Novel. Allan Massie. Sceptre 1994.

Caesar. Christian Meir. Fontana 1996.

Caesar. The Civil War. Translated by Janet F. Gardner. Penguin Books 1982.

Caesar. The Conquest of Gaul. Penguin Classics translated by S.A. Handford revised by Jane F. Gardiner. Penguin Books 1982.

Chambers Twentieth Centry Dictionary edited A.M. Macdonald OBE BA Oxon. 1974.*

Chronicle of the Roman Emperors. Chris Scarre. Thames and Hudson 1995.*

Cicero. Anthony Everitt. John Murray 2002.

Cicero and the Roman Republic. F.R. Cowell. Pelican Books 1956.

Claremont Dictionary of Quotations. Claremont Books. London 1995.

Cleopatra of Egypt. Edited by Susan Walker and Peter Higgs. British Museum Press 2001.

Coin Collecting. J. G. Milne and C.H.V. Sutherland. OUP 1951.

Complete Works of Shakespeare. Printed in England under the direction of The Shakespeare Head Press, St. Aldates, Oxford by Billing and Sons Ltd., Guildford and Esher 1938.

De Titini and Miluli. Facinoribus. Casterman 1990.

Domesday. Michael Wood. Book Club Associates. London 1986.

Eats Shoots & Leaves. Lynn Truss. Profile Books Ltd 2003.

Egmont. Goethe. George Harrap and Co. in association with D.C. Heath and company 1955.

Elementary Latin Exercises by the Rev. A.E. Hillard and C.G.Botting, Rivingtons 1947.

Elements of Roman Law. R.W. Lee. Sweet and Maxwell 1956.

Elizabeth. Dr. David Starkey. Vintage 2000.

Enemy of Rome. Leonard Cottrell. Pan Books 1960.

English Quotations. Robinson Smith. George Routledge and Sons Ltd. 1907 (1937).

Epitaphs. Nigel Rees. Bloomsbury 1993.

Everyman's Book of Evergreen Verse edited by David Herbert. J. M. Dent and Sons Ltd. 1991.

Fabulae Faciles. F. Ritchie MA. revised J.W Bertram. Longmans Green and Co. 1951.

Freshwater Fishes. Dr. Jiri Cihar. Octopus Books 1981.

Gibbon's Decline and Fall of the Roman Empire Abridged and Illustrated. Bison Books Corp 1984.

Gladiators and Caesars. Eckhart Kohne and Cornelia Ewigleben. British Museum Press.

Graffiti Latini. Biblioteca Universale Rizzoli 1999.

G. K. Chesterton. Stories, Essays and Poems. Everyman's Library. Dent. London 1965.

Hannibal. Ross Leckie. Abacus 1996.

Harry Potter and the Philosopher's Stone. J.K. Rowling. Bloomsbury 1997. Latin edition translated by Peter Needham.

History of the English Speaking Peoples. Winston. S. Churchill. Cassell and Company 1956.

Holy Bible. Authorised King James version printed 1934.

How to Insult, Abuse and Insinuate in Classical Latin. Michelle Lovric and Nikiforos Doxiadis Mardas. Ebury Press 1998.

Hymns Old and New. Anglican Edition. Compiled and edited by Geoffrey Moore, Susan Sayers, Michael Forster and Kevin Mayhew. Kevin Mayhew Ltd. 1996.

I Claudius. Robert Graves. Penguin books 1966.

James Elroy Flecker's Poems. John Baker (Publishers) Ltd. For the Richard's Press 1964.

Kennedy's Revised Latin Primer. Edited and revised by Sir James Mountford D. Litt. DCL. LLD. Longman 1987.

Kings and Queens of England and G. B. Devides and edited by Eric R. Delderfield. David and Charles 1999.

Latin for the Illiterati. Jon R. Stone Routledge 1996.

Latin in Oxford. Compiled by Reginald H. Adams. Perpetua Press. Oxford 1996.

Latin Prose Composition. M.A. North and A.E. Hillard. Rivingtons 1950.

Langenscheidt's Pocket Latin Dictionary. S.A. Handford. Methuen and Co., Ltd.1955.

Le Fils d'Asterix. Editions Albert Rene. Goscinny and Uderzo, 1983.

Le Mot Juste. The Penguin Dictionary of Foreign Words and Phrases. C. O. Sylvester Mawson revised Eugene Ehrlich 1987.

Loeb Classical Library. 1992. Cicero xiv. Translated by N.H. Watts. Harvard University Press.

Longer English Poems. From Spenser to Alfred Noyes. Edited by Ben R. Gibbs BA. George G. Harrap and Co Ltd. 1953.

Marcus Aurelius Meditations. Oxford World Classics translated by A.S L. Farquharson. Introduction and notes by R.B.Rutherford. OUP 1998.

Memoirs of Hadrian. Marguerite Yourcenar. Penguin books 1986.

Mushrooms and Other Fungi. Aurel Dermek. Byeway Books 1982.

Oxford Colleges. E.H. New and F.G. Withycombe. Basil Blackwell 1946.

Oxford in the History of the Nation. A.L.Rowse. Weidenfeld and Nicholson 1975.

Paginae Primae. Dale and Henderson. Blackie and Son Ltd. 1932.

Pears Cyclopaedia. 90th edition edited Christopher Cook 1987.

Penguin Dictionary of Proverbs. Rosalind Fergusson. Penguin Books 1983.

Poems of Tennyson 1830-1870. Intro. Sir Herbert Warren OUP 1950.

Pope. Poetical Works. Edited Herbert Davis. OUP 1966.

Roman Law and Common Law. W.W. Buckland and Arnold D. McNair. 2nd edition revised by F.H. Lawson. Cambridge University Press 1952.

Roman Records from Vindolanda on Hadrian's Wall. Robin Birley. Roman Army Museum Publications 1999.

Seaby's Standard Catalogue of British Coins 1971. Seaby's Numismatic Publications.

Sir Gawain and the Green Knight. Penguin Classics. Second edition 1974. Translated by Brian Stone.

Suetonius. The Twelve Caesars. Translated by Robert Graves. Penguin Books 1967.

Tacitus. The Annals of Imperial Rome. Translated by Michael Grant. Penguin Classics 1989.

The Agricola and the Germania. Tacitus. Translated by H. Mattingly and S.A. Handford. Penguin Classics 1988.

The Book of Common Prayer and English Hymnal (a collection of the best hymns in the English Language – see preface thereof) OUP 1969.

The Book of Unusual Quotations. Ed. Rudolph Flesch. Cassell and Co. Ltd. 1959.

The College Graces of Oxford and Cambridge. Compiled by Reginald Adams. Perpetua Press. Oxford 1999.

The Concise Oxford Companion to Classical Literature. Margaret Howatson and Ian Chilvers. OUP 1996.*

The Concise Oxford Companion to English Literature. Margaret Drabble and Jenny Stringer OUP 1993.

The Dream of Gerontius. Cardinal Newman. M.F. Egan. Longman's Green and Co. 1912.

The E.F.G. New Pocket Dictionary of the Latin and English languages. J. McFarlane. Eyre and Spottiswoode. Circa 1950.

The Great Siege of Malta 1565. Ernle Bradford. Hodder and Stoughton 1961.

The Gun. C.S. Forester. Cassell and Co. 2000.

The Illustrated Poets. William Blake. Edited Peter Porter. Aurum Press 1994.

The Institutes of Gaius. Text and notes by F. de Zulueta. Oxford Clarendon Press 1958.

The Institutes of Justinian. Thomas Sandars MA. Longmans Green and Co. 1956.

The language report. Susie Dent OUP 2003.

The Little Book of Misericords. Mike Harding. Aurum Press 1998.

The Little Oxford Dictionary of Quotations. Ed. Susan Ratcliffe OUP 1994.

The Longest Journey. E.M. Forster. Penguin Classics 1964.

The Lost World of Pompeii. Colin Amery and Brian Curran Jnr. In association with the World Monuments Fund. Frances Lincoln.

The Modern Encyclopaedia for Children. Odham's Press Ltd. C.1949.

The Nuttall Dictionary of Quotations Compiled James Wood. Frederick Warne and Co. 1934.*

The Oxford Dictionary of Modern Quotations edited Tony Augarde OUP 1996.

The Oxford Dictionary of Quotations third edition OUP 1987.*

The Oxford Dictionary of the Popes. J.N.D. Kelly. OUP. 1988.

The Oxford Dictionary of the Saints. David Hugh Farmer. OUP 1984.

The Oxford Modern English Dictionary edited Julia Swannell. Clarendon Press 1992.*

The Oxford Writer's Dictionary. Compiled by R.E. Allen. OUP 1981.

The Roman Empire. Colin Wells. Second edition 1984. Fontana Press.

The Usborne Internet- Linked Encyclopaedia of the Roman World by Fiona Chandler, Sam Taplin and Jane Bingham.

Tiberius. Allan Massie. Sceptre 1992.

Tolstoy on Divorce 4th edition Sweet and Maxwell 1958.

Vergil Aeneid II. Bristol Classical Press (by arrangement with Macmillan Education Ltd) 1991 edited by H.E.Gould and J.L. Whitely.

Virgil Aeneid. Penguin Classics. Translated by W.F. Jackson Knight 1958.

Virgil. Aeneid I. Macmillan and Co Ltd 1954. Edited by T.E. Page, M.A., Litt. D.

Virgil Aeneid. World Classics. Translated by C. Day Lewis OUP 1989.

Vulgate. Wurstembergische Bibelanstalt. Stuttgart 1969.

Wordsworth Dictionary of Bible Quotations. Martin H. Mansor. Wordsworth Reference 1995.

INDEX OF ENTRIES UNDER
SUBJECT MATTER HEADS

1) Archaeological, letters, curses inscriptions
Avete, cave canem, Claudius Karus, C.L. Severa, defixio, liquam, M. Casellium, nullum quod tetigit, pax possessori, pereunt et imputantur, qui mihi Vilbiam, renuntium, Rufus Callisuni, silentium dormiant tauri, si monumentum, tene me ne, ubique navigabimus, Vegetus Montani, vesper in ambiguo.

2) Bible, church, ecclesiastical and religion
Ab alio, accepta aqua, adeste fidelis, ad majorem Dei Gloria, advocatus diaboli, aedes Christi, afflavit Deus, Agnus Dei, anathema sit, apologia pro, Ave Maria, beatae memoriae, beati immaculati, benedicite, benedicto benedicatur, benedictus, benedictus benedicat, biblia sacra, cantate Domino, Cantuar, capitulum hujus, cena Domini, contritionem praecedit, corpus Christi, credo, da mihi castitatem, de heretico, Dei gratia, Deo volenti, de profundis, Deus dat, Deus deorum, Deus misereatur, Deus vobiscum, Deus vult, dies annorum, dies irae, Domine dirige, Dominus custodiat, Dominus illuminatio, Dominus labia, Dominus vobiscum, Domus Dei, Ebor, ecce Agnus Dei, ecce homo, Ego sum pastor, Ego sum via, esurientes, et regat illas, ex cathedra, exurgat Deus, facito aliquid, fiat lux, Gloria in excelsis, habendum et, Hegira, hic jacet, hic sepultus, humanae vitae, idcirco ipse, in cauda venenum, index expurgatorius, index librorum prohibitorum, in eadem hora, in hoc signo, in memoriam, in nomine patris, in pace, in Paradisum, in principio, ite missa est, Jesus Nazarenus, jubilate Deo, lacrima Christi, laudate Dominum, legatus a latere, levari oculos, libenter enim, lux mundi, magna est veritas, Magnificat, maior e longinquo, mappa mundi, mea culpa, Miserere, misericordia, Missa, Missa in Dominica Resurrectionis, Missa in tempore bello, Missa solemnis, muscae morientes, natus, nihil sine Deo, nihil sub solum, nisi Dominus frustra, noli me tangere, nolite thesaurisare, non est pax, novissima hora, novum opus, nulli malum, nullum quod tetigit, Nunc dimittis, nunc scripsi totum, obit, oculi omnium, oportet ergo, Opus Dei, panis angelicus, Pater Noster, pax vobiscum, pelli meae, per omnia saecula, placebo, profiscere anima Christiana, quadragesima, quaecumque sunt vera, quae Deus conjunxit, quare fremuerunt gentes, quaesivit sibi Dominus, quic-

quid appositum, quicunque vult, quinque viae, quod scripsi scripsi, quo vadis, radix malorum, reddite ergo quae, requiem aeterna, requiescat in pace, retro me satana, RIP, Roma semel, sanctus, scio enim quod, scrutamini scripturas, sed et benignitatis, sepultus, sic transit gloria mundi, sicut erat in principio, sicut pastor, stabat Mater, super flumina Babylonis, super montem, sursum corda, tantum religio, Te Deum Laudamus, tempus tacendi, ubi caritas, ubi saeva indignatio, vade in pace, vanitas vanitatum, veni creator spiritus, venite exsultemus Domino, vox clamantis in deserto, Vulgate.

3 Classificatory names of animals, plants etc.

Agaricus campestris, amanita phalloides, bellis perennis, bufo bufo, coccinella septempunctata, digitalis, esox lucius, gasterosteus aculeatus, hyacinthoides, lactrodectus mactans, narcissus obvallaris, platanus hybrida, prunella modularis, quercus, ricinus communis, ulmus procera, vipera beris.

4) Coinage and its inscriptions

Amor populi, aureus, civium industria, decus et tutamen, Dei gratia, denarius, dum spiro, e mare libertas, exurgat Deus, fidei defensor, follis, florent concordia, has nisi, Indiae imperator, justitia thronam, post mortem patris, redde cuique, quae Deus conjunxit, rutilans, scutum fidei, voce populi.

5) Graffiti

Apolllinaris medici, Avete, Caesaris Augustus, Cestilia, fullones, Julius necuam, Lucilla ex corpore, M. Mirenius, Nonis Februariis, quisque me cenam, Romani ite domum, salve lucrum, sum tua aeribus assibus II.

6) Historical or legendary. Roman and other

Ab urbe condita, AD., ad caelendas, aedes Christi, aenei nasi, afflavit Deus, agricola, AH., anno Domini, Arcadia, Boudicca, Britannia, Brittunculi, capitulum huius, Caractacus, Carausius, Cassivellaunus, cave canem, circus, Classicianus, cloaca maxima, Clodius Albinus, commentarii, consule Planco, Corpus Christi, cunctator, cursus honorum, de excido, delenda est Carthago, de vita Caesarum, dis aliter visum, ditior in toto, Domitianus, domus Dei, duas tantum, ego et rex meus, est in Britannia, exurgat Deus, fidei defensor, fides Punica, Gallia est, Hannibal ante portas, Harold rex, Horatius, incipit, in consimili casu, item is, laus est facere, lictor, Magna Carta, mappa mundi, Masada, munera nunc, nam tua res, non Angli, non ipsa pericula, non placet, novus homo, nullum quod, nullus amor populis, occasionem cognosce, oderint dum metuant, omne ignotum, oportet ergo, opus Dei, paterfamilias, patria potestas, pax, pecunia non olet, pontifex maximus, portant armas, post mortem patris, praetor, prescriptio, prima luce, pro Rege, quae Deus conjunxit, qualis artifex pereo, Romulus, Rubicon, salus generis, salus publica, sic semper tyrannis, soles occidere, Spartacus, SPQR., super flumina, tanquam in speculo, tarpeian rock, triumviri, ut rex noster, Vare redde legiones, veni vidi vici, verbosa et grandis epistula, viridis, vivat Hispania.

7) Literature

Andronicus, apud Lapidomurenses, arcades ambo, Argus, arma virumque, Asterix Gallus, atque in perpetuum, auditque vocatus, ave Dea, caput draconis, commentarii, conscia mens, cor cordium, Coriolanus, de Excidio, de Jure Belli, de Officiis, de Titini, de vita Caesarum, Domus Anguli, domus Dei, draco dormiens, Draco Malfoy, dulce et decorum, dux femina, ecce Agnus, et tu Brute, et vera incessu, exegi monumentum, Gallia est, Graecum est, haec studia, integer vitae, intolerabilius nihil, latet anguis, mens sibi, muscosi fontes, nemo aspicit, nescit vox, non omnis moriar, nullus amor populis, o lente, placet, puella Carthaginis, quis umquam, quomodo sedet, signa inferre, soles occidere, spectatum veniunt, summa sedes, sunt lacrimae rerum, Titus Andronicus, tu regere imperio, ubi saeva indignatio, vae victis, verbum non amplius, vivat Hispania, Winnie ille pu.

8) Military, gladiatorial, war and Roman entertainment.

Asterix Gallus, ave Caesar, bellaque matribus, bellum maxime, Boudicca, campus martius, casus belli, circus, Colosseum, Coriolanus, decimare, delenda est Carthago, duas tantum, fasces, in hoc signo, munera nunc, naufragia, plus quam valor, retiarius, secutor, signa inferre, SPQR, triumviri, una salus, vae victis, Vare reddi legiones, veni vidi vici, vivat Hispania.

9) Miscellaneous.

Ab incunabilis, ab origine, a capite, acu rem tangere, ad eundem gradum, ad gustum, ad hominem, aenei nasi, aere perennius, albus, annus horribilis, a posse ad, apostrophus, aqua regia, Aquae Sulis, aqua scutum, arbiter elegantiae, Arcadia, arcana imperii, arcus (pluvius), ars gratia, atrium, augur, aurora borealis, ave atque vale, BD., belua multorum, bonis avibus, brutum fulmen, cani ingenti, canis ingens, cantabrigiensis, capistrum maritale, caries, certum est quod, cloaca maxima, commune bonum, concubina, condimentum, corona civica, corpus Christi, cum grano salis, damnatio memoriae, deciens repetita, de die in diem, de gustibus, delirium tremens, de novo, Deus dat, deus ex machina, dictum factum, digito monstrari, ecce cor meum, ecce gubernator, e mare libertas, et in Arcadia ego, exacta diligentia, ex abundante cautela, ex cathedra, exordium et praefatio, fabulae faciles, faex populi, fama clamosa, fecit, felo de se, fiat justitia, filius nullius, filius terrae, floribus Anna, fluctus in simpulo, foenum habet, fons et origo, fortunae filius, Gallice, hic es, hic liber est meus, his non, Hispania, hominis vis, homo, homo cui vivere, homo erectus, homo sapiens, ides, illegitimi, illiterati, impedimenta, imprimatur, in aeternum, in loco parentis, in nuce, in statu pupillari, in vitro, lapsus linguae, Latine dictum, Latium, lege feliciter, libinosissima, libra, lignum vitae, lingua Franca, lingua Latina, literae humaniores, lux et veritas, lux gentium lex, magister artium, magister juris, magna cum laude, magnum opus, majusculae, malum in se, margarita, mea culpa, me consule, medicinae doctor, me judice, melita, meo periculo, mero motu, merobibus, meum est propositum, minusculae, misericordia, mobile vulgus, natura abhorret, natura nihil agit, nemo me impune, niger, nihil ad rem, nimbus, nocte, nolens volens, nones, norma, novacor, novi, novus homo, numerus, obit, oculi omnium, odium, odora, o fortunatos, oleum, omnem movere, omnia tuta, opinio juris, oratio congratulatoria, oratio obliqua, Oxoniensis, Pater Noster, patria potestas, pax possessori, pecunia in arboribus, pelliparii, perfecto in spiritu, piscator-non, placebo, placet, plebs, positura, post cibum, post mortem, potius sero quam, Principia Mathematica, pro bono publico, profanum vulgus, pro patria, pro rege, pruritis ani, quaestor, quercus, quicquid appositum, quid ais, qui me tangit, quis umquam, quoad hanc, quomodo vales, rara avis, regius, res perit domino, ricinis communis, ridiculum acri, ruat caelum, Rubicon, ruber, rus in urbe, sagittarius, salus factori, salve, salve lucrum, scintilla, scriptio continua, semen, senatus, senex, si monumentum, simulatio maxima, sine dubio, sine mora, sinistra manu, solis terraeque, solus, spectatum veniunt, stabit quocunque, stilus, stipendium, subfuscus, sub specie aeternitatis, suggestio falsi, summa cum laude, suo gladio jugulatus, super montem, symposium, tabula in naufragio, tangere ulcus, tanquam in speculo, tempus abire tibi, tenere lupum, terminus a quo, terminus ad quem, ter quaterque beatus, terra filius, terra marique, terra nullius, Thomas Edwardus Lawrence, ubi lapsus, una voce, uno animo, uno flatu, unus et idem, ut amem et, utinam noster, uxor, vade mecum, vale, veritas, victor ludorum, vivat, vivat Latina, vivat lingua Latina, vivat Regina, viva voce, volans, vox populi.

10) Mottos

alta pete, ars gratia, audentes fortuna, bene merentibus, cavendo tutus, cave paratus, consilio et prudentia, citius, Deus dat, Domine dirige, Dominus illuminatio, e pluribus unum, excelsior, facta non verba, fortis est veritas, hic et *ubique, hinc lucem, hostis honori, in principio erat verbum, laborare est orare, lege feliciter, lege refertus, lux et veritas, meliores priores, multum in parvo, nec prece nec pretio, nisi Dominus frustra, non bene pro toto aureo, non revertar inultus, nunquam non paratus, per ardua ad astra, piscator-non, potius mori quam foedari, praemonitus praemunitus, progressus per peritiam, pro mundi beneficio, semper eadem, semper fidelis, semper paratus, sit sine labe decus, tarde sed tute, tenex propositi, utilius sensoria, veritas, vincit veritas, virtute fortuna.*

11) Music
Credo, exsultate jubilate, gaudeamus igitur, jubilate Deo, laudate Dominum, Magnificat, missa in Dominica, missa solemnis, muscosi fontes, novissima hora, nunc dimittis, placebo, quam pulchra es, requiem aeterna, sicut pastor, tacet, te Deum laudamus, venite exsultemus Domino, vivat regina, vox humana.

12) Personalities
Agricola, Andronicus Livius, Augustus, Boudicca, Caesar, Caractacus, Carausius, Cassivellaunus, Cicero, Classicianus, Clodius Albinus, Coriolanus, Draco Malfoy, Gaius, Hannibal, Horatius, Justinianus, plus quam valor valet Valette, Romulus, si monumentum (Sir Christopher Wren), *Spartacus, Titus Andronicus, Thomas Edwardus Lawrence, Trajan, Vercingetorix.*

13) Proverbial, wisdom, philosophical, advisory
Ab alio, ab asino, ab honesto, a bove, absit invidia, absit omen, ad captandum vulgus, adolescentem verecundum, ad poenitendum properat, age dum, age quod agis, alium excute, amore est sapere, amor nummi, amor vincit, aquila non, ars longa, at spes, audentes fortuna, beatus illi qui, beneficium accipere, bis dat qui, bis pueri senes, blandae mendacia, boni viri, bono animo, caeca invidia, canes timidi, canis in praesepi, cantabit vacuus, carpe diem, casta est qui, cave ne cadas, cave quid dicis, cedant arma togae, certum est qui, certum est quod, cogito ergo sum, corpora lente, credite posteri, credo quia, crescit amor nummi, cucullus non, cui licitus, de mortuis nil, desine de quoquam, dies annorum, dimidium facti, discite justitiam, domus et placens, dona clandestina, donec eris, draco dormiens, dummodo sit dives, dum spiro spero, dum vivimus, ego ero, egomet mihi, eheu fugaces, esse quam videri, est modus, et adulescentis, etiamsi tacent, et semel emissum, et vera incessu, experientia docet, faber est, facit indignatio, facito aliquid, facultas, fama nihil, fas est, fecundi calices, felicitas multos, felix heu, felix qui nihil debet, felix qui potuit, fere libenter, fertilior seges, fide sed cui vide, fidem qui perdit,

finem respice, flamma fumo, forsan et haec, fortiter in re, fortuna favet, fronti nulla fides, gaudeamus igitur, haec studia, hodie mihi, homines enim, homini fidelissimi, honores mutant, ille potens, immortalia ne speres, in articulo mortis, iniqua nunquam, iniquum est, in rerum natura, insanus omnis, in silvam ligna, inter arma silent leges, interdum stultus, in vino veritas, ira furor brevis est, irritabis crabrones, justitia est, labor omnia vincit, laudator temporis acti, laus est facere, legem brevem, legum idcirco, lex talionis, litus arare, longissime a sapientia, lucri bonus, lupus in fabula, macte nova, major e longinquo, medici causa, medio tutissimus, memento mori, mens sana, militat omnis, mirabile dictu, misce stultitiam, mortui non mordent, multis timere, nam et ipsa, nam in omni, nam risu inepto, ne cede malis, nemo aspicit, ne quid nimis, nescis mi fili, nescit vox, ne sutor ultra, nihil est ab omnia parte, nihil illegitimi, nil desperandum, nil obstat, non bene pro toto aureo, non olet, non omnia possumus, non omnis moriar, non semper erit aestas, non sum qualis eram, nosce te ipsum, nunc bibemus, nunc demum redit animus, nunc est bibendum, nunc scripsi totum, nunc vino, nunquam minus solus, omne ignotum, omnem crede diem tibi, omne trinum, omnia mors aequat, omnia tuta timens, opus artificem probat, orandum est, o tempora, ovem lupo, pallida mors, panem et circenses, pares cum paribus, parva domus, parva leves capiunt animo, patris est filius, pax quaeritur bello, pecunia in arboribus, pecunia non olet, pereunt et imputantur, pervenire ad summa, plenus et optabilis, pons asinorum, possunt quia posse videntur, potius sero quam nunquam, primum non nocere, primus inter pares, probitas laudatur, pulvis et umbra sumus, puto Deus fio, quae fuerant vitia, quae fuit durum, quae nocent docent, qualis rex, quem di diligent adolescens moritur, quicquid agas, quid enim proderit homini, quid est futurum, quid est veritas, quid faciam, quid faciant leges, quid faciendum, quid leges, quieta non movere, qui fugiebat rursus proeliabitur, qui maxime clamat, quis custodiet, quis umquam, qui timide rogat, quomodo adulator, quot homines, quo vadis, radix malorum, rapiamus amici, rem tene, rescripsit boni pastoris, res loquitur ipsa, respice finem, ridiculum acri, sapere aude, sapientis est proprium, satis diu vel, senex, sic volo sic jubeo, sine amicitia, si possis, si vis pacem, spero meliora, suae quisque fortunae faber, summarum summa, summa sedes non capit duos, sum quod eris, suo cuique, suus cuique, tantum religio, tecum habita, tempora mutantur, tempora si fuerint, tempori cedere, temporis ars medicina, tempus edax rerum, tempus fugit, timeo Danaos, trahit sua quemque, tu ne cede malis, ubi mel ibi apes, ubi solitudinem faciunt, ultima ratio regum, una salus victis, Utopia, ut saepe summa, ut sementem feceris, varium et mutabile, vel capillus habet, verbum non amplius.

ENGLISH INDEX
Not comprehensive, relating to main alphabetical text only